Linguistic Identities
through Translation

APPROACHES TO TRANSLATION STUDIES
Founded by James S. Holmes

Edited by Henri Bloemen
            Dirk Delabastita
            Ton Naaijkens

Volume 23

Linguistic Identities through Translation

Maria Sidiropoulou
National and Kapodistrian
University of Athens

Amsterdam – New York, NY 2004

The paper on which this book is printed meets the requirements of
"ISO 9706:1994, Information and documentation - Paper for documents -
Requirements for permanence".

ISBN: 90-420-0990-X
©Editions Rodopi B.V., Amsterdam - New York, NY 2004
Printed in The Netherlands

Contents

PART III
Intercultural Variation in Literature and Theatre Translation

Identities in the English-Greek Translational Paradigm:
Concluding Remarks

Table of Figures

Acknowledgements

This book owes a great debt to the international community in translation, linguistics and cultural studies for the tools and inspiration it has offered me in pursuing the goals in this study.

Grateful thanks to those friends and colleagues at the Faculty of English, School of Philosophy, National and Kapodistrian University of Athens, who have kindly discussed issues with me and offered their own insight into the study of identity, in the English – Greek context. I would like to thank Prof. Marios-Byron Raizis and Prof. Robert Crist for allowing me to use their translations for the purposes of the present research. Our students have always been an invaluable company in the study of identities for more than ten years: they have assisted with the questionnaires and offered suggestions on practical issues through their insight into Greek (and English).

I am particularly indebted to Marieke Schilling, Editions Rodopi, for generously providing editorial assistance in this project

Preface

This study looks at whether translation can provide data and insights for the study of linguistic identities. It explores diversity in three genres, in the English-Greek translation paradigm, and claims that STs and TTs are invaluable resources for the study of identities. Varying ideological perspectives and culture specific preference in the structure of discourses are reflected in ST/TT pairs to reveal intercultural difference manifested in terms of (a) linguistic preference across cultures in contact and (b) varying conceptualizations of the world as part of readership/ audience identity. The explicitation tendency in translation, which is assumed to be blurring the reflection of identities in discourses, is claimed to reveal the 'truth of the subconscious'. Translators, in their attempt to produce contextually appropriate versions of texts, activate readily available linguistic options in their minds, which have an increased potential to express meaning in the target language. The book attempts to exploit a situation which is described in terms of the gate keeping metaphor in translation theory. Mediators' attempt to remould texts into contextually appropriate shapes leaves traces on target texts that allow conclusions about linguistic preference, the reflection of an identity.

The study comprises author's research in the English-Greek paradigm. It shifts attention to linguistic preference to claim that translational data can contribute to the study of linguistic identities. It has a consciousness-raising goal in that it aims at enforcing linguistic identity awareness across cultures, in multilingual societies, and points towards novel research directions and applications.

Maria Sidiropoulou
Athens 2004

Diversity Manifested through Translation

1. On Translation and Identity

Translation is a conscious, planned activity, performed in a controlled manner and aims at establishing communication between different cultural environments (Wilss 1999). On a par with the commonplace view that ability to translate is a gift, there is the conviction that there are professional routines and concepts which regulate effective language mediation. Operational procedures, rules and principles that govern language mediation, let alone professional routines and generic conventions, usually go unnoticed, unless STs and TTs are juxtaposed. Genre discourses are often highly conventionalized with "more or less pre-structured lexical resources which denote distinct fields of reality" (ibid : 81) which minimize the role of sender and receiver as subjective agents in the production and reception of texts.

The idea that initiated this book is that these conventionalized environments with the pre-structured resources exhibit some regularity in discourse construction which can give translation researchers an opportunity to explore aspects of linguistic preference across cultures.

Not all texts are equally pre-structured and conventionalized. Literary texts are assumed to be relatively open, others are relatively standardized in terms of syntax and lexis. However, even the openness of the literary text is not to be seen as a "chaos of genius, but as a result of a strategy which creates a fusion between art and craft" (ibid: 77). No matter the degree of conventionality and regularity in various genres, translation research can fruitfully focus on production conventions across cultures to pursue its own theoretical goals and provide tools to this effect.

Identities is an important issue in theoretical translation thinking. Whether purely linguistic, class, social, gender, age, national, colonial, hegemonic, the issue of identity boils down to linguistically inscribed preference in the choice and construction of discourses. Thus, regularities are claimed in this book to be identifiable and – to some extent – measurable.

Translation theories make use of regularities in a number of ways. Theories which have a linguistic orientation or those working within the framework of M.A.K. Halliday's systemic grammar draw on ideas from register analysis, pragmatics and sociolinguistics to account for conventionally established phenomena across cultures.

Polysystem theories of translation also value convention highly. Toury's (1995) concern for reconstructing the norms at work, in translation process, focuses on conventional patterns of translation behaviour to uncover probabilistic laws that ensure appropriateness across cultures and at particular times.

Cultural theories of translation have focused attention on cultural transfer in translation. Lefevere (1998) considers interaction between poetics and ideology in a translation context, namely, the ideology of the translator or the ideology imposed upon the translation by patrons. The gender-and-translation Canadian feminist project (Simon 1996, von Flotow 1997) is concerned with making the feminist identity visible in translation. In the translation and postcolonialism trend, attention is directed to how identities of politically less powerful cultures and literatures are eliminated in their translated version, the "translationese" (Spivak 2000, in Munday 2001), which cater for flawed concepts underlying Western Translation Theory. Translation, Bassnett and Trivedi (1999) claim,

has been at the heart of the colonial encounter, and has been used in all kinds of ways to establish and perpetuate the superiority of some cultures over others. But now, with increasing awareness of unequal power relations involved in the transfer of texts across cultures, we are in the position to rethink both the history of translation and contemporary practice (ibid: 17).

Venuti (1995, 1998) discusses how translations into English make foreign identities invisible by too forcefully assimilating them into the domestic English culture. In all varieties of cultural studies approaches to translation, attention does not seem to be primarily directed to the linguistic level. However, the ideological, ethical and philosophical considerations underlying the cultural studies approaches, assume and are manifested in terms of linguistically realized traits and preferences reflected in colonial, hegemonic or cannibalistic discourses.

Interdisciplinary approaches to translation combine interests in the area of translation studies and other disciplines like discourse analysis, critical discourse analysis, cognitive studies, psychology, philosophy, sociology, history, terminological studies etc. Moreover, they are concerned with assumptions following from source and target textual structures.

2. Equivalence in Translation Theoretical Accounts

'It can be argued that all theories of translation –formal, pragmatic, chronological – are only variants of a single, inescapable question. In what ways can or ought fidelity be achieved? What is the optimal correlation between the A text in the source-language and the B text in the receptor-language?' (Steiner, 1975/1992: 275).

Establishing equivalence between STs and TTs was a central issue in translation studies for quite some time. The issue of equivalence is discussed here because it foregrounds translators' agonizing effort to achieve an appropriate degree of regularity, systematic behaviour and standardization in a target version, in order to make discourse appropriate for a particular target readership at a specific time. What is assumed to be an equivalent version in a target environment may allow observation of preferred patterns of linguistic behaviour, as part of a target language identity.

Academic training in translation has incorporated recent research in linguistics, discourse studies, pragmatics, semiotics, communication and comparative literature studies. The theoretical component in academic translation courses, all over the world, is intended to widen trainees' perspective, to promote understanding about how languages function and, thus, facilitate decisions to be made in the process of translation. Two main trends have had a powerful influence on translation theory. Linguistics and related disciplines, on the one hand, have been sources of insight about what would the appropriate tools and methodology be to account for translation practices. The product and process of translation have been analyzed in terms of findings in the areas of linguistic semantics and pragmatics, semiotics, sociolinguistics, discourse studies and communication studies. On the other hand, comparative literature tradition has provided another set of extremely interesting insights for the process and product of translation to be accounted for. As Venuti (1998) claims, there are two prevalent approaches in translation studies which can be divided into "a linguistics-based orientation, aiming to construct an empirical science, and an aesthetics-based orientation that emphasizes the cultural and political values informing translation practice and research" (ibid: 8).

The linguistically oriented branch of translation theory, Snell-Hornby (1988) notes, both in England (e.g. Nida, Catford) and in Germany (e.g. Neubert, Wilss, Reiß, Vermeer) was concerned with the central concept of translation equivalence which "shifted the focus of attention of translation theory away from the traditional dichotomy of "faithful" or "free" to a presupposed interlingual tertium comparationis" (ibid:15). By contrast, the comparative literature tradition in the Dutch-speaking area (Lefevere, Lambert, Hermans) and in England (Bassnett-McGuire) or Israel (Toury), viewed translation as manipulation drawing back on Russian formalists and the Prague Structuralists. In this view,

> ...literary translation is seen as one of the elements participating in the constant struggle for survival and domination, and the Israeli scholars emphasize that translations have frequently played a primary, creative and innovative role within their literary systems. Hence in this approach, translation is seen essentially as a text-type of its own right, as an integral part of the target culture and not merely as a reproduction of another text....Their emphasis on the target text naturally leads to a primarily *descriptive* approach which explicitly rejects the normative and evaluative attitudes of both traditional translation theory and linguistically oriented translatology (ibid: 24, emphasis in original).

Although this differentiation among translation scholars, as belonging to one or the other trend, may not be absolute since a lot of merging of ideas has occurred, it does outline a diverging tendency in translation theory.

Translation equivalence is related to the translation approach adopted. Catford (1965) distinguishes between *literal* vs. *free* translation approaches, and quite a few versions of this distinction have appeared since then. Newmark (1981) prefers the distinction between *semantic* and *communicative* approaches to translation, Toury (1995) introduces the distinction *source-* vs. *target-orientedness* in translation, whereas Hatim and Mason (1990) prefer the terms *author-centered, text-centered* and *reader-centered* translating. If translation approaches are to be seen as standing on a continuum between *literal* vs. *free, semantic* vs. *communicative, author-centered* vs. *reader-centered* ends, the approaches towards the left end of the continuum are considered to be pursuing a rather *formal* type of equivalence. By contrast, those on the right end of the continuum are concerned about *dynamic* equivalence. Formal equivalence (Nida 1964) is the closest possible match in form and content between original (source) text and translated (target) version. Dynamic equivalence, on the other hand, is based on the idea of *equivalent effect* on addressees, i.e. the impact of the target text on target readers should be the same as that of the source text on original receivers. Similarly, Nord (1995) outlines the general considerations in (a version of) a *functional* approach to translation which takes into consideration the *skopos* of the discourse:

> The functional approach in translation which I subscribe to hinges on a double concept of "functionality plus loyalty" (Nord 1991a: 28ff). This means that
> (a) the translation of any text is determined by its purpose (or "skopos", Vermeer 1978, Reiß and Vermeer 1984), the purpose being defined by the *communicative functions* for which the target text is intended, and
> (b) the range of purposes or functions which are "possible" or "legitimate" for a particular translation of a particular source text is limited by the conventional, *often genre-specific concepts of translation prevailing in the culture(s) involved* and

determining the expectations of clients, ST authors and TT recipients with regard to the relationship holding between source-texts and target texts. (ibid: 269-270, emphasis added)

Within the comparative literature tradition, Venuti (1995) distinguishes between *domesticating* and *foreignizing* translation. A domesticating strategy involves reflecting dominant target cultural values of society at the time of translating, whereas a foreignizing strategy preserves source values undermining target ones. An important parameter in this view is the *status* of the source/target languages and the notion of cultural hegemony. In a translation situation in which the direction of the translation is from a *dominant* towards a *minority*-status language, domestication is viewed positively (Hatim & Mason, 1997: 145-146) in that the minority-status language is being protected against its tendency to absorb. By contrast, if the target language is culturally dominant, domesticating creates an illusion of transparency.

The issue of dominant cultures and *power relations* in translation was explored within a cultural studies approach to translation originating from the comparative literature tradition. Because cultures are so different, attention should be drawn to language as a means of shaping experience, thus drawing attention to ideologies and identity. In discussing gender in translation, Simon (1996) argues that

...'the turn to culture' implies adding an important dimension to translation studies. Instead of asking the traditional question which has preoccupied translation theorists – "how should we translate, what is a correct translation?" – the emphasis is placed in a *descriptive* approach: "what do translators do, how do they circulate in the world and elicit response?" (ibid: 7, emphasis added)

Whatever the approach to translation theory, or whatever type of 'translation equivalence' is sought after, some of the thinking about successful translation processes seems to be similar. As Snell-Hornby (1988) argues, "it is striking how repetitive some of the thinking, the concepts and the terms have been" (ibid: 26).

For instance, within the comparative literature tradition, Bassnett (1980: 27), in discussing translation equivalence, refers to an instance of translating Italian or Spanish blasphemous expressions in terms of expressions with sexual overtones, which in English would produce a comparable shock effect (eg. *Porca Madonna→fucking hell*). On a par, within the linguistic tradition, a very interesting illustration of the translator's varying orientation in making choices, in the context of Bible translation, appears in Hatim and Mason (1990:17). The way a sum of money is treated in the three versions of Bible translation reflects this differing orientation of the translator. The sum of money[1] was rendered as *a penny a day* in the Authorised Version (1611). In the Revised Standard Version (1881 and 1954), it was turned into a *denarius* a day* (followed by a comment: * *the denarius was worth about seventeen pence),* whereas in the New English Bible (1961), it appeared as *the usual day's wage.* This third rendering of the sum of money is an instance of what Hatim and Mason have called *reader-centered* translating, where the translator's concern is about ensuring an adequate communicative response in readers. In this case, a communicative response can be ensured if quantities are assigned their value in the readers' own time. The implication that *a penny* (Authorized Version 1611) was the usual day's wage is missed because present day target readers do not share the same cognitive environment with 1611 readers and, thus, cannot 'infer' or 'calculate' its value, unless this piece of information is provided.

In fact, modifications in translation versions of a literary work that reflect a different orientation in translation may be due to the fact that the equivalent effect pursued in translation varies with respect to the *norms* prevalent in the target language at a certain time. Weissbrod (1996) reports that the differences observed in the treatment of wordplay in three different translation versions into Hebrew (1923, 1951, 1987) of Carroll's *Alice's Adventures in Wonderland* resulted not only from the rapid development of the Hebrew language itself, but also from changes in the norms of literary translation into Hebrew. In the 1923 version (Siman's translation), original instances of wordplay were replaced by completely new ones, which were rooted in a different cultural and textual space. In this version, *acceptability at a socio-cultural level* was the predominant concern, and thus socio-cultural aspects were manipulated: Alice, for instance, not only had a Hebrew name (*Alissa*) but she also became a "Jewish girl whose world was filled with Jewish holidays, daily prayers, etc." (ibid: 225). Also, the Duchess' baby who turns into a pig, was turned to a fish, because for Jews a pig is ritually unclean and its eating is prohibited. In the 1951 version (Amir's translation), the strive is for *stylistic achievement in target-culture terms* (an elevated style was preferred) rather than for adequacy. Many instances of wordplay were not only completely ignored but also the loss was compensated nowhere else in the text. One of the instances of wordplay that resisted being transferred into Hebrew was Carroll's exploitation of the *well* (adverb)/*well* (noun) homonymy in English (: "they were *in the well*... Of course they were, *well in*"), whereas a bit later in the text, Caroll activates two completely different meanings of *to draw* (water from a well, and pictures). In this latter instance, too, Amir sacrificed the pun. By contrast, in the 1987 version (Ofek's translation), the norm in literary translation into Hebrew had shifted again and required *adequacy at both the socio-cultural and the linguistic level*, and

---

[1] (referred to in the Parable of the Labourers in the Vineyard, Matthew 20, 1-16).

this norm had already reached children's literature. In this version, elements which were foreign to Carroll's world were introduced only insofar as they helped the translator replace the original wordplay. On a number of occasions, Weissbrod reports, Ofek replaced a single polysemous English word by two different Hebrew words, and then used one of them to create a new wordplay. In the trial scene, the King tells the Queen: "You never had *fits* my dear... Then the words don't *fit* you". The translator used a Hebrew word in the sense of 'outburst' as the previous translator had done, but did not elaborate on the word for the sake of wordplay. He created a new wordplay by activating two meanings of another Hebrew word (*holem*) which means both *fit* in the sense of 'suitable' and 'a strong sound', in this case, the sound made by the inkstand which the Queen throws at Bill the Lizard (ibid: 230). Thus, examination of the treatment of wordplay in three translation versions of a literary work shows that the definition of the equivalent effect varies with respect to norms operating in translation practice at a certain time.

The issue of equivalent effect on target readership led translation theorists to consider equivalence at various levels of linguistic expression. Notions from the theoretical linguistic apparatus are employed to describe equivalence conditions at these levels. Thus, notions like *semantic, pragmatic, cognitive, discoursal, textual, semiotic* equivalence account for types of the translator's goals (Hatim and Mason 1990, 1997, Baker 1992).

3. Why Linguistic Preference?

This book borrows insights from current translation theoretical accounts to look at the notion of identity with a view to exploring how (and to what extent) identities may be studied through translation. Linguistic identities are tackled through the notion of *linguistic preference*. They are taken to be linguistically manifested preferences reflected in target discourses. They are worth studying in this context, because they are assumed to be contributing information about target readership distinct profiles, thus, foregrounding ST and TT identities and promoting intercultural understanding.

Linguistic preference, in this book, may be assumed to relate to

- grammatical preference in message construction,
- assumptions prevalent in the culture-specific way a target language conceptualizes universal notions,
- gender-sensitive assumptions that affect discourse construction in intercultural communication,
- assumptions about culturally effective persuasion strategies in a target environment,
- assumptions about some culturally appropriate discourse style relative to such cognitive notions as audience participation and involvement, etc.

Preference is reflected in target discourses and is assumed to constitute part of a target linguistic identity. A goal of this book is to show that target discourses can point to culture specific assumptions in alternative conceptualizations of reality, with a view to target linguistic identity preservation and formation, in multicultural societies, thereby resisting globalization.

Varying assumptions about appropriately structured discourses may be contrastively reached at in translation, in a particular ST-TT paradigm, as they do in parallel text situations or original production.

Politeness and impersonality, for instance, are variables which adjust tenor in discourses (Bell 1991). In translation, varying politeness or im-/personality patterns across cultures should be reflected in the target version for pragmatic equivalence to be achieved. Brown and Levinson (1978/1987) show that the notion and patterns of politeness vary from culture to culture: there are *positive* vs. *negative* politeness patterns or *solidarity* vs. *deference* ones. Sifianou (1992: 214) argues that the main difference between the Greek and English systems of politeness is a matter of orientation rather than degree: more negative politeness orientation in English and more positive orientation in Greek. In discussing external modification with respect to requests in Greek, Sifianou (1992) argues that the main difference between Greek and English seems to be the Greek tendency to *give reasons* for the requests more frequently than in English, which is a feature of positive politeness. What is essential in understanding this differential choice among the devices available in the two languages is that different social norms and values bring about different conventionalized patterns for the realization of *speech acts* in each language (ibid:199, emphasis added).

In translation across cultures which favour a different politeness behaviour, linguistic options associated with one type of politeness, in a source version, might have to be adjusted to conform to the preferred politeness orientation in a target version. This allows the potential of studying politeness preferences (as part of linguistic identities) through translation.

A linguistic manifestation of positive politeness is a reason giving tendency in discourse (Brown and Levinson 1978/1987). The reason giving tendency may be observed in parallel text situations as well as in translational contexts. A reason giving tendency may be observed in air travel announcements (parallel texts) on board Olympic Airways aircraft. The following example quoted from Marmaridou (1987) illustrates the preference.

Greek   If you continue your trip with us, *we inform you that because* you'll pass through passport and currency control at Rome Airport, you have to take your hand luggage and personal items with you.
Αν συνεχίζετε το ταξίδι σας μαζί μας, σας πληροφορούμε οτι, επειδή θα περάσετε έλεγχο διαβατηρίων και συναλλάγματος στο αεροδρόμιο της Ρώμης, πρέπει να πάρετε μαζί σας όλα τα προσωπικά σας είδη.

English If you continue your flight with us, you will pass passport and currency control here at Rome Airport. Kindly take your hand luggage and personal items with you. (ibid: 730)

The *reason giving* tendency observed in requests in Greek, seems to have a parallel in English-Greek news translation practice. The translator is concerned with 'explicitating' causal relations in the Greek version, specifically at points of evaluation or estimation. This is a reason giving tendency which echoes positive politeness preferences on the part of text producers and a 'denier' attitude on the part of receivers. The example, below, illustrates an instance of causal link explicitation at a point of estimation in the news structure (my emphasis).

Instances of positive politeness manifestations are numerous in other parallel text situations. *I/we personalizations* and *direct questioning,* which reduce social distance, as positive politeness devices, were more frequent in abstracts written by Greek researchers than in abstracts written by researchers from the English-speaking world (Sidiropoulou, 1995c: 585-586). No cultural group can be considered as purely positively or negatively polite and thus translators must draw on their 'knowledge base' in order to adjust patterns accordingly.

English ST
..it is no use counting on organized Christianity to combat this spread of witchcraft... [] This is organized Christianity...
(*Sunday Telegraph*, October 17, 1993)

Greek TT
..*it is no use*[2] hoping that organized Christianity can combat this new witchcraft movement. *The reason is that* Christianity has produced the movement... (*Mesimvrini,* October 30, 1993) [my translation]

..*Είναι μάταιο να ελπίζει κανείς οτι η Χριστιανοσύνη μπορεί να καταπολεμήσει αυτή την νέα κίνηση υπέρ της μαγείας. Ο λόγος είναι οτι η κίνηση προέρχεται ακριβώς μέσα απο τους κόλπους του Χριστιανισμού των ΗΠΑ...*
(*Μεσημβρινή,* 30.10.93)

English ST
Ritzy Manhattan soirees were spiced with debates about what was real and what fantasy in Resnais's *Last Year at Marienbad* or Fellini's *8½*, about Antonioni's seductive use of existential ennui.
('Fellini Go Home!', *Time*, January 20, 1997)

Greek TT
Cinema goers spent whole evenings in Manhattan sitting-rooms talking about what is real and what is fantacy in Resnais's *Last Year at Marienbad* or Fellini's *8½*, about Antonioni's seductive use of existential ennui.
('European cinema outside cinema halls in the US', *I Kathimerini*, March 27, 1997) [my translation]

Οι φιλοθεάμονες περνούσαν ολόκληρες βραδιές στα σαλόνια του Μανχάταν συζητώντας για το τί είναι αλήθεια και τί φαντασία στο «Πέρυσι στο Μάριεμπαντ» του Ρενέ ή στο «8 ½» του Φελίνι και για την πλήξη της ύπαρξης του Αντονιόνι.
('Το ευρωπαϊκό σινεμά εκτός αιθουσών στις ΗΠΑ', Η Καθημερινή, 27.3.1997)

Another instance of varying preference may be observed in the system of *transitivity* in translational contexts and parallel texts alike. Grammatical

---

[2] *It's no use* (*Είναι μάταιο*)..: a point of estimation in the news structure schema.

preference in the system of transitivity may be reflected in Greek target news reporting texts to adjust tenor levels.

A preference for active constructions in Greek was also observed (Marmaridou, 1987: 726) in a set of announcements delivered in English and in Greek to passengers on board Olympic Airways aircraft. The rendering of

English: You *are* kindly *requested* to observe the non-smoking sign
as
Greek :   Please, *do not smoke* until the non-smoking sign is off
          Παρακαλούμε να μην καπνίζετε μέχρι να σβήσει η φωτεινή επιγραφή

illustrates the point. This is a difference related to the pragmatic level of meaning encoded in text messages, which attempt to ensure socio-cultural appropriateness in a particular context.

The following shifts attention to another pragmatic variable, namely the appropriate *quantity* of information to be allowed in a TT. It illustrates a varying preference in the assumption about the appropriate quantity of information to be allowed in a news headline.

Varying news-reporting conventions about the amount of information to be included in headlines are likely to have a parallel in various language pairs. In Hatim and Mason (1990), reference is made to a political news article which appeared in *Le Monde* (18.9.1985) and was translated in the *Guardian* (18.9.1985). It was about a third team which was alleged to have been involved in sinking the 'Rainbow Warrior', the Greenpeace flagship, in the harbour of Auckland Islands. Hatim and Mason draw attention to the difference in the preferred quantity of information between the French-English headline pair (1990: 84-87): target language news reporting conventions have trimmed information from target headline version.

ST
Le «Rainbow Warrior» aurait été coulé par une troisième équipe de militaires français (*Le Monde*, 18.9.1985)
TT
Third military team involved in sinking (*Guardian*, 18.9.1985)

A question arises as to what the appropriate quantity of information would have been, had the headline been translated for a Greek newspaper. The question of how much information can conventionally be allowed in Greek headline versions has been addressed elsewhere (Sidiropoulou 1995a) and conclusions will be referred to below, but, in the present context, a target preference has been identified in terms of a test conducted with Athens University translator-trainees. The test has revealed that a Greek version of the headline would have required more information, than the one presented in the English version. One group of translation students was asked to translate the *Guardian* title for a news item which was to appear in a high-circulation Greek newspaper. Another group (37 university students) was asked to evaluate some of their colleagues' versions as to which were the most appealing ones to appear in a Greek context. Headline versions were presented in pairs with gradually increasing amount of information and preference was eventually shown for the most informative headlines.

Results indicate that 1a was preferred over 1b by 100%, 2b over 2a by 94,5%, 3b was over 3a by 67,5% and 4a over 4b by 86,5%. The preferred information increase, in pairs 1-3, allows for some pessimistic assumptions to be made explicit, which may have accorded with the audiences ideological presuppositions. One assumption was that having a third team involved in sinking (rather than the two already mentioned) is *beyond expectations* (this is triggered by the appearance of και (*and*) in 1a), just as reality underlying political surface might be. Another assumption is that there is *officially* (triggered by *sinking mission* in 4b) *organized* planning beneath the surface (triggered by *sinking plan* in 3b).

The claim in this book is that awareness of preferences like the ones described above can contribute to linguistic identity awareness in multicultural environments. Translation is an extremely rich area of application which may contribute to identification of intercultural difference.

GREEK NEWS HEADLINE VERSIONS
EVALUATED BY STUDENTS

1a. *And* (=another) third military team involved in sinking
    Και τρίτη στρατιωτική μονάδα εμπλεκόμενη σε βύθιση
    vs.
1b. [ ]Third military team involved in sinking
    [ ]*Τρίτη στρατιωτική μονάδα εμπλεκόμενη σε βύθιση.*

2a. Third military team involved <u>in sinking</u>
    Τρίτη στρατιωτική μονάδα εμπλεκόμενη σε βύθιση
    vs.
2b. Third military team involved <u>in sinking plan</u>
    Τρίτη στρατιωτική μονάδα εμπλεκόμενη σε σχέδιο βύθισης.

3a. Third military team involved in a sinking <u>plan</u>
    Τρίτη στρατιωτική μονάδα εμπλεκόμενη σε σχέδιο βύθισης
    vs.
3b. Third military team involved in sinking <u>mission</u>
    *Τρίτη στρατιωτική μονάδα εμπλεκόμενη σε αποστολή
    βύθισης πλοίου.*

4a. Third military team involved <u>in sinking the Greenpeace
    ship</u>.
    *Τρίτη στρατιωτική μονάδα αναμεμιγμένη στη βύθιση του
    πλοίου της Greenpeace.*
    vs.
4b. Third military team involved <u>in sinking plan</u>
    *Τρίτη στρατιωτική μονάδα αναμεμιγμένη σε σχέδιο
    βύθισης.*

4. Preference across Genres

Linguistic preference is to be identified relative to particular genres, because it may be genre-specific. Variables have been shown to vary across genres, within the same language. Two instances of generic variation with respect to a particular variable (e.g. a linguistic phenomenon) are presented below to illustrate the point, namely, to illustrate (a) fluctuation in the quantity of information to be included in a news headline and (b) the treatment of taboo issues across genres.

In the English-Greek news reporting context, information quantity increase in political headlines has been anticipated in Sidiropoulou (1995a). Diversity in the translator's behaviour was observed with reference to the genre the text belongs to. This can be illustrated in the way political, economic and medical article headlines are treated in translation. The quantity of information transferred in the Greek (target) version of political, economic and medical headlines was shown to differ in a 1991-1993 random sample of a 100 source-and-target headline pairs. There was a tendency for *more* information to be allowed in the target version of political article headlines. By contrast, the Greek version of *economic* and *medical* article headlines showed a tendency for *less* and almost *equal* –respectively– amount of information with reference to the source headline versions (ibid: 298). It is as if there is a genre-specific constraint operating, in Greek news reporting, which regulates the amount of information to be included in the category "headline" of the news reporting schema (van Dijk 1985).

Generic variation with respect to the treatment of taboo issues may be a manifestation of some aspect of a linguistic identity. Along with Grice's maxims and the notion of politeness which may vary across cultures, taboo issues are not universal. A translator may omit parts of texts in order to avoid giving offence in a target culture. In an English-Greek translation context, the translator has been shown to interfere with the interpersonal distance (between text producer and reader) when taboo issues are dealt with. Taboo issues, in translated Greek press material, are associated with *indirectness,* a linguistic device creating distance (Sidiropoulou, 1995a: 294). In the following target headline version, a nominalization[3], *treatment of impotence* (*αντιμετώπιση ανικανότητας*), is preferred over a literal translation version of the source title, which would have been grammatical but not appropriate[4] in the particular context

---

[3] i.e. a distance creating device (Brown and Levinson 1978/1987).
[4] a literal translation version would have given offence in Greek: *to help some impotent men..* (*να βοηθήσει μερικούς ανίκανους άνδρες*).

ST   Pelvis exercises may help some impotent men
        (*The New York Times*, 10.2.1993)
TT   Special exercises *for the treatment of impotence.*
        Ειδικές ασκήσεις για την αντιμετώπιση της ανικανότητας
        (Τα Νέα, 25.2.1993)

Further research on the treatment of taboo issues in three translation contexts revealed that translator behaviour differed with respect to the genre variable. Translators tended to omit taboo items to avoid giving offence in the Greek news reporting context, they tended to elaborate on taboo issues in performance translation contexts and retained an equal amount of taboo items in literary translation (Sidiropoulou 1998d). Greek showed varying preferences in the treatment of taboo items relative to English, and this may be assumed to be part of its identity – which would have gone unnoticed if it had not been identified in a translation context.

5. About this Book

English-Greek cross-cultural variation, in this book, will be observed across genres, the news reporting genre (Part I), the EU genre (Part II) and the literary/theatre genre (Part III).

The book explores the potential of outlining linguistic identities through contrastive analysis of source and target versions of texts. In multilingual European societies attribution of linguistic preference to specific cultural/national groups is of paramount importance, as it contributes to intercultural understanding. Moreover, globalization intensifies the need for focusing on diversity across languages, with a view to cultural identity awareness, formation or preservation. It focuses on systematic preference observed in target versions of texts in translation situations between English and Greek and expands on diversification across other language pairs. It intends to claim that preferred linguistic traits that may contribute to outlining a linguistic identity are identifiable and measurable in order to be exploited in various linguistic applications such as translation training, the EFL classroom, machine translation etc.

The present introductory chapter is intended to explore the potential of translational data to foreground preferred linguistic behaviour that would be part of a linguistic identity. Part I (The Inscription of an Ideology in Press Translation) examines linguistic preference in the rendition of particular linguistic phenomena from the English to the Greek Press. It aims at showing a different ideology negotiated through the construction of Greek target discourse which will be claimed to be part of the target linguistic identity. The phenomena to be tackled are

- how logical connections are handled for readership response to be ensured
- how temporal adverbials are treated in Greek target versions of press material
- how testimonial discourse may be modified to appeal to target readerships
- what local constraints seem to regulate the rendition of metaphors etc.

Part II (Readership Identities through EU Discourse Diversity) examines diversity in the construction of EU discourses. Although EU versions of texts may not be translations from the same EU official language – they may even be 'parallel texts' rather than translations – the diversity encountered across text versions can foreground linguistic preference. Examination of thematization preference, for instance, between English and Greek, may reveal that language is employed to appeal to and control a readership which is assumed to have a distinct profile.

Part III (Intercultural Variation through Literature and Theatre Translation) examines how translators' concern about ensuring readership/audience response may reveal aspects of the linguistic identity of an intended readership or audience. For instance, in examining Lord Byron's translation into Greek, it is observed that rendition of metaphorical mappings reveals diversity in the Idealized Cognitive Models (ICMs) assumed in the target language and the constraints that regulate their use, which is argued to be part of a linguistic identity. Prose translation from Greek to English (G>E), allows for a set of modifications that reveals projection of translator internal preference in target discourses. Theatre translation for the stage, where translator's main concern is to ensure immediate audience response in the communicative situation, allows for intercultural variation that may be outlining a cultural identity in a fairly accurate and immediate manner. Theatre translation for the page and for the stage along with such variables as translation directionality are employed, in Part III, to suggest that translational contexts are sources for intercultural diversity identification. In any case, the book also intends to show that the theoretical apparatus in pragmatics and cognitive semantics is most operative in ensuring linguistic identity awareness in languages, whether hegemonic or not, through contrastive analysis of source and target versions of texts.

6. Explicitation: an Obstacle?

Translators tend to be more analytical than source authors and make things explicit for their readerships. Steiner comments on explicitation as follows:

… the mechanics of translation are primarily explicative, they explicate (or, strictly speaking, 'explicitate') and make graphic as much as they can of the semantic inherence of the original (1975/1992: 291).

Munday (2001), in discussing how translation can reduce variation, refers to Berman's twelve 'deforming tendencies' in translation. Tendencies 2 and 3 describe explicitation tendencies:

2. *Clarification*: This includes explicitation, which 'aims to render "clear" what does not wish to be clear in the original'...
3. *Expansion*: Like other theories (…), Berman says that TTs tend to be longer than STs. This is due to 'empty' explicitation that unshapes its rhythm to 'overtranslation' and to 'flattening'. These additions only serve to reduce the clarity of the work's 'voice' (ibid: 150)

It is not definite what manifestations explicitation may have in a TT. It may be strengthening cohesive and collocational networks in a TT, making pragmatically opaque expressions transparent, making illocutionary force of utterances explicit, expressing evaluation and speaker attitudes towards people and situations, recovering ellipsis.

ST   But, out of everybody, *she* could stand Erasmia least of all. She stewed inside and fumed at the sight of her. And when she would arrive with her friends to show off our house – I could barely keep *her* from throwing her out of the door. [my translation]

Αλλ' απ' όλους λιγότερο χώνευε την Ερασμία. Στο στομάχι της καθόταν. Την έβλεπε κι ανακατεύονταν τ' άντερά της. Κι όταν κουβαλούσε μαζί της και τις φιληνάδες της για να κάνει επίδειξη του σπιτιού μας, με το ζόρι τη συγκρατούσα να μην τη διώξει. (*Το Τρίτο Στεφάνι*, p. 19)

TT   But it was Erasmia *our Marietta* could stomach least of all. She stewed inside and fumed at the sight of her. Particularly when she would arrive with her friends to show off our house – it was all I could do to keep *Marietta* from throwing her out of the door then.
(*The Third Wedding Wreath*, p. 13, transl. by John Chioles)

The example above is from Kostas Taktsis' novel *To Trito Stefani* (*The Third Wreath*, 1987 [my translation]) translated into English by John Chioles (*The Third Wedding Wreath*). The name of *Marietta* is made explicit in the English TT: it occurs twice in the English version, whereas in Greek pronominal reference (*she, her*) suffices. There are many instances of translator interference, in the novel, that may be taken as manifestations of an explicitation tendency. This example above can be more dubious as to whether the interference can be a manifestation of translator's explicitation tendency or whether it is motivated by the target language system (i.e. by linguistic rules or simply preferences prevalent in the target context).

The question arises as to whether explicitation can allow accurate reflection of preference in target versions. Translation scholars (e.g. Toury 1995) have doubted the reliability of translational data as resources that can allow safe conclusions about original production. Other scholars (Malmkjaer 1999) maintain that in literary translation contexts, target versions of texts may allow fairly safe linguistic conclusions about a target language. There may be variance, she claims, in the treatment of phenomena in translation (e.g. Malmkjaer explores the treatment of deixis, in Danish versions of H.C. Andersen's stories), but quantitative research is expected to be more fruitful in this respect, than qualitative research.

Malmkjaer has spotted the usefulness of doing linguistic research through translation. What linguistics, she claims, can perhaps learn from translation studies is to

check the results of its 'bottom-up' analyses of lexical and systemic cross-linguistic differences and similarities against results obtained from translational cross-textual analysis (ibid: 17).

In her empirically-based analysis, Malmkjaer points to two approaches to translational data: on the one hand, she claims, "translational contrastive linguistics" examine "equivalence in difference", and on the other, "translational comparative linguistics" uses translational data to bring to light relationships between languages which might be less "conducive to observation by descriptive linguistic means alone" (ibid: 12).

As mentioned above, the book examines diversity through translational data across English and Greek. It draws attention to issues which would not have been easily identified through descriptive linguistic means alone. Translational contexts, despite potential drawbacks, are employed to foreground identities in source and target linguistic systems.

Translation explicitation is not considered an obstacle in 'extracting' identities from target discourses. Although explicitation may be blurring measurement results, it is assumed to be contributing to the project, in that it is taken to reveal the truth of the subconscious, in the mind of the language user, i.e. of the translator. Through explicitation, translators are assumed to project internalized TL conceptualizations of reality on the TT, which promote, rather than cancel goals of the project.

The following examples show instances of making pragmatic aspects of meaning explicit in the English TT by making values and attitudes assigned to situations explicit or by explicitating inferences following from expressions. The '[]' sign in ST indicate points of translator interference.

ST   ...in those days he'd fallen head first for the religious life. [] When we got married, he was more godless than the Devil. [my translation]

        ...την εποχή εκείνη είχε πέσει με τα μούτρα στα θεία. [] Τον καιρό που παντρευτήκαμε ήταν πιό άθεος κι απ' τον εξαποδώ.
        (Το Τρίτο Στεφάνι, p. 21)

TT   ...in those days he'd fallen head first for the religious life. *Funny thing is*, he was the one more godless than the Devil when we first got married. (*The Third Wedding Wreath*, p. 15)

ST   If I wanted to be a nurse, I could do it without marrying.[] 'He's an old man, he won't live much longer, you'll be left with the houses'.
    [my translation]

        Αν ήθελα να κάνω τη νοσοκόμα, την έκανα χωρίς να παντρευτώ. 'Είναι γέρος, δε θα ζήσει πολύ, θα σου μείνουν τα σπίτια' ...
        (Το Τρίτο Στεφάνι, p. 37)

TT   If I wanted to be a nurse, I could do it without marrying. *That way I'd at least be independent.* 'Marry him' they'd say to me, 'He's an old man, he won't live much longer, you'll inherit the houses'
    (*The Third Wedding Wreath*, p. 31)

These instances of interference are assumed to be manifestations of an explicitation tendency which registers translator agonizing effort to render the strength of the original in another language. To what extent, such tendencies are manifestations of pragmatically motivated rules and principles of the source or target language remains unspecified.

The book explores the treatment of a range of phenomena within or across genres. *Connectivity* (mainly adversative and causal) is examined in E>G news reporting, as well as in E>G and G>E literary/theatre translational data, to bring to light the pros and cons of the linguistic-identities-through-translation project. Metaphor treatment and conditions on metaphor use are tackled in E>G news reporting and G>E literary prose translation. Observation of phenomena across genres and translation directions is expected to yield more reliable conclusions about linguistic identities. A plausible assumption is that quantitative studies and machine-aided research will do the job better, because accurate measurement will allow insights as to how much of the interference is due to such factors as explicitation and how much of it may be due to TL specific preferences in message construction.

PART I
Inscription of Ideology in Press Translation

1. Ideology in Discourse

Events are perceived and reported through a specific ideological perspective (Hodge and Kress 1979, Kress 1985, Fairclough 1989 & 1995, Lee 1992, Dendrinos 1992) which interact with "a whole range of socially regulated way of speaking (and writing)" (Lee, 1992: 107).

An issue bound up with the question of perspective in discourse construction is that of social identity – social class, ethnicity, gender, age etc. Research on sexist language mostly carried out in the 1970s originated from the observation that there were a number of lexical, grammatical and phonological features that characterized women's language (Labov 1972, Trudgill 1972, Lakoff 1975). In translation, male/female registers, gender-specific codes, ethnicity and national identity are reflected in source and target versions of texts. It is in the translator's power to reflect identities in favour of or against a particular ideological perspective.

Critical Discourse Analysis influential position that language is a carrier of ideological meaning (Hodge and Kress 1979: 208) had significant consequences in translation studies. Schäffner (2003) has employed concepts of linguistics and critical discourse analysis "to link textual features and ideological context of text production and reception" (ibid: 41) in a comparative analysis of the English and the German text of a Blair/Schröder political paper. Similarly, Harvey (2003) has analyzed the material and contextual factors that contribute to rendering three gay fictional texts translated from American English into French in the late 1970s. He concludes that – among others – the texts are interfaces between competing ideological positions (ibid: 43). Issues of gender, cultural identity and nationalism in translation studies have been an ongoing field of research. As Mason claims,

...consciously or subconsciously, text users bring their own assumptions predisposition and general world-views to bear on their processing of text at all levels...The translator, as both receiver and producer of text, has the double duty of perceiving the meaning potential of particular choices within the cultural and linguistic community of the source text and relaying the same potential, by suitable linguistic means, to a target readership (Mason, 1994: 23)

Ideology has also been tackled in the area of cultural studies and literary translation. "Because there is no total equivalence between cultural systems", Simon (1996) points out in her discussion of gender and translation, "the alignment of source and target text is necessarily skewed". She further draws attention to "language as a force through which experience is shaped" (ibid: 136) – hence ideology. In accounts of translation which put emphasis on forms of identities, as feminism, ideology is accounted for in terms of the notion of *mediation*. Simon, for instance, argues that the cultural turn in translation "defines translation as a process of *mediation* which does not stand above *ideology* but works through it" (ibid: 8, emphasis added).

Ideological perspectives are inscribed in texts, in terms of linguistic devices, the carriers of ideological meaning. Lexical choice, style-shifting, cohesion and transitivity are textual devices, examined in Hatim and Mason (1997), as to whether or how they contribute to constructing ideologies in translation. In discourse studies, the significance of more discourse features as vehicles of ideological meaning has been examined in Hodge and Kress (1979, e.g. negation, time), in Lee (1992, e.g. thematic selection, nominalization), in Simpson (1993, e.g. modality, transitivity, spatial and temporal point of view).

This part examines mediation and the inscription of ideology in target versions of data, as manifested through modifications in the rendition of certain linguistic devices in press news translation. These devices are adversative, causal connection, temporal adverbials etc. The points of variation are shown to be part of a linguistic identity which is claimed to be fairly safely approached and studied through contrastive analysis of source and target versions of texts.

2. Connectives: an Ideologically Loaded Network

Halliday and Hasan (1976) have considered cohesive devices, within and between sentences of a text, as the primary determinants that create texture. These are reference, substitution, ellipsis and lexical cohesive devices. Explicitly marked cohesive devices in a text can also be signalled in terms of formal markers such as *and, but, so, then*. In this case, the actual cohesive power lies in the underlying semantic relation (whether additive, adversative, causal or temporal) rather than in the surface realization of the cohesive relation, namely, the formal marker, the connective. Connectives may be

> additive: *and, or, furthermore, similarly, in addition*, etc.
> adversative: *but, however, on the other hand, nevertheless*, etc.
> causal: *so, consequently, for this reason, it follows from this*, etc.
> temporal: *then, after that, an hour later, finally, at last*, etc.

or other.

Focusing on connectives as cohesive devices, in a translation context, is significant because there is considerable variation across languages in the connectives to be preferred and in their relative frequency in discourses. Baker (1992:192) claims that "compared to Arabic, English generally prefers to present information in relatively *small* chunks and to signal the relationship between these chunks in *unambiguous* ways" (emphasis added). A difference between English and Greek in the use of connectives may be identified in errors of EFL learners, in composition writing. A constant advice of EFL teachers to Greek learners is that they should avoid long winding sentences in their written production. Evidently, mother tongue interference allows a preference for winding subordination in Greek to cross the intercultural filter and be imprinted on learners' written production in EFL.

Translator trainees need to be made aware of aspects of differences in the way connective devices operate across languages, because difference in the use of such devices may not be straightforwardly identifiable.

The benefit from the interaction between linguistic research and contrastive analysis of translational data, in the study of cohesion, can be bi-directional. Linguistic research may increase awareness of intercultural difference and block unnatural effects from target discourses. Contrastive analysis of translational data, on the other hand, can point to research directions, in the study of cohesion, for instance, which may not have attracted researchers' attention, in the first place.

Linguistic research ↔ Contrastive analysis of translational data

This section, explores the benefit of examining intercultural difference between English and Greek with respect to the use of conjunctive cohesive devices. It examines the use of adversative, causal and temporal cohesive devices through contrastive analysis of samples of news reporting translational data. The goal is tracing differences in the treatment of conjunctive cohesive devices that ensure appropriateness in a target discourse. The ideological significance attributed to these linguistic preferences is expected to enhance awareness of the range of potential differences between language pairs and to broaden translator-trainees' perspective as to what might be wrong with seemingly appropriate versions of target texts, in translation assessment.

Language variation in translation studies is considered in relation to specific genres. This is because there are generic conventions or constraints operating to make discourses appropriate in particular cultures. The question is whether varying generic conventions leave space for conclusions about what might constitute a linguistic preference in a target language. The assumption is that even if linguistic preference is attributed to generic conventions, it is still a preference that may be part of a linguistic identity, let alone that certain types of linguistic preference may override generic difference.

Translational data, both in studies of cohesion and elsewhere, offer researchers the opportunity to examine phenomena in texts which assume similar, if not identical, threads of discourse. Differences in the use of linguistic phenomena may be made clearer in translational contexts, because source and target bodies of data, unlike monolingual corpora, do not simply tackle the same topic in a discourse segment, but may share same discourse intentions, lines of argument etc. Researchers examining linguistic phenomena across cultures, through independently created bodies of data (e.g. independently created texts about disasters or war incidents), may run greater risk, in that conclusions may be blurred by diversified approaches to topics that multiply reasons for variation.

3. Argumentation Formats in Persuasion Strategies

This section examines aspects of adversative (contrastive/concessive) connections between English and Greek press discourses. It highlights ideological meaning differences the use of the adversative connective networks conveys and the different social roles presupposed of the target readership, in the mind of text producer. A 20.300-word sample of Greek articles that appeared in high circulation Greek newspapers (*To Vima, I Kathimerini, Economikos Tachidromos*) has been contrasted to its source version from the English press (*Newsweek, Time, The Economist*). The English (source) articles have almost always been much longer as only parts of them are often transferred in the Greek TTs.

Adversative connectives are employed in argumentation. Preference for argumentation patterns may vary across cultures. Hatim (1991: 192-194) examines the pragmatics of argumentation in Arabic and claims that Arabic exhibits a preference towards one of the following argumentation type models, in contrast to English which prefers the other part of the pair. He distinguishes between 'through-argumentation' and 'counter-argumentation'. 'Through-argumentation' adopts the format

thesis to be supported, substantiation , conclusion

whereas 'counter argumentation' assumes the format

thesis to be opposed, opposition, substantiation of counter-claim, conclusion.

In the latter argumentation format, counter argumentation, two further sub-types may be distinguished. One sub-type is (a) the 'balance' format in which the text producer signals the contrastive shift between what may be viewed as a claim and a counter claim, either explicitly (by making use of a contrastive connective) or implicitly (no connective used). The other sub-type is (b) the 'lop-sided' format. The counter-proposition, in the present 'lop-sided' format, Mason claims, is anticipated in terms of a concessive clause or phrase (*while, although, despite* etc.). Hatim's research (1991) into the argumentative text-type in English and Arabic, from a translation perspective, points to a noticeable tendency in English towards counter-argumentation. By contrast, Modern Standard Arabic is claimed to favour 'through argumentation'. The following diagram summarizes the argumentative options referred to in Mason. These argumentative options can account for some of the preferences in the use of adversative connectives in English and Greek news reporting data. Issues to be addressed are how contrastive and concessive relations are signalled in English and Greek, from a translation perspective, what counter-argumentation sub-types English (source) and

Greek (target) versions favour or what the implications are of this preference in terms of the ideological assumptions created.

ARGUMENTATION FORMATS

<u>*THROUGH-argument*</u>	<u>*COUNTER-argument*</u>
(thesis cited to be argued through)	(thesis cited to be opposed)

<u>*balance argument*</u>   <u>*lop-sided argument*</u>

explicit/implicit

contrastive connections   concessive connections

but, however etc.   *although, while* etc.

(adapted from Hatim and Mason (1990: 158) & Hatim (1991)).

3.1. A Preference for Adversative Connection

The adversative connective network has been modified in the Greek TT in various ways. Cross-examination of the source and target versions has revealed the following statistics: out of the 129 ST shifts signalled in terms of an adversative connective (contrastive or concessive), 12 have been rendered implicitly in Greek. For the rest 117 ST explicit shifts, an explicit connective has been employed in Greek, but the contrastive or concessive gloss of the shift has not always been preserved in the TT:

(a) source contrastive connectives were occasionally turned into concessive ones in the TT,

(b) considerably fewer source concessive connectives were turned into contrastive connectives in the TT, and

(c) a considerable number of mostly contrastive (rather than concessive) connectives were added to the Greek target version making explicit source implicit shifts.

The Greek target version exhibits a stronger tendency for a contrastive/concessive network[1] than the source version does.

ST   ...In the former Yugoslav republics of Croatia and Serbia, where gypsies are at the bottom of a vicious ethnic pecking order, Roma from Bosnia are driven out of refugee camps by fellow victims of the civil war there...

('The Romani Enigma', *Newsweek*, March 1, 1993)

---

[1] 129 instances of counter-argumentation have been traced in English vs. 175 in Greek, while the target ratio of added vs. omitted connectives has been 58 vs. 12.

> TT ...In the former Yugoslav republics of Croatia and Serbia, gypsies are targeted for national purification, *while* Roma from Bosnia are driven out of refugee camps by the very victims of the civil war...
> ('The Romani Enigma', *To Vima*, February 28, 1993) [my translation]
>
> ...*Στις πρώην γιουγκοσλαβικές δημοκρατίες της Κροατίας και της Σερβίας, οι Τσιγγάνοι βρίσκονται στο στόχαστρο της «εθνοκάθαρσης», ενω στη Βοσνια τους εκδιώκουν από τα στρατόπεδα προσφύγων τα ίδια τα θύματα του εμφυλίου πολέμου...*
> ('*Το αίνιγμα των Τσιγγάνων', Το Βήμα, 28 Φεβρουαρίου 1993*)

Moreover,
(d) shifts made explicit in TT are often supported by additional contrastive elements (transferred or added) to the source version, or
(e) contrasts are actually *created* in the TT rather than simply enforced.

If 'x', 'y' and 'z' are propositions, the following formulas show types of modifications allowed in the TT, which enforce the contrastive cohesive network. The first part of the formulas describes ST structure, the latter part of the formulas describes TT structure (ST>TT). Greek connectives are transliterated in the formulas below; additional elements in the target part of the formula have been back translated into English:

- *But* has been rendered in terms of (a) coordinative and longer distance connectives, or (b) subordinatives in the Greek TT.

(a)	English STs:	x *but* y	Greek TTs:	x *omos* y
		x *but* y		x *pantos* y
		x *but* y		x *ostoso* y

| (b) | | x *but* y | | x *molonoti* y |
| | | x *but* y | | x *eno* y |

- *Though* has been rendered in terms of (c) coordinative and longer distance connectives or (d) subordinative ones

| (c) | English STs: | x *though* y | Greek TTs: | x *omos* y |
| | | x *though* y | | x *pantos* y |

(d)		x *though* y		x *molonoti* y
		x *though* y		x *an ke* y
		x *though* y		x *parolo pou* y

- Coordinative (e) or subordinative (f) connectives have been added to the Greek TT

(e) English STs: x. y   Greek TTs: x *alla* y
                   x. y   x *pantos* y
                   x. y   x *ostoso* y

(f)   x . y   x *an ke* y
                   x . y   x *eno* y
                   x . y   x *molonoti* y

- Contrastive shifts in the TT have been enforced in terms of additional elements, i.e. (g) contrastive adverbs such as *on the other hand, in contrast*, or (h) adjectives and expressions

(g) English STs: x *but* y   Greek TTs: *May* x *but, on the other hand,* y
                   x *but* y   x *eno, in contrast,* y

(h)   x. y   *The issue has a contradiction it it*: x *but* y

- Implicit contrastive shifts in the ST, which have been made explicit in terms of an explicit coordinative connective, are further enforced in terms of evaluative items such as *already* (ήδη), *unfortunately* (δυστυχώς), *even* (μάλιστα) etc.

(i) English STs: x... y. z Greek TTs: *Already* x ...*Pantos* y. *already* z

                   z. x *and* y   *Unfortunately* z. *Even* x, *while, at the same time,* y

                   x *but* y...z   x *omos* y. *Pantos* z.
                   x. y. z   x, *in contrast* y. *Pantos* z.

Source material is often restructured in TT, for information to be presented contrastively. The following example shows
(1) an instance of a contrast-creating intention manifested in the TT, in terms of a phrase such as *the strange thing is*, which makes explicit that the propositions to follow stand in a contrastive relation to each other, and

(2) an 'x...y. z > x ...*Pantos* y. z' formula enriched with two occurences of an evaluative item (*already*). Additions are italicized in the back translated TT.

Mason (1991) claims that Modern Standard Arabic tends to favour through-argumentation, in contrast to English, which tends to favour counter-argumentation. If languages were to be placed on a continuum relative to the degree of contrastiveness they tolerate, enforcing the contrastive/concessive network, in the Greek version of the present data, suggests that Greek would be placed closer to the argumentative end of the continuum, with English someplace in between:

←---Modern Standard Arabic ----English---- Greek---→

Fig. 1 summarizes rendition of explicit and implicit contrastive shifts in the Greek TT. It shows rendition of English ST adversative connectives in the Greek TT. The most popular adversative connective seems to be *omos* (*however/yet*, 71 instances) and second on the list is *alla* (*but*, 50 instances). The next most popular connective is *eno* (*while*, 22 instances) evidently because it can have both subordinative and coordinative functions (Kitis 2000). In the English ST, the most popular connective is *but* (78 instances). It will be claimed, in this book, that despite warnings about the misleading role of explicitation (Mason 1998), these numbers indicate some genuine preference for adversative junction on the Greek side, which is assumed to reveal appreciation for and respect for logical thinking.

ST   For centuries Wuhan's location has made it a key link in China's
      internal trade;...
      ...Last year Beijing authorized Wuhan to offer foreign investors
      the same package of tax breaks and other concessions they enjoy
      in the coastal provinces...
      ...The construction can barely keep pace with Wuhan ambitions.
      In 1990 work started on a new domestic airport budgeted at $58
      million...
      ('Woo Sees the Future in Wuhan', *Newsweek*, March 8, 1993)

TT   *The strange thing is that* Wuhan, *a rather dull city today*, has
      once and for many centuries been an important crossroads for
      China's internal trade...
      ...Wuhan has *already* got permission from Beijing to provide
      foreign investors with the same tax breaks and other concessions
      made in the coastal areas.
      ...*However*, the leaders' ambitions seem endless in Wuhan. In
      1990 the construction of a new domestic airport, budgeted at $58
      million, had *already* began...[my translation]
      ('Chinese people form the basis for a huge internal market', *To
      Vima*, March 7, 2003)

      *Το αξιοπερίεργο είναι ότι το Ουχάν, μια μάλλον καταθληπτική
      πόλη σήμερα, ήταν κάποτε και επί πολλούς αιώνες ένα σημαντικό
      σταυροδρόμι στο εσωτερικό εμπόριο της Κίνας...
      ...Το Ουχάν έχει ήδη λάβει από το Πεκίνο την άδεια να χορηγήσει
      σε ξένους επενδυτές τα ίδια φορολογικά και άλλα κίνητρα που
      παρέχονται στις παράκτιες επαρχίες...
      ...Πάντως, οι φιλοδοξίες των ιθυνόντων του Ουχάν φαίνεται να
      είναι ατελείωτες. Το 1990 είχε ήδη αρχίσει η κατασκευή ενός
      νέου αεροδρομίου για γειτονικές πτήσεις, προϋπολογισμού 58
      εκατ. δολαρίων...
      ('Οι Κινέζοι δημιουργούν υποδομή μιάς τεράστιας εσωτερικής
      αγοράς', Το Βήμα, 7 Μαρτίου 2003)*

Fig.1. Instances of transferred and added contrastive and concessive connectives in the Greek (target) version of a 20.300-word sample of news reporting material.

ADVERSATIVE CONNECTIVES IN A SAMPLE OF GREEK NEWS TTs

	T R A N S F E R R E D							ADDED
	however	yet	but	though	although	while	despite	
(however/yet)								
Omos	4	3	33	2	2	4	-	23
Ostoso	-	-	3	-	-	-	-	3
Pantos	-	-	1	1	-	-	-	8
(but)								
Alla	-	1	38	-	-	1	-	10
(although)								
An ke	-	-	-	3	1	-	1	1
Parolo pou	-	-	-	1	-	-	-	-
Molonoti	-	-	1	2	1	-	-	1
(while)	-	-	2	-	-	8	-	12
Eno[2]	-	-	-	1	-	-	2	-
*(despite)*Para								

3.2. A Preference for Counter-Argumentation Subtypes

Another question has been what the preference might be with respect to the ratio between balance and lop-sided argumentative formats in the two versions of the data. Statistics indicate that about 25% of the English lop-sided formats have been 'balancized' in Greek (see top shaded area in Fig 1), whereas only about 4% of the balance formats have been turned into lop-sided ones (bottom shaded area in Fig. 1). Greek shows a clear preference for balance formats. This tendency is enforced even further by added Greek connectives (44 added balance format connectives vs. 14 lop-sided ones). In English, the lop-sided shifts have been 1/4 of the total number of explicit

---

[2] Kitis (2000) maintains that there is a shift towards coordination in the traditionally subordinative connective *eno* in everyday speech.

adversative shifts, whereas in Greek the ratio is 1/5. Results are summarized in Fig.2.

Fig. 2. Counter-argumentation and subtypes in the ST and   TT news reporting sample.

	ENGLISH	GREEK
Instances of explicit counter-argumentation in the two versions	129	177
Ratio of lop-sided formats vs. explicit counter-argumentation formats	1/4	1/5

The preference in the Greek version for explicit counter-argumentation formats may be a realization of a general tendency in translation, namely explicitation. Explicitation relates to the intention of the communicative translator to 'explain' (Newmark, 1988: 48) things for the readership. Translators make the text easily 'digestible' in the TT context, by making contrastive relations explicit.

3.3. Distinct Readership Profile

My intention here is to claim that apart from the suggestion that the preference for counter-argumentation, in the target data, is a mere instantiation of a general explicitation process, it is meaningful in that it constitutes part of target linguistic identity. The level of evaluativeness in a text and the way the connective cohesive network has been constructed is claimed to relate to the character of a social or cultural group. Theories of text and context in ancient Arabic rhetoric suggest that texts reflect what text producers assume of readerships/ audiences. In examining argumentation formulas in Arabic, Hatim (1991: 196) claims that in ancient Arabic rhetoric there may be three possible contexts distinguished, in terms of
- the assumed state of the receiver, i.e. in terms of the receivers' preparedness to accept the propositions put forward, and
- the degree of evaluativeness the producer uses in the text.
The three possible contexts are:
   a. a context in which the receiver is a denier. Utterances, in this case, *must* be made maximally evaluative. The degree of evaluativeness depends on the degree of denial assumed or displayed,

b.   a context in which the receiver is uncertain or hesitant. In this context, evaluative items *may* (rather than *must*) be used, and

c.   a context in which the receiver is assumed to be open-minded. Utterances, in this context, *must not* be made evaluative.

Degrees of evaluativeness are associated to graded values on a scale from denial to open-endedness. A parallel may be drawn here: as degrees, of evaluativeness signal a particular state of receiver, varying degrees in the contrast-creating intention may be assumed to reflect a differentiation in the ideological stance presupposed of the reader in the news reporting context. The claim is that making source implicit shifts explicit, in a target version, presupposes that translators are aware that they are addressing readers who

- are more willing to take up the role of a denier,
- are used to perceiving the world in terms of contrasts, which they are expected to decode and process, and
- appreciate or are fascinated by tracing logical sequencing and contrasts in discourses.

This contrastive view of reality is not unique to Greek news reporting. In investigating ideology and power in press and TV news, Hartley and Montgomery (1985) argue that media journalism often operates with an oppositional view of the world. Events are constructed in terms of binary oppositions. Eco (1981) has claimed that popular discourses may resolve around fundamental oppositions.

There are items in discourse which are particularly sensitive carriers of ideological meaning. As suggested in Halliday (1978/1990), Kress (1989) and Dendrinos (1992), textual devices are among the elements which are ideologically loaded and which can construct a very different reality, if used differently. In determining the set of features in which language may be ideologically invested, Fairclough (1989) refers to cohesive devices, lexical meanings, presuppositions, implicatures and metaphors. Furthermore, Halliday (1978/1990: 144) claims that there are certain second-order social roles which come into being through language. They relate to variation on the tenor level and are differences in the selection of certain interpersonal options in the system of intensity, evaluation etc. One such social role is that of a contradicter, as determined by role relationships in the situation and reflected in discourse structure preferences.

It is assumed that the present target version displays a richer contrastive-concessive network, because the producer addresses people who seem to be willing to take up denier and contradicter roles more openly. The claim that target receivers are assumed to be contradicters is supported by additional linguistic elements in the target version, which relate to the systems of intensity and evaluation. The trait is not unique to Greek news reporting. EU parallel texts display this contrast-creating intention in the Greek version of the data, in this volume. The reflection of contrast-creating intention in the news reporting genre seems to be a two-way process: it both mirrors the type of readership addressed (contradicters) *and* constructs target reader positions, thus, enforcing ideology through language.

Fig. 1 shows that there is a preference for balance argumentation rather than lop-sided one. In the present data, 25% of the lopsided formats were balancized vs. 4% of the balance formats which were turned into lop-sided ones. No matter the semantic/pragmatic differences between coordinative and subordinative connectives, the preference for balance formats may be attributed to translator intention to maintain an unexpectedness effect which the balance format creates, as opposed to the lop-sided format (concession: *although*, *while* etc.). By contrast, in *although x, y* formulas, when the subordinate clause precedes the main clause, the reader is actually 'warned' that an opposition is to follow and the unexpectedness effect is cancelled.

Concern for unexpectedness has also been encountered in the Greek target version of E>G literary translation. For instance, a number of *suddenly* adverbs have occasionally been added in the Greek TT to enforce unexpectedness effects in narratives (Sidiropoulou 2003). Enforcing unexpectedness implies a suspense-creating intention which can be assumed to be a manifestation of an interpersonal, rather than transactional, approach in interaction. Interpersonal approaches to interaction are often claimed to be preferred in Greek rather than in English (Sifianou 1992, Sidiropoulou 1994).

Research on source and target versions of texts can support claims made in monolingual linguistic research, as suggested above, but it may also point to quantitative research directions. The present data shows a preference for the *omos* (*however*) subordinative connective, rather than the *alla* (*but*) one. The 72 instances of the source *but* connections have been rendered in terms of 33 instances of *omos* vs. 38 instances of *alla*. If it is taken into consideration that *omos* does not allow phrasal connection and that the ratio of added connectives in the Greek data has been 23 instances of *omos* vs. 10 instances of *alla*, the preference for *omos* in the news reporting genre is indisputable, in contrast to English.

Contrasting source and target versions of texts in translation may thus reveal intercultural preference in the construction of discourses to be taken into account in linguistic research on identities. Even if linguistic conclusions from target versions of texts are partly distorted because of the explicitation tendency in translation, the fact that there are specific items which are systematically mis/preferred reveals their crucial or insignificant contribution to constituting part of the target identity.

Mason has identified recognisable tendencies in the construction of French news discourse. In examining the use of discourse connectives and markedness in English-French news reporting data, he claims that ellipsis of junction "is sufficiently frequent in French for it to be a recognisable text strategy". The markedness of the structure seems normal in French, Mason claims, but in the translation into English there is a tendency for translators to restore explicit junction (1998: 172).

If languages were to be placed on a continuum with respect to the degree of junction ellipsis they allow in discourses, English, French and Greek would be ordered as follows:

ESTABLISHED PATTERNS OF ADVERSATIVE DISCOURSE CONNECTION

junction				explicit
ellipsis	FRENCH	ENGLISH	GREEK	junction

----------------------|----------------------|----------------------|----------------------|----------------------

Mason (ibid: 175) refers to Blum-Kulka [1986: 19] and the explicitation hypothesis which weakens the reliability of translational data in providing evidence for differences between language systems. The claim is that "the rise in the level of cohesive explicitness" in the TT is regardless of "the increase traceable to differences between the two cultures and textual systems involved". However, Mason claims that instances of junction ellipsis are far fewer in the F>E translation direction, than otherwise.

In the literature/theatre part of this book, the issue of connectivity is further explored in samples of E>G and G>E data. The suggestion is that, no matter the relative diversity in translator behaviour, there are clearly discernible tendencies in message construction that can enlighten the study of linguistic identities.

SUMMARY OF 3 (I)
The section examined adversative connectives in a 20.300-word sample of target versions of articles that appeared in Greek press. Preferred options in TT, as manifested through juxtaposition of source and target versions of texts, are claimed to reveal aspects of linguistic identities in the source and target environments, thus contributing to studies of intercultural variation. The stronger preference in Greek for one of the two argumentation formats referred to in Hatim (1991) and the social roles it implies contrastively reveal aspects of source and target preferences in the construction of discourses, that may be part of a linguistic identity. The preference for one of the target coordinative (balance) connectives, as opposed to source preferences, supports conclusions drawn in (target) monolingual research. Contrastive analysis of source and target versions of data is claimed to point to research directions that contribute to the study of linguistic identities through translation.

4. Reasoning in Translating Persuasion

Kinneavy (1990: 200) claims that the most obvious function of journalism is to produce a news story, a factual report. Research on journalistic rhetoric assumes that the referent, 'the news', is a recognisable, unambiguous entity. However, researchers have devoted much of their effort in presenting and interpreting the news items. A lot of attention has been directed to the notion of subjectivity and the relation of journalists to the facts. The notion of subjectivity, in the news, points to persuasive strategies preferred in discourses and the verbal techniques human beings can be manipulated by. Rhetoricians describe strategies of topic development in the four types of discourse: exposition, argumentation, description, narration. Corbett (1965/1971/ 1990: 97) identifies four "common topics" in discourse. These are "definition", "comparison", "relationship", "circumstance" and "testimony". Transferring information to readerships involves considerations about what the nature of things might be (definition), likeness and differences (comparison), reasons for consequences (relationship), feasibility of action (circumstance) and evidence (testimony). Persuasive strategies in news reporting often involve manipulation of these devices, in order for the strategies to become maximally effective. Because intercultural difference in the persuasion strategies preferred in particular languages is likely to leave unintended traces of foreignness in target persuasive discourses, press translators often interfere with discourse organisation to cater for intercultural preference and enhance appropriateness in target discourses. Juxtaposition of source and target versions of press items may thus allow for observations that point to aspects of intercultural difference to be considered in linguistic research.

The present section explores the potential of identifying and studying intercultural differences between English ST and Greek TT, with reference to one of the above 'common topics' in strategies of topic development, namely, relationship. "Relationship" involves types of reasoning techniques like "cause-and-effect", "antecedent-consequent", "contraries" and "contradictories" (ibid: 111-119).

STRATEGIES OF TOPIC DEVELOPMENT (Kinneavy 1990)
Definition   Comparison   Relationship   Circumstance   Testimony
↓

| Cause-and-effect |
| Antecedent-consequent |
| Contraries |
| Contradictories |

Contraries and contradictories have been focused upon in the previous section under adversative connection. The claim has been that there are different social roles assumed of target readers, namely, those of contradicters, and that the target discourse presupposed a different ideological stance, a stronger oppositional view of the world. The following section explores the cause-and-effect type of the "Relationship" strategy of topic development.

4.1. Elaborating on Causal Connection

The present section focuses on the how cause-and-effect relations have been manipulated in news reporting material, in translation, and the significance these modifications may have for enhancing awareness of intercultural difference between languages. The distinction between deductive and inductive meaning has not been tackled in this study, because variation is minimal and cannot be theoretically significant. Besides, Scollon (1993: 56) argues that the choice of either pattern in persuasion is not a matter of cultural tradition. It rather depends upon the speaker's need to clarify the relationship with the hearer. Aristotle has shown (ibid: 57) that a deductive pattern of topic introduction is to be preferred in situations in which the relationships between interlocutors can be taken for granted, whereas an inductive pattern is most effective in situations where consideration should be given to the relationships between interlocutors. Variation in terms of deduction or induction is not immediately relevant for the purposes of the present research.

Relevant to this study is the preference for creating causal links in the TT out of pieces of content scattered all over the ST. In addition, there is a tendency for making a number of implicit source causal connections explicit, in the TT. Translators are shown to be inventing a result or a cause, through interpretation of source information. The modifications in the target Greek news reporting sample may be summarised as follows:

The 12.000-word sample of the present TT indicates that

- explicit source cause-and-effect relationships are almost always transferred intact in the TT. Translators are not prepared to 'miss' any of the causal relations, unless there is some local constraint disallowing their use.
- Implicit source causal relations are made explicit in the Greek TT, in terms of making explicit the result ((a) below) or the cause part ((b) below) of the connection.

(a)   English STs: x. y   Greek TTs: x. *So* y
                        x. y   x *so that* y
                        x. y   x *with the result that* y
                        x, *and* y   x. y *was the consequence*

(b)   x. y   y. *The reason is* x
                        y. x   y *because* x
                        y. x   y *since* x
                        y, x   y *given that* x

- Explicitation becomes fairly strong at points. When source information is omitted (due to such factors as space limitations, renegotiation of the maxims of quantity and relevance), text restructuring often involves causal constructions. Information may be added to the TT in order to contribute to creating some causal formula. If the cause (x) or the result (y) of the assumed causal connection are not present in the ST, translators may invent some cause or result by manipulating pragmatic/cognitive aspects of ST fragments. In order to set up intended arguments, translators may exploit pieces of ST information to arrive at some inference that would facilitate processing in TT. For instance *x* or *y*

x: [having bought a second and third soccer team]
y: [white–collar crime in post-communist countries from China to Russia}

may be assumed to imply x′ or y′

x′: [having attempted an infinite number of money laundering tricks]
y′: [organised crime has no local boundaries]

Formulas, in this case, take the form

(c)   English STs: y. x   Greek TTs: y *since* x′
                        as x, *so* y   *given* x, y′

- There are instances in which both propositions *x* and *y* are a result of translators' inference drawing mechanism, as in (d)

(d)   English ST: z. But y. x   Greek TT: z. However y′ *given* x′

The following example makes the reason part of the causal connection explicit and shows instances of content renegotiation and inferencing. It also presents a *but>however [+ evaluation]* modification which was discussed in the previous section. The formula is

z. *But* y. x > z. *Unfortunately however,* y′ *given* x′. x

x′ and y′ stand for inferences derived from x and y, respectively.

ST   ...Boris Yeltsin insists that only Moscow should keep the peace for the 'near abroad', the term Russians use for the republics of the old Soviet Union. [] But judging from the debacle in Georgia, neither Yeltsin's government nor the decaying and demoralized Russian Army is up to the job. Equipment is in disrepair. Armories are so vulnerable to attack and theft that many soldiers have to be detached from other duties simply to guard them...
('Russia's Army – Tiger or Teddy Bear?', *Newsweek*, October 31, 1993)

TT   ...Boris Yeltsin believes that only Russia can impose peace on what he calls 'near abroad', that is, the republics of the old Soviet Union *that now are independent countries. Unfortunately, however, disposition is not enough:* [y′: *the mission is impossible*] *given* [x′: the state of the Russian Armed Forces]. Russian Army is in disrepair. The army is demoralised and the equipment almost useless. Armories are so vulnerable that many soldiers have to be detached from other duties for guards to be enforced. [my translation]
('Russian Army – Tiger or Teddy Bear?', *To Vima*, October 31, 1993)

....Ο Μπορις Γιέλτσιν πιστεύει ότι μόνο η Ρωσία είναι αρμόδια να επιβάλει την ειρήνη σε αυτό που ονομάζει 'εγγύς εξωτερικό', δηλαδή, τις πρώην σοβιετικές δημοκρατίες που είναι σήμερα ανεξάρτητα κράτη. Δυστυχώς όμως οι προθέσεις δεν αρκούν: η αποστολή είναι ανέφικτη με δεδομένη την κατάσταση των ρωσικών ενόπλων δυνάμεων. Ο ρωσικός στρατός βρίσκεται στα πρόθυρα διάλυσης. Ηθικό πεσμένο και υλικό σχεδόν άχρηστο. Οι αποθήκες του στρατού είναι τόσο τρωτές ώστε πολλοί στρατιώτες αποσπώνται από άλλες υπηρεσίες για να ενισχυθούν οι φρουρές των οπλοστασίων.
('Ρωσικός Στρατός – Τίγρης ή αρκουδάκι;', Το Βήμα, 31 Οκτωβρίου 1993)

The most common types of added cause-and-effect connectives in the data are: a rather formal version of *because* (*dioti*/διότι, 24,4%), *since* (*afou*/αφου, 9,75%), *given that* (*dedomenou oti*/δεδομένου ότι, 9.75%), *because of* (*logo*/λόγω, 5%), *so* (*etsi*/έτσι, 12%), *with the result that* (*me apotelesma na/με αποτέλεσμα να*, 9,75%), and *so..that* (*toso..oste/ τόσο ώστε*, 5%). The rest c. 25% of the target cause-and-effect markers is constructions that may be interpreted causally, *and* connectives signalling cause-and-effect relations, etc. The density of the target cause-and-effect cohesive network is enforced by an average of 3 instances per article. The following number pairs, in Fig. 3, show number of words per target article vs. number of instances of added connectives:

Fig. 3. Number of words per target news item vs. instances of added cause-and-effect connectives

600 /3	720 /2	888 /3	204 /1
406 /3	896 /2	555 /2	1160 /2
1100 /5	1065 /5	545 /2	630 /2
600 /3	628 /3	576 /1	1135 /2

Translators consider cause-and-effect connectives a cohesive device which contributes to making TT appropriate and thus make every effort in signalling them.

Research on the structure of textual rhetoric, in non-translated narrative Greek texts, points to the use of explicit devices ("semantically rich forms", Kostouli (1992: 381) at points of discontinuity. Implicit relations and evaluation were observed at points of continuity and were signalled in terms of "semantically minimal forms". Although evidence mostly concerns temporal markers, it raises the question where in the rhetorical structure of the news data the translator tends to interfere with making causal relations explicit. In the present data, translator intervention is not random; most of the points the interference occurs at relate to some kind of evaluation or estimation. ST evaluation or estimation seems to trigger interference in the TT which makes causal cohesive devices explicit.

ST	...it is no use counting on organized Christianity to combat this spread of witchcraft. [] This is organized Christianity... ('Every witch way to the Goddess', *Sunday Telegraph*, October 17, 1993).

> TT   ...*it is no use* for someone to hope that Christianity can combat this new movement of witchcraft. *The reason is that* this movement *precisely* originates from US Christianity...[my translation]
> ('Modern "witches"', *Messimvrini*, October 30, 1993)
>
> ...*είναι μάταιο να ελπίζει κανείς ότι η χριστιανοσύνη μπορεί να καταπολεμήσει αυτή την νέα κίνηση υπέρ της μαγείας. Ο λόγος είναι ότι η κίνηση προέρχεται ακριβώς μέσα από τους κόλπους του χριστιανισμού των ΗΠΑ.*
> *('Οι σύγχρονες «μάγισσες»', Μεσημβρινή, 30 Οκτωβρίου 1993)*

4.2. Reasoning and Responsibility for Specifying Discourse Connection

The present target data show that in van Dijk's (1985) superstructure schema of news discourse, translator intervention relates to the 'comments' part of the schema.

Greek is a language in which positively polite patterns prevail (Sifianou 1992) and reason giving is one of them (Levinson 1978/1987). The present news data indicates some overt cultural/linguistic interest in reasoning, in the target context. It is in accordance with the social roles of contradicters or deniers attributed to Greek readers in the previous section. The reader is assumed to be reluctant to accept the validity of arguments, at least at points of estimation or evaluation, and, thus, translators tend to make explicit the parts of discourse that will contribute to reasoning, in order to facilitate persuasion.

                    NEWS DISCOURSE
          SUMMARY --------------------NEWS STORY
        Headline Lead   EPISODE-------------COMMENT
                          Events Consequences   Expectation Evaluation
                                Relations

(The superstructure schema of news discourse, adapted from van Dijk (1985: 86)

The tendency of the translator to interfere with adversative and causal connection signals a preference for a different persuasion strategy. Robin Lakoff (1990:216) claims that persuasion strategy is not the same everywhere and that when members of two cultures want to persuade an audience to the same decision, they might use different means to achieve that end. Besides, the way abstract relations are signalled in discourses is a point of cross-cultural variation. This has been claimed in Tytler (1992: 15) who examined discourse structure and the specification of relations in two highly constrained parallel texts, one produced by a native speaker of English and another one by a native speaker of Korean. Discourses differed in the degree of speaker/listener responsibility for specifying connections between ideas. American English have developed distinct norms or degrees of expected explicitness from Korean: American English is represented as lying at the extreme end of *speaker* responsibility for specifying discourse relations between ideas. Languages like Japanese, Chinese, Athapaskan are represented as lying at the opposite end of the continuum, assigning more responsibility for specifying discourse relations to the *listener*.

If the difference between English and Greek in signalling cause-and-effect relations in the present data was to be shown along the same axis, the continuum would have to be extended towards the opposite end to include Greek, leaving English in the middle.

RESPONSIBILITY FOR SPECIFYING DISCOURSE CONNECTIONS ON SPEAKER:

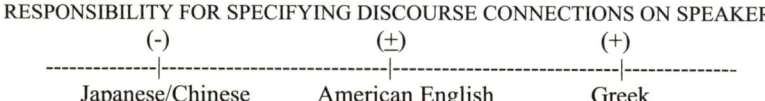

```
        (-)                      (±)                       (+)
-------------|----------------------------|----------------------------|-------------
  Japanese/Chinese        American English              Greek
```

Target production in the news reporting genre also points to a preference with respect to whether causal information is to be presented as old or new (Halliday 1978). Absence of cause-and-effect connectives in the source version leaves this aspect of meaning unspecified. Distinctions between given and new information in discourses carry some ideological significance. Information presented as given in discourse is assumed to be non-negotiable and, thus, issues to be presented as non-negotiable in political discourse or advertising, are usually conveyed through items which have that potential.

The management of given vs. new information is an active constraint on causal link usage. Abraham (1991: 335) claims that *because* tends to encode new information, whereas *because of* tends to encode given information. The relative infrequency of *because of*, she claims, is a consequence of the interlocutors' cautious assessment of the new/given character of what is presented as causal information. In Greek, the equivalent connective to *since* (*afou/αφου*), presupposes some kind of consensus that x is a unique and obvious cause for y (Sidiropoulou, 1989: 292)

In the present target news data, the ratio between added causal connectives which assume givenness to those which carry new information is comparable. The three most common added causal connectives which assume givenness in TT, *due to* (*logo/λόγω*), *given that* (*dedomenou oti/δεδομένου ότι*) and *since* (*afou/αφου*), are as many as the added ones which presuppose new causes (24,5% vs. 24,4%). Compared to English where the presence of causals which assume givenness is "relatively infrequent" (Abraham, ibid), the degree of givenness assumed through added causal connectives in the Greek TT is quite strong. Translators have preferred to assume giveness, in reason giving, in an attempt to presuppose shared conviction and thus make argumentation more convincing.

Ensuring givenness seems to be indispensable in persuasion strategies developed in discourses which address a wide Greek readership. The preference for downgrading causal knowledge as guaranteed and given will be paralleled to a tendency for adverbializing in the Greek version of the EU material, in the following sections.

The next section examines rendition of temporal adverbials in English STs and Greek TTs in the press, with a view to revealing culture-specific preferences in temporal conceptualizations of reality that can constitute part of a linguistic and cultural identity.

SUMMARY OF 4 (I)
This section examined rendition of cause-and-effect relations in Greek target versions of news discourses. On the one hand, results have coincided with evidence from monolingual research on Greek and contrastive studies between English-Greek (reason-giving tendency). On the other, juxtaposition of source and target versions has pointed to degrees of preference with respect to a particular tendency (opting for givenness in reasons for consequences).

Even though the strength of individual linguistic tendencies may somehow be distorted because of translators' mediating effort, differences still reveal the direction (or even the extent) to which intercultural preference may potentially point to. The assumption is that contrasting source and target versions of texts can contribute fairly safe insights into drawing conclusions about linguistic identities.

5. Time across Cultures

Although the concept of time is shared among cultures, there are specific attitudes towards it (Khairoullin 1993). Time is a universal concept in that time units exist independently of the grammar of any particular language (Quirk *et al*, 1972: 84). Reference to these extra-linguistic realities is made through the language specific categories of tense (event location in time), aspect (temporal event distribution) and certain adverbials (time indicators).

   The way temporal specification is conceptualized varies cross-culturally. A contrastive lexical semantic analysis may indicate that the manner the 24-hour period of the day is divided up into spans may be fuzzy and vague or differ cross-culturally. Moreover, tense and aspect systems vary considerably across languages and therefore time adverbials are expected to conform to language-specific constraints creating problems of equivalence in translation.

   In discourse, temporal adverbials may function as topic-shift markers or other discourse organizers (Brown and Yule, 1983: 96). Because cross-cultural preferences in discourse organization vary across cultures, temporal adverbials may need to conform to language-specific constraints operating at discourse level. For instance, temporal clauses in narrative texts, originally written in Modern Greek, have been argued to function as essential guideposts that regulate the flow of information within the text (Kostouli, 1989: 350). Empirical examination of these narrative texts showed regularities in the use of temporal clauses which were accounted for by particular principles.

   In translation, difference in the treatment of temporal adverbial constituents across languages may reveal linguistic preferences in the use of this grammatical category. Although observation of translated material has been doubted as to whether is allows safe conclusions about original production, the present section intends to show that it does provide some basis for observation in this direction. One reason for this is that genre membership, similarity of content and other factors influencing linguistic production are more easily controlled in translation and thus irrelevant variation may be eliminated. Awareness of these differences evidently makes translators aware of the type of difference they are entitled to, and assist with organizing the structure of target discourses, effectively.

5.1. An Appropriate Temporal Structure through Time Adverbials

   An 18.000-word sample of 1992-1995 Greek news material translated from the English press has been contrasted to its source version with respect to the way temporal adverbial constituents are rendered in the target version. The modifications introduced in the target text are assumed to be conforming to translators' or editors' insights about what the appropriate temporal structure might be in the target situation. They are, thus, assumed to be dictated by professional routines which are intended to ensure communicative equivalence and make the text appealing to Greek readerships.

1.038 source-and-target pairs of time expressions were encountered in the present data. About two thirds (i.e. 678) of the source time expressions were transferred intact, whereas a little more than one third of the total number of the time expressions (i.e. 360) appeared modified in the target version, in various ways. The differences between the translated Greek news material and the English source version reveal two varying tendencies with respect to time specification in this genre. On the one hand, modifications introduced in the target version reveal an intensification intention of the translator conveying a particular ideological force. On the other, a relative tendency for future orientation is observed in Greek, as opposed to a clear preference for past time reference in English. Ideological perspectives are, thus, reflected in the way time is treated in the news reporting genre.

Following Fowler (1996), it is assumed that there is not necessarily any true reality which can be unveiled by critical practice, but simply relatively *varying representations*, which I would like to highlight for the purposes of the present research.

A point of variation in the rendition of time expressions is that journalist-translators tend to eliminate elements indicating time approximation and accuracy: English ST expressions such as *almost* overnight are likely to be rendered as Greek TT *overnight*, and English ST *less than* three months as Greek TT *three months*.

ST   Most important, does Mexican President Ernesto Zedillo Ponce de Leon, *less than* three months into his six-year term, have a consistent strategy for dealing with political and financial crises...?
('Riding Off in All Directions', *Time*, February 27, 1995)

TT   Most important, does Mexican President Ernesto Zedillo, [] *three months* after the election, have a consistent strategy for facing the political and financial crisis...? [my translation] ('Mexico: What is the case with Zapatistas and Zendillo?', *I Kathimerini*, February 26, 1995)

Και, το σπουδαιότερο, ο Μεξικανός πρόεδρος Ερνέστο Σεντίλιο, τρεις μήνες μετά την εκλογή του, έχει άραγε κάποια συνεπή στρατηγική για να αντιμετωπίσει την πολιτική και οικονομική κρίση...; ('Μεξικό: τί γίνεται με τους Ζαπατίστας και τον Σεντίλιο;', Η Καθημερινή, 26.2.95)

The opposite phenomenon, instances of temporal specification relativized in the Greek version (e.g. *a century ago* > *about a century ago*), is extremely rare in the data.

The tendency for eliminating time approximation or additional temporal specifications, in favour of more general time indicators in Greek, points to the stronger oppositional view of reality promoted in Greek, as shown above. Accuracy in time specification is assumed to be a rather marginal issue, irrelevant to the ideological message intended. Grice's maxim of relevance is being renegotiated in the new context. Drawing readers' attention on such 'unimportant' temporal details or using up readers' processing effort would not only be useless but also contrary to promoting the view of a world constructed in terms of strong binary oppositions.

This relative lack of accuracy in time specification, may be paralleled to an interpersonal involvement between speakers and audience, observed in the study of Greek and American narratives (Tannen, 1984: 27-28). While Greeks had an interpersonal attitude when engaged in telling what happened in a film, Americans seemed to be performing a memory task, echoing some more transactional attitude. Greeks used details to support an interpretation of the message in the films and tended to judge the behaviour of characters. A similar difference has been observed elsewhere in contrastive studies. Greek researchers have been shown to adopt an interactional attitude in abstract writing, whereas researchers from English-speaking countries exhibited a more transactional behaviour in organizing and presenting information in their abstracts (Sidiropoulou 1995c).

Despite the fact that lack of accuracy in time specification is favoured, to some extent, in the Greek version of the data, there is another feature which might suggest concern for detail. In contrast to the English version, which favours relatively longer time units when referring to time periods, the Greek version shows a preference for shorter time spans when referring to the same periods of time. English time expressions like *last week, over the past fortnight, for more than a decade* etc. are rendered in Greek as follows:

English STs:	Greek TTs:
Last week, x	*Some days ago*, x
Over the past fortnight, x	*In the last weeks*, x
For more than a decade, x	*About 10 years ago*, x

The following example shows an instance of the shorter-time-span preference. The next one shows the opposite phenomenon and is an exception to the rule: whenever instances of longer or more general time units appear in Greek, they always contribute to a local intention in the text. A more general time unit is employed in the second example, because translator wishes to imply that a ten day period is too much time for someone to wait until a coherent explanation of a massacre emerges.

ST   Ruby did make a flurry of calls to his underworld contacts *in the months* before the Kennedy assassination...
('I wanted to be a hero', *Newsweek*, November 22, 1993)

TT   The relationships of Ruby with Cuba and Mafia were suspect and indeed he had made a lot of phone calls *in the weeks* that preceded the assassination. [my translation]
('Jack Ruby "I wanted to be a Hero"', *To Vima*, November 21, 1993)

Οι σχέσεις του Ρούμπι με την Κούβα και τη Μαφία ήταν ύποπτες και πράγματι έκανε πάρα πολλά τηλεφωνήματα τις εβδομάδες που προηγήθηκαν της δολοφονίας...
('Τζάκ Ρούμπι «Ήθελα να γίνω ήρωας»', To Βήμα, 21.11.93)

ST   It took *ten days* for a coherent explanation of the massacre to emerge... ('Rain-Forest Genocide', *Time*, September 6, 1993)

TT   It took a *ten-day-period*, before researchers had managed to provide a satisfactory explanation for the atrocious event...[my translation]
('Indians are being murdered', *I Kathimerini*, September 5, 1993)

Χρειάστηκε να περάσει ένα δεκαήμερο, προτού οι ερευνητές μπορέσουν να δώσουν ικανοποιητική ερμηνεία για το αποτρόπαιο γεγονός...
('Δολοφονούν τους Ινδιάνους', Η Καθημερινή, 5.9.93)

This concern for detailed accounts of time periods, in the Greek version, contributes to a dramatic effect intended by translators, in accordance with the prevailing ideological message described earlier, that we live in a world constructed in terms of strong oppositions.

A number of intensifying modifications has also been allowed in the Greek version, which contribute to the intended dramatic effect. Temporal conjunctions like *when* or *while* are rendered in terms of intensifying target items, although there are readily available target equivalent items: English ST *when* may be rendered as Greek TT *the moment that* (τη στιγμή κατα την οποία, see following example), or English ST *when* may be rendered as Greek TT *and suddenly* (και ξαφνικά).

Moreover, temporal adverbials are intensified in the target version although there IS a readily available target language equivalent: they are rendered in terms of adverbials showing higher frequency and immediacy

---

ST   *When* one of those single-celled embryos divided into two cells, ...,
        the scientists *quickly* separated the cells.
        ('Cloning:Where Do We Draw the Line?', *Time*, October 8, 1993)

TT   *The moment that* one of those single-celled embryos divided into two
        cells, ..., the scientists *immediately* separated the cells, creating two
        different embryos with the same genetic information[my translation]
        ('An experiment that...shook the World', *I Kathimerini*, November
        14, 1993)
        *Τη στιγμή κατα την οποία ένα απ' αυτά τα μονοκύτταρα έμβρυα
        διαιρέθηκε σε δύο κύτταρα, ..., οι επιστήμονες διαχώρησαν αμέσως
        τα κύτταρα, δημιουργώντας δύο διαφορετικά έμβρυα με την ίδια
        γενετική πληροφορία. ('Ένα πείραμα που...κλόνισε τον κόσμο', Η
        Καθημερινή, 14. 11.93)*

English STs:	*Quickly*	Greek TTs:	*Immediately*
	Eventually		*Soon*
	Sometimes		*Often*
	For weeks		*For many weeks*

Occasionally, the pragmatic reading of English ST dates is made transparent in the Greek TT:

English STs:	*on Oct. 25*	Greek TTs:	*recently*
	last month		*Soon*
	On September 10th		*Soon...*
	Nov. 26, 1963.		*just Nov. 26, 1963.*

The devices of intensification in the present target data, namely,
- raising the target evaluativeness level by making the reading of certain time expressions transparent,
- making use of shorter time units,
- replacing temporal connectives or time adverbials with others denoting higher frequency or immediacy,

create a dramatic effect which contributes to a different conceptualization of social reality constructed for the target reader, i.e. the stronger oppositional view of the world.
- Lack of accuracy in time specification

is attributed to an interpersonal involvement between translator and target readership, as opposed to a more transactional involvement observed in source version situations.

5.2. Hardening Soft News

The articles are 'feature articles' in the press, i.e. stories with background and personal opinion, by-lined by the author's name, soft news. Bell (1991) argues that for both newsworkers and researchers the boundaries between *soft* and *hard* (reports of accidents, conflicts, crimes, announcements, discoveries) news are unclear, and that journalists "spend much of their energy to find an angle which will present what is essentially soft news in hard news terms" (ibid:14). The differences between source and target texts seem to suggest that Greek translator-journalists are strongly concerned with hardening soft news.

A different social meaning was also promoted in the target version of English-Greek press news translation with respect to the treatment of quantities (Sidiropoulou 1998c). An examination of an 80.000-word translated press material revealed a number of systematic modifications which contributed to generating an *intensified* version of the presupposed –in the press– social/political conflict. These were *upgrading* modifications and *surface negation removal* types of interference which established differing identities, and presupposed different values and models, in the target version. On a par, *quantification adjustment* and *approximation elimination* modifications showed disregard for accuracy, in favour of highlighting ideologically significant events and processes. This disregard for accuracy in quantity presentation (which is also reflected in the time approximation elimination tendency observed in the time data, in this section) must have been very strong, because it occurred even in cases where it was contrary to the implied message. Eliminating details in quantity specification, even when they run 'contrary' to the intended message, can be viewed as a realization of the *interpersonal/ interactional* attitude that Greeks adopted in the film-story-narrating situation, as opposed to the more *transactional* attitude of the Americans who seemed to be performing a memory task (Tannen 1984).

There seems to be a negotiation between two conflicting translator intentions, namely, between

- adopting the appropriate interpersonal attitude in Greek (e.g. through eliminating details even when contrary to the intended message), and
- intensifying the presupposed –in the press– social/political conflict (e.g. through introduction of intensifying modifications),

which the translator will have to take into account. These conflicting intentions are probably an instance of a situation anticipated in Lee's (1992) account of the operation of ideology:

Given the way in which *perspective* is *mediated* through textual processes, it would appear that those who control the production of text *control* the operation of ideology.

It is important to recognize however, the extensive *social* and *generic constraints* that impinge on textual production – constraints which impose severe limitations on the power of the producer of text (ibid:107, emphasis added).

The former intention, above seems to be an instance of a social constraint having a limitation effect on the latter intention (i.e. the producer's intention to intensify the social/political conflict).

In what follows, attention is directed to a relative tendency for future orientation manifested through treatment of temporal adverbials in the Greek version of the data, as opposed to a clear preference for past time reference in English.

5.3. English and Greek Temporal Adverbials in News Items

Khairullin (1993: 247) has examined time reference in Russian and English, through Russian translations of 20th century English writers. He has claimed that English "tends to describe the future moment by referring to the past or present moment", whereas Russian exhibits a kind of future orientation in time reference. The future orientation preferred in Russian temporal reference, as opposed to the past-time orientation of English expressions, is illustrated in Khairullin (1993: 244) in terms of examples like the following:

English STs:	Russian TTs:
eleven-fifteen (11.15')	*a quarter of twelve*
late afternoon	*it was coming to the evening*

The tendency is observed not only in the description of time proper, but also in 'the referential classification of personal subjects'. Khairullin (1993) refers to the following examples to illustrate differences in the referential classification of personal subjects:

English STs:	Russian TTs:
He was forty-one years old	*to him was coming the forty second year*
When he reached the middle forties	*After forty-five years with him..*
The father of Andrew's fiancée	*The future father-in-law of Andrew*

In the present target version of the data, the modified expressions show that translators view time from a different perspective. Occasionally, there is a future orientation in the description of time, in the Greek version, which may be contrasted to some reluctance of the English to refer to the future. *Never before* has been rendered as *for the first time*, more than twice in the present data. Other modifications showing a future orientation in temporal reference involve modifications along the following formulas

English ST: *By 1981*, x   Greek TT: *In 1981*, x

                   x *were using* y   x *started receiving*[3] y

Although such instances are not numerous in the present data, the reverse phenomenon has not been encountered except once.

ST   His wife Barbara was shocked to see her husband burst into tears. She had *never* seen him cry *before...*
('The JFK Assassination: A nation of doubters', *Newsweek*, November 22, 1993)

TT   His wife Barbara was shocked to see *for the first time in her lifetime* her husband burst into tears...[my translation]
('Thirty Years Later: The Unknown File of the Keneddy Assassination', *To Vima*, November 21, 1993)

Η σύζυγός του Μπάρμπαρα έπαθε σόκ όταν είδε για πρώτη φορά στη ζωή της τον άντρα της να βάζει τα κλάματα...
('Τριάντα χρόνια μετά: Ο άγνωστος φάκελος της δολοφονίας του Τζον Κένεντυ', Το Βήμα, 21.11.93)

The preference for future orientation, in the present TT data, is enforced by instances of time points replaced, in the target version, by time expressions referring to beginning of time spans. This could be seen as a variant future orientation attitude, since the end of time spans is left unspecified and open to the future.

ST   *In* the euphoria of *1989 and 1990*, many people in Central and Eastern Europe hoped that a new group of rulers, untainted by communism, would emerge.
('Former communists – A phoenix phenomenon', *The Economist*, February 25, 1995)

---

[3] The transition from English ST *x were <u>using</u> y* to the Greek TT *x started <u>receiving</u> y* is justified on ideological grounds: the text fragment is about a politically weak country receiving guns from an economically powerful one. Rendition in Greek foregrounds the passive nature of x's contribution to the interaction, while the English text is neutral in this respect.

> TT   According to the euphoria that prevailed *after 1989*, many people in Central and Eastern Europe hoped that a new group of rulers would emerge, which would be untainted by communism. [my translation]
> ('Are the Former Communists Coming back?', *I Kathimerini*, February 26, 1995)
>
> *Κατα την ευφορία που επικράτησε μετά το 1989, πολλοί κάτοικοι της κεντρικής και της ανατολικής Ευρώπης ήλπιζαν οτι θα επικρατούσε μια νέα ηγετική ομάδα η οποία θα είναι αποκομμένη απο τον κομμουνισμό...*
> *('Επιστρέφουν οι πρώην κομμουνιστές', Η Καθημερινή, 26.2.95)*

The preference also reflected modifications along the following lines:

English STs:		Greek TTs:	
	x was assigned y *back in March*		*since March*, z has assigned x y
	In 1986, x did y		x having done y *since 1986...*

    Preference for beginning of time spans over time points reveals a dynamic vs. static approach to time, which may be further supported by a preference, in the Greek target version, for referring to processes rather than static events. It is as if Greeks are particularly sensitive to the fact that time flows and that events could be seen in relation to periods extending towards the future or future in the past

> ST   With Europe's nerves stretched to breaking point *before* France's Maastricht referendum on September 20th, Scandinavia's were the first to snap... ('Nordic currencies – In shock', *The Economist*, Sept. 12, 1992)
> TT   The nerves of Europeans are about to break *as* the French referendum on Maastricht on September 20th *is approaching*. They have already in the Scandinavian countries...[my translation]
> ('Currencies in Shock', *Economikos Tachidromos*, September 17, 1992)
>
> *Τα νεύρα των Ευρωπαίων κινδυνεύουν να σπάσουν καθώς πλησιάζει το γαλλικό δημοψήφισμα της 20ης Σεπτεμβρίου για το Μάαστριχτ. Εσπασαν ήδη στις Σκανδιναυικές χώρες... ('Σοκ στα Νομίσματα', Οικονομικός Ταχυδρόμος, 17.9.92)*

Similar types of modifications in the English-Greek translational context, may be observed along the following lines:

English ST: x *was* 52 (years old)   Greek TT: x *had reached* 52

              Just a few years ago, x   *And up to just a few years ago*, x

The future orientation tendency in time specification may be paralleled with some vagueness in specifying ends of periods, also observed in the Greek TT. English seem to be concerned with not exceeding time limits, whereas Greeks can either be relatively less precise about specifying ends of periods or specify them by treating them as been exceeded, which again suggests concern for the future.

ST   ...it is pressing ahead with preparations for a presidential election *before the end of this year*...
      ('Many loses, no victories in Algerian war', *Guardian*, February 17, 1995)

TT   ...Instead the military are planning presidential election *towards the end of the year*... [my translation]
      ('Algeria: Deadlock extended', *I Kathimerini*, February 18, 1995)

      Αντ'αυτού οι στρατιωτικοί προγραμματίζουν προεδρικές εκλογές για τα τέλη του έτους...
      ('Αλγερία: παράταση αδιεξόδου', Η Καθημερινή, 18.2.95)

Other modifications involve formulas like

English ST: *Before* the end of x   Greek TT: *up until* the end of x

              x ... did y *for at least 36 weeks*...   x... did y *for more than 36 weeks*...

The preference for past time reference in English vs. concern about the future and the more dynamic conception of time in the Greek version, should be widened to include the present moment, on the Greek side. There are instances of time specification in the data, in which the focus on past time reference in English is switched to present time reference in Greek.

ST   *Thirty years later*, it is still hard to persuade conspiracists of the simplest explanation...
('I wanted to be a hero', *Newsweek*, November 22, 1993)

TT   For this reason *even today* the simplest explanation seems slightly convincing for those who want to believe the conspiracy version...[my translation]
('Jack Ruby 'I wanted to be a Hero', *To Vima*, Nov. 21, 1993)

       Γι αυτό ακόμη και σήμερα η απλούστερη εξήγηση μοιάζει ελάχιστα πειστική για όσους θέλουν να πιστεύουν τη θεωρία της συνομωσίας...
('Τζακ Ρούμπι «Ηθελα να γίνω ήρωας»', Το Βήμα, 21.11.93)

Modifications along this vein are

English STs: *four years later, x*   Greek TTs: *even today, x*
                   x never before   *x never up to this moment*

5.4. Temporal Structures: Different Viewpoints

One motivation for this piece of research has been the conviction that the concept of time, although shared among cultures, is associated with culture specific attitudes which constitute linguistic and cultural identities. The differences between the source and target versions of the data with respect to time specification have been accounted for in terms of

- a general tendency of the translator to intensify the oppositional view of the world assumed in the press (Eco 1981, Hartley and Montgomery 1985),

and in terms of

- an interpersonal attitude adopted between translator and readership which affected time specification accuracy, as opposed to a more transactional involvement observed between source author and readership. The relevance of accuracy in time specification was, in fact, reevaluated in the target situations.

Raising the target evaluativeness level, employing shorter time units, replacing temporal conjunctions or adverbials with others which have a more dramatic impact on target readership are steps taken towards an *intensification* goal in the target version. On a par, the future orientation preference in the target version, in addition to the preference for specifying beginnings of periods (over time points), the preference for the durative aspects of events and the rather vague specification for ends of periods, are contributing towards an *open-endedness* view with regard to time, in this genre, and a positive, open-ended attitude towards futurity.

One third of the total number of time expressions, in the present set of data, appeared modified in the target version. Figure 4 summarises the types of modifications between source and target versions and indicates percentages in the portion of time expressions which appeared modified in the target version.

Fig. 4. Percentages per type of modifications found in the portion of time expressions which appeared modified in the target version.

> (Dashes do not signify that English has no interest in intensification or present time reference. They mean that, in the present set of data, there are no instances of counterexamples as far as the indicated preference is concerned)

English STs	Greek TTs	Types of modifications
%	%	
		INTENSIFICATION
1.6	30.5	Evaluation
1.1	10	Lack of accuracy
1.6	6.6	Shorter/more specific time units
-	10.5	Other intensifying modifications
		OPEN-ENDEDNESS
-	7.7	Focus on present moment
0.5	5.5	Future orientation
1.1	6.1	Focus on beginning of periods
0.5	1.1	Processes preferred

Open-endedness in time specification could be paralleled with the one claimed in Khairullin (1993) between English and Russian, but the categories of differentiation are not identical, in the English-Russian and English-Greek paradigms. Generic conventions and professional routines may impose varying temporal perspectives on discourses, across cultures, which are assumed to be part of linguistic identities.

The translator interference pattern cannot be systematic. As Toury points out

...a translator's behaviour <u>cannot be expected to be fully systematic.</u> Not only can his/her decision-making be differently motivated in different problem areas, but it can also be unevenly distinguished throughout an assignment problem area. Consistency in translational behaviour is a *graded* notion which is neither nil (i.e. total erraticness) nor 1 (i.e. absolute regularity); its extent should emerge at the end of the study as one of its conclusions, rather than being presupposed (ibid: 69, emphasis in original, my underlining).

In Toury's (1995) terms, the type and intensity of translator intervention, in the rendition of temporal adverbials, may be described as an instance of a *secondary norm or tendency* determining a favourable behaviour, rather than a *basic (primary) norm* (:one exhibiting maximum intensity) or a *tolerated (permitted) behaviour* (:one exhibiting minimal intensity).

In Hatim and Mason's terms (1997:146), the rendition of time adverbials in press news would involve *partial* rather than *maximal* or *minimal* mediation, since about one third of the total number of time expressions encountered in the data appear modified in the target version - constructing an appropriately intensified version of the source ideological message.

Awareness of how versions of ideologies may work through discourses sensitivizes translator-trainees to the types (and intensity) of variation involved in information transfer across languages. This further allows them to adjust translational behaviour accordingly, in order to achieve the appropriate degree of *domestication* (Venuti 1995, 1998) and level of *mediation* (Hatim and Mason 1990, 1997).

SUMMARY OF 5 (I)
This section examined variation in the rendition of temporal adverbials in source and target versions of press news items between English and Greek. Translator interference has revealed distinct ideological profiles through linguistically inscribed patterns of behaviour in the news items. The open-endedness in time specification tendency in Greek (as opposed to English which showed greater concern for past time reference) points to research directions that can elaborate on the means and the extent to which linguistic identities can be defined in cultural and subcultural environments. In the age of electronic communication, culture-specific views on time may more than ever before become an impediment to intercultural understanding and cooperation. Whether motivated by audience profiles or intended to module audience beliefs, the inscription of linguistic preferences in discourses provides useful insights into linguistic identity awareness and intercultural understanding. Translation data is an invaluable tool to this effect through the opportunity it provides for contrastive analysis.

6. Inscription of Identities in Ad Translating

Traces of ideological and cultural/linguistic practices in discourse –as shown in the translation of time adverbials above– have been anticipated in Simpson (1993), among others. In a chapter devoted to *Gender, Ideology and Point of View*, he contends the linguistic determinist position and refers to cultural and ideological practices reflected in discourse:

A more realistic alternative to Whorfianism is to propose that the language system is shaped by functions which it serves. In this sense, language reflects and to some extent re-inforces the *cultural* and *ideological practices* which it describes (ibid: 164, emphasis added).

Simpson analyzes *gender bias* in language by taking a critical linguistic approach to gender. He uncovers asymmetries and inconsistencies in the way language is used by "investigating the gender-related assumptions which underlie texts" (ibid:174). Inconsistencies in translation practice are attributed to gender-related assumptions underlying translator behaviour.

Translator behaviour was shown to vary, in advertisement translation with respect to the persuasion strategies preferred. A data set of 55 English-Greek advertisement pairs indicated that translators are sensitive not only to conventions applying across genres in a particular culture, but also to conventions associated with genre-internal variation (Sidiropoulou 1998b). 'Soft-sell' (cosmetics, liquor, etc.) and 'hard-sell' (business-oriented commodities, e.g. office equipment) approaches in advertising trigger different types of translator interference which cater for different social needs attributed to men and women. English-Greek adverising data showed that a common type of modification is adjusting tenor across cultures (Sidiropoulou 2004a). This was done in a gender-diased manner. Greek translators tended to raise tenor in business-oriented ad translation, while tended to lower tenor in cosmetics ad translation. Raising and lowering tenor may be a manifestation of translators' concern to cater for different social needs attributed to males and females. Fowles (1996) reports on a national survey which revealed a hierarchy of values attributed to American consumers. Self-respect and security were top priority personal needs followed by personal needs like warm relationships with others and a sense of belonging. Raising tenor in business-oriented ads (male audiences) caters for top priority needs like self-respect, while lowering tenor (in cosmetics ads – female audiences) catered for secondary needs like warm relationships with others. The data indicated that different gender groups were attributed different social needs in the target environment, conforming to socio-cultural stereotypes.

Diversity in the Greek target version of advertisements involved decisions of a *strategic* type (*what* is to be said): content was reorganized or modified in various ways to fit cultural preferences in constructing identities. Séguinot (1994) outlines cultural perspectives and conventional ideologies which affect the way values are promoted in advertising across cultural settings. She identifies types of distinctions made between cultures as far as advertising is concerned. One such distinction, she argues, is the "tendency to prefer either style and visuals – like France and Japan – to text and argumentation, as in North America" (1994: 258). This latter preference echoes the Greek translator's concern for reorganizing the content of a hair shampoo advertisement to foreground health issues as a top priority in the ad, as opposed to appearance, thus reflecting the 'denier' attitude of target audience and emphasizing text and argumentation (Sidiropoulou 1998b). There may be cultural norms, Séguinot claims, which are not written down and need to be taken into account in ad translating.

On a par, the modifications in English-Greek translation involved decisions of a *technical* type (*how* it is to be said): certainty was raised, contrasts highlighted, evaluativeness intensified etc., according to target language specific preferences. This latter set of modifications was more or less *expected* in the E-G context, because it shows up almost everywhere in English-Greek media translation (see, for instance translators raising the level of evaluativeness, in time specification or the contrast-creating intention in adversative connection, above).

However, juxtaposition of ST and TT showed that there were some *unexpected* modifications. Linguistic features which have been systematically opted for in English were now promoted in the Greek TT, not following some source feature, but introducing unexpected features in the TT: imperatives, personal pronouns and definiteness/ informativity were *avoided* (although they have been systematically preferred elsewhere in English-Greek press translation). Figure 5, adapted from Sidiropoulou (1998b: 203) summarizes diversity per commodity type allowed in the target version.

It appears that cosmetics is the most tolerant product type with respect to the modificationsallowed in the TT. Following Rotzoll (1985: 102/104), I have argued that varying translator behaviour was due to factors associated with *potential readers* or the *product* itself: variation in translator behaviour with respect to the product advertised would not be surprising because, in 'soft-sell' approaches (perfumes, cosmetics, beers, liquor), impression is more important than in 'hard-sell' approaches (e.g. office equipment) where the advertiser assumes the addressee to be more information sensitive.

This section, draws attention to the identity of *potential readers* as a variable creating a motivation for variation in translator behaviour: it claims that the variation in target advertising material can be attributed to the gender of intended readership. Following Vestergaard and Schrøder (1985:10) and Milapides (1994: 410), it is assumed that the method of persuasion in advertising varies with product type and age, sex and social class of intended readers. Translators have been dis/allowing sets of modifications in target versions, relative to whether the advertised commodity is exclusively addressed to female readerships or not. The issue of variation in the strategies employed in interaction, in men-addressing-women vs. men-addressing-men situations, has often been addressed in monolingual reserch and translation studies (Cameron 1986, Dendrinos and Ribeiro-Pedro 1997, Makri-Tsilipakou 1998, Simon 1996, von Flotow 1997). Women are among the groups whose voice has been systematically silenced in interaction. As Makri-Tsilipakou (1998) puts it, "they are often recipients of silencing interactional practices on the part of men" (ibid: 267). The claim here is that the variation in the strategies employed in interaction is reflected in the present target version of advertising material. Unexpected modifications are instances of silenced interactional strategies addressed to women.

Fig. 5. Selected set of modifications introduced in English-Greek advertisement translating (adapted from Sidiropoulou 1998b: 203)

Modifications	Cosmetics	Watches	Airlines	Cars
Strategic				
Content info (modified)	+	+	+	+
Content (reorganized)	+	+	+	+
Humourous effects (adjusted)	-	-	+	+
Technical- *EXPECTED*				
certainty (raised)	+	+	±	+
contrasts (highlighted)	+	±	±	±
evaluativeness (intensified)	+	±	+	±
Technical– *UNEXPECTED*				
Imperatives (avoided)	+	-	-	-
Personal pronouns (avoided)	+	-	-	-
Definitiveness/ informativity (avoided)	+	-	-	-

What is occasionally *unexpectedly* avoided, in cosmetics advertisements in E>G translation, has a distance-minimizing effect in interpersonal communication. It is as if modifications are occasionally intended to reduce (rather than increase) the amount of positive politeness devices employed, when addressing Greek female consumers. The intention is claimed to conform to gender-specific features of assumed social identities and patterns of behaviour, for the sake of persuasion.

It is as if women in the Greek target environment occasionally need more interpersonal distance in the act of persuasion, thus, strengthening the stereotype of delicacy with respect to females. As mentioned above, the tendency in E>G cosmetics ad translation has been to lower tenor in order to adjust interpersonal distance between advertiser and consumer to culturally preferred patterns of behaviour (Sidiropoulou 2004a). This distance-creating interference is intended to moderate interpersonal proximity. Exploiting sex-role stereotyping is commonplace in advertising practices. As Drossou (1997) claims, in investigating the social roles promoted in British advertising, "sex-role stereotyping is frequently exploited as a manipulative device" (ibid: 99).

By contrast, 'hard-sell' products which do not necessarily address women or do not appeal to the value of sensual pleasure (as in the case of cosmetics and perfumes) need not employ this positively-polite-device elimination technique, as they need not ensure more interpersonal distance between advertiser and consumer. In business-oriented ads, translators tend to raise tenor (rather than lower it) to increase interpersonal distance between consumer and advertiser.

Gender is, thus, another variable constructing identity profiles and ideological meanings to be reflected in target versions of texts. It motivates change across languages and complicates the notion of linguistic identity. In other words, studies of linguistic identity profiles should be assumed to cater for gender-related (or gender-biased) variation. If "masculinity and femininity of gender is culturally determined" (Fowles, 1996: 199), its reflection in such public discourses as advertising is likely to be manifested through the subtle practices involved in identity representation (or formation) in discourse.

The next section further elaborates on differences in cultural assumptions and institutional practices operating on news discourses across cultures. Varying norms prevalent in target discourse types are reflected in target production to enhance appropriateness. Varying linguistic preferences become evident through observation of systematic variation between source press production and target versions of it.

SUMMARY OF 6 (I)

The present section has drawn attention to and elaborated on gender sensitive aspects of linguistic variation in English-Greek advertising data (Sidiropoulou 1998a/b). The challenges of localisation which reshuffle representation of experience in target versions of texts trigger – among others – gender-imposed aspects of linguistic variation which enlighten specification of linguistic identities through translation.

7. Varying Assumptions through Testimonies

7.1. Translating Testimonial Discourse in the Press

Studies of ideological predispositions in monolingual research have often stressed the significance of cultural assumptions which shape experience:

Cultural assumptions, values and attitudes are not a conceptual overlay which we may or may not place upon experience as we choose. It would be correct to say that *all experience is cultural* through and through, that we experience our 'world' in such a way that our culture is present in the very experience itself (Lakoff and Johnson, 1980: 57, emphasis added).

In translation studies, systematic differences between languages and textual traditions have often been attributed to the operation of socio-cultural constraints. As Toury (1995) claims, such socio-cultural constraints, *norms*, "are acquired during the socialization and always imply *sanctions*" or "serve as criteria according to which actual instances of behaviour are *evaluated*" (ibid: 55). The very notion of equivalence in translation may be determined by norms, which form a graded continuum along a scale: it is norms that "determine the (type and extent of) equivalence manifested by actual translations" (ibid: 61).

Machill (1998), for instance, in examining the programme design at a transnational news station (Euronews) in the U.S., gives examples of differences in textual devices employed in the construction of the lead paragraph in news items. Machill observes content related shifts due to length of paragraphs, journalistic styles and conceptions of journalism. The same image sequence of a Euronews news item is supplemented by different texts, in five language versions (German, French, English, Spanish, Italian):

Comparison of the five language versions reveals what are, in part, considerable differences in the design of the news item. Wide variations are to be found, especially in connection with the lead-in. Whereas the classical lead-in (the central element of the report –who and what – is presented in one sentence) is employed in the German and the English versions, the French version begins by telling a short 'story'... The Spanish version even begins with a sentence offering a value judgement and a comment... The Italian version also starts with a value judgement...before moving on to the key statement in the second part of a sentence which must be regarded as too long for a news item lead-in...(ibid: 433)

Within the descriptive translation studies approach, there are two difficulties inherent in the notion of norm: their *socio-cultural specificity* and their basic *instability*. Toury (ibid: 67) suggests a tripartite division, namely, *basic* (primary) norms, i.e. more or less obligatory preferences, *secondary* norms or tendencies determining a favourable behaviour and simply *tolerated* (permitted) norms exhibiting minimal intensity. Besides norms may be modified through time.

Socio-cultural specificity points to the notion of *cultural assumption* or *cultural presupposition* in cognitive theory. In fact, socio-cultural factors can be so strong that they influence or even modify cognition itself. In the present section, normative and cognitive parameters merge to modify the structure of discourse in the Greek version of target news data.

Cognitive scientists (whether linguists, psychologists, anthropologists, philosophers, computer scientists or literary critics) have viewed language as a reflection of general-purpose cognitive abilities, governed by neural processes (Barcelona 1998). Thus, language has been viewed as providing data that can lead to general principles of understanding. An important hypothesis, in this cognitive view, is that concepts can organize the world differently. The same sense data can be viewed in different conceptual ways. For instance, Whorf ([1950], in Indurkhya, 1947/1992:100) has argued that even the most basic concepts (like time or space) can be different across cultures and can lead to radically different world views. An instance of this is reflected in the way temporal adverbials are treated in the target version of English-Greek press news translation (section 5). One way translation is connected to cognition is through processes involved in translator mediation: it involves awareness of cross-cultural differences which are to be reflected in translation products.

The present and the following section are intended to show that, due to varying conceptual world views, translators' perception of (differing) cultural presuppositions modifies the outcome of translation process. In rendering testimonial material in press news translation into Greek, translators' awareness of differing cultural presuppositions assigns a [± *interest/ importance*] feature to news topics, which is shown to regulate the treatment of testimonial material in the Greek version of the text. Similarly, translators' awareness of varying psychological distance between target readership and topic dealt with in the news item, in the next section, is shown to affect the treatment of metaphorical expressions in the target news version.

Such varied discourse formulations reflect awareness of norms operating in language and their significance in constructing discourses. In this section, the two norm-system sets operating across cultures, associated with the above phenomena, namely,

- the norms regulating the treatment of testimonial material in E>G press news translation, and
- those regulating the treatment of metaphors,

are shown to be preferred non-randomly in English and Greek cultural tradition. To a great extent such differences go unnoticed, except when particular source discourse structures are clearly alien in target environments. Observation of source and target data, however, can reveal numerous (systematically preferred) types of variation in the treatment of phenomena across languages, that would otherwise have gone unnoticed. This consciousness-raising intention with respect to normative preferences across English and Greek enriches translators' viewpoint by showing varied preferences across cultures and measuring them.

7.2. Variation in Translating Testimonial Discourse

Testimony is one of the five general lines of argument in persuasive discourse, among Definition, Comparison, Relationship, and Circumstance (Corbett 1965/1971/1990). It is a general term for various types of 'evidence', like *informed opinion* and *authority*, *statistics*, *maxims* or *laws* and *examples*. It relates to 'invented' (rather than 'created') material brought into discourse from external sources, in the process of argument construction. Testimony, in this section, is examined on the grounds that, among the general lines of argument, testimony exhibits the most interesting diversity, in English-Greek press news translation, in the types of modification introduced in the target text.

One goal in the news reporting business is making the story or argument as convincing as possible. This is often pursued through bringing testimonial material into the discourse. The main function of testimonial material is to show that the general opinion formulated in the text is not 'invented' but based on facts and experiences. The way testimony is constructed frequently contributes to producers' intentions to effectively manage readers' inferences about reliability of the information put forward. Since audiences vary considerably with respect to the persuasion strategies they respond to (Lakoff 1990), testimony is, likewise, expected to be presented differently. Awareness of cross-cultural differences in testimonial discourse construction is crucial in news translation because target persuasion strategies are adjusted in order to be made maximally effective.

The present section intends to show that apart from ideological considerations to be taken into account when adjusting discourse techniques in translation, there are some normative and cognitive variables which regulate performance. Out of the subtopics discussed under the general heading of testimony,

informed opinion, statistics, examples, laws, maxims,

informed opinion and *statistics* were most frequently interfered with by translators. By contrast, reference to *laws* and *maxims* was extremely restricted and, therefore, preferences with respect to the treatment of these items in translation could not be safely identified. Maxims and proverbs rarely appear in the present news data and when they do, they are neutralised in the target version, apparently due to their culture-bound nature, e.g.

ST   "Wronged souls don't vanish" a Chinese proverb says and many
        survivors of the Tiananmen crackdown silently agree.
        ('Ghost Stories Come to Life', *Newsweek*, March 25, 1996)

TT   This corner of Asia is not an angel land and those who experienced the
        tragic events of Tiananmen square would agree. [my translation]
        ('Two presidents in the dock', *To Vima*, March 24, 1996)

        Δεν είναι η γωνιά αυτή της Ασίας τόπος αγγέλων και σε αυτό θα
        μπορούσαν να συμφωνήσουν όσοι έζησαν τα τραγικά γεγονότα της
        πλατείας Τιανανμέν.
        ('Δύο πρόεδροι στο εδώλιο', Το Βήμα, 24.3.96).

Similarly, *examples* did not present considerable cross-cultural variation, apart from the expected explicitation tendency with respect to the treatment of cohesive links. The focus here will be on the treatment of *informed opinion*. Although informed opinion may be carrying less weight than mere facts and statistics, it is extensively used in news reporting, because "knowledge is so diversified and specialized in our age that... people are obliged to take the 'word' of some expert about the facts" (Corbett 1965/1971/1990). Thus, although informed opinion is not infallible, it seems to have a great persuasive force and is extensively used in news reporting.

7.3. Preference in Treating Testimony

Three major types of modifications are selected and discussed in this section, in a set of 45 English-Greek article pairs (Greek version: c. 32.300 words), between 1995-1996.

One systematic modification was adverbializing and thematizing the part of the sentence which makes reference to the source of the information. Part of the content which was placed sentence-finally has been adverbialized and thematized as in the example below:

ST   US military involvement is essential to the credibility of the continuing Balkan "watch group," composed of Russia, the United States, Britain, France, Germany and Italy, *which the commission proposes.*
('The Balkan Ailments are Political, thus Treatable', *Herald Tribune*, October 8, 1996)

TT   *According to the comission,* the latter [the international military presence in Bosnia and particularly the American one] is necessary for the credibility of the 'watch team' to which Russia, Britain, France, Germany and Italy contribute. [my translation]
('Balkan diseases are political', *To Vima*, November 10, 1996)

Σύμφωνα με την επιτροπή η τελευταία [η διεθνής στρατιωτική παρουσία στη Βοσνία και κυρίως η αμερικανική] είναι απαραίτητη για την αξιοπιστία της «ομάδας παρακολούθησης» την οποία συμπληρώνουν οι Ρωσία, Βρετανία, Γαλλία, Γερμανία και Ιταλία.
('Οι ασθένειες των Βαλκανίων είναι πολιτικές', Το Βήμα, 10.11.96)

The tendency is manifested in modifications described in terms of the following formulas

English ST: y, *experts say, is* x   Greek TT: *According to expert analysts*, x is y

               x *says Bois-feuillet Jones, president of the 'Washington Post'*   As for *'Washington Post', for instance, the argument is* x

In the former formula, part of the source content is preposed in an adverbialized form, whereas in the latter, adverbialization and thematization are combined to allow
- modification of the identity of the source the opinion comes from, and
- explicitation of the exemplification relationship between parts of discourse in terms of a cohesive marker (*for instance*).

Adverbializing and thematizing constituents will be dealt with in English-Greek EU translating (Part II, this volume) to suggest that it ia a relatively strong discursive preference in Greek political texts. Van Dijk (1981: 21) argues that thematisation can be associated with cognitive notions such as *actualization*, i.e. with a preference to indicate concepts which are actualized in working memory. In treating testimonial material, that is, translators are concerned with establishing a different level of communicative importance with respect to the source of informed opinion. Because informed opinion has a great persuasive force, its source has to be ensured as 'given' and 'actualized' for its argumentative value to be calculated in the reader's mind.

A second difference, in the presentation of testimonial material, is a varied level of generalization preferred in the two versions of the data, with respect to informed opinion and examples. Renegotiating the relevance or the quantity of information, in the new context, results in omitting names of informed opinion sources TTs. In the second formula above, for instance, the name and position of the President of the *Washington Post*, who is the testimonial source, is omitted in the target version. This is because it is highly unlikely for members of the target readership to be familiar with the person referred to or because the particular name is difficult to pronounce. Most instances of personal reference by name are omitted in the target version of the present set of data. Names of family associates and places are omitted, in favour of highlighting social positions and services.

Evidently, there is a relative lack of interest, in the target version, for detailed attribution of statements. The source level of generalization, with respect to the source of informed opinion, is raised in the target version. Positions and social roles are preferred over specific names and when a source of informed opinion is rather vaguely referred to in the source version, it is likely to be omitted in the target version and quotation marks to disappear. Van Dijk (1977: 107) argues that "perhaps each type of discourse, given a certain topic of conversation, has an upper bound of generalization and a lower bound of particularization or specification". He also makes use of the notion of *selective incompleteness* to refer to the fact that discourses may omit reference to certain facts...because these facts are not relevant, in the conversational context.

ST   ...they want to rebuild their lives elsewhere.
'What hope do I have in Bosnia?' asks Haso Osmanovic, 55, a Muslim who with his wife *Ramiza* has lived in Berlin for three years...
Nenad Zuho, a Muslim lives in *Hanau,* near Frankfurt, with his *Serbian* wife *Dragina*, and his sons *Dario*, 12, and *Goran*, 18.
('Invitation to Return', *Time,* October 7, 1996)

TT   ...so that they want to restart their lives somewhere else.
        'What hope do I have in Bosnia?' wonders 55 year-old Muslim Haso
        Osmanovic, who has lived with his wife in Berlin for three years...
        .... says Muslim Nenad Zuho, who lives with his [] wife [] and two
        sons [] [] in a city near Frankfurt. [my translation]
        ('Obligatory refugee return to Bosnia', *I Kathimerini*, October 13,
        1996)

        ...ωστε να θέλουν να ξεκινήσουν τη ζωή τους κάπου αλλού.
        «Τί ελπίδα έχω στη Βοσνία;» αναρωτιέται ο 55χρονος   μουσουλμάνος
        Χάσο Οσμάνοβιτς που ζεί με την γυναίκα του τρία χρόνια στο
        Βερολίνο...
        «...», λέει ο μουσουλμάνος Νενάντ Ζούγιο που ζεί με την γυναίκα του
        και τους δύο γιούς του, 12 και 18, σε κοντινή πόλη της Φρανκφούρτης.
        ('"Υποχρεωτική επιστροφή" προσφύγων στη Βοσνία', Η Καθημερινή,
        13.10.96)

The data in this section, shows that despite translator concern for
actualizing sources of informed opinion, which implies that they are highly
valued in the argumentative structure of the news reporting discourse, these
sources are presented in a selectively incomplete way regulated by
considerations like what may be contextually significant and relevant. What
is selected to be maintained is information about positions and social roles
which can build up on the ideological conflict. Details (like names of
individuals and places) may obscure the presentation of that conflict and,
thus, tend to be omitted. Modifications introduced in the presentation of
numerals in press news translation (like elimination of approximation devices
in the presentation of quantities, Sidiropoulou 1998c) were attributed to this
highlighting-the-conflict intention.

A third noticeable difference relates to rendering verbs of saying in the
Greek TT. There is a strong tendency for the illocutionary force of
authoritative utterances to be made explicit in the target text, by modifying
the reporting verb and eliminating quotation marks. English ST *say* very
often turns into Greek TT items like *assure, state, confess, decide, protest,
complain, accuse, describe, explain* etc.

ST   "This is not yet a disaster for the airline industry, but it is fast
        becoming more than just a blip," *said* Chris Avery, an analyst with
        Paribas Capital Markets.
        ('Fuel Prices Pinch Airlines and Travelers may feel it', *Herald
        Tribune*, October 13, 1996)

TT   Analysts face the issue with moderate optimism and claim that – at
      least for the moment – the increase in fuel prices is not a disaster,
      although they admit   that it is a problem that is fast becoming
      worse and worse. [my translation]
      ('Air-fares at take off position', *I Kathimerini,* October 13, 1996)

*Αναλυτές του κλάδου αντιμετωπίζουν το θέμα με συγκρατημένη
αισιοδοξία και υποστηρίζουν οτι – τουλάχιστον προς το παρόν – η
αύξηση της τιμής των καυσίμων δεν αποτελεί καταστροφή, αν και
παραδέχονται οτι είναι ένα πρόβλημα που διογκώνεται με ταχείς
ρυθμούς.*
*('Σε θέση απογείωσης οι τιμές των αεροπορικών εισητηρίων', Η
Καθημερινή, 17.10.96)*

In the example above, the name of the source is eliminated in favour of
highlighting the person's position, the verb of saying takes on two different
'values', e.g. *claim* '*υποστηρίζουν*' and *admit* '*παραδέχονται*', whereas the
attitude of the authority is evaluated (see *moderate optimism*, '*συγκρατημένη
αισιοδοξία*', and *at least*, '*τουλάχιστον*').

The choice between direct vs. indirect speech, in news reporting, has been
argued to be an issue of ideological importance. Roeh and Nir (1990), in
examining how different techniques of speech presentation colour the news
ideologically on the Israeli radio, argue that varieties of indirect speech
(enriched with parallelisms, repetitions, figurative, idiomatic expressions,
colloqualisms, intensifiers etc.) "contribute to a rhetoric of authenticity, even
though the news register typically tends toward a high degree of narrator
mediation and control" (ibid: 233). Patterns of speech presentation, thus, are
said to be clues for a system of values for cultural hierarchies.

In the present English-Greek translation context, indirect speech is
extensively preferred, in the target version, over direct presentation of
opinions. This is realized through explicitating the illocutionary force of
verbs of saying and making evaluative and intensifying additions. The
tendency of translator for assigning verbs of saying different 'values' is
perceived to be (a) strengthening the argumentative force of the target
discourse and (b) raising the degree of *personal involvement* of the
authoritative source. This contributes to a directness effect (also observed
elsewhere in news translation) through interpersonal interactional patterns
preferred in Greek.

In terms of politeness strategies (Brown and Levinson 1978/1987),
• a distance-creating technique (i.e. indirect speech implying lack of bias,
  in the target version)
is, once again, 'balanced' by

- a distance-reducing device (i.e. manipulation of the illocutionary potential of verbs of saying, to imply active involvement of the authoritative source)

to allow a culture-specific pattern of politeness in news discourse.

The three types of target modifications in the 45 pairs of English-Greek articles, i.e. the tendency for

a. actualizing the sources of authoritative opinion in working memory,
b. omitting details with respect to the source's identity, in favour of highlighting elements of social and political structure, and
c. raising the level of speaker involvement by manipulating the argumentative 'value' of reporting verbs

were not the only modifications observed. There are more modifications which relate to the presentation of the authority and may be argued to be ideologically motivated, but they have been encountered less extensively in the data (e.g. preferring the party (e.g. *Tory*) over the leader (e.g. *Mr. Blair*) etc).

7.4. Constraints on Performance

A question arises as to what the conditions are that dis/allow these modifications in authoritative opinion presentation in the Greek TT. The ratio of the intact-modified expressions was calculated against the *importance* of the topics dealt with in the articles. Results showed that the most frequent modifications appeared in the *low*-importance article category, bearing consequences for the nature of translator mediation.

Thirty-five university students, not familiar with the research conducted, were exposed to a list of topics dealt with in the 45 article pairs examined in this section. They were given a questionnaire with a list of news topics. The topics were described either in terms of the Greek headline (Greek versions of news headlines are not allusive, they are high in information content (Sidiropoulou 1995a) so they provided clues about the topic to be dealt with in the article) or in terms of the lead in the target version, or –where necessary – in terms of parts of the article content itself. Students were asked to place themselves in the position of the average news reader who shares a feeling of insecurity about living in a world where inequalities affect people's lives. They were asked to mark each one of the topics as '*high*-impotrance' (H), '*moderate*-importance' (M) or '*low*-importance' (L) topics. The *high*-interest/importance feature was assigned to articles dealing with issues like sexual exploitation of children in Belgium, the declining number of population in Europe, children in Bosnia, a TWA accident. The *moderate*-and *low*- interest/importance feature were assigned to articles on how a secret deal with France helped Britain defeat Argentina in the Falklands back in 1982, or on imposing the islamic law in Grozny, capital of Chechnya, respectively. Fig. 6 summarizes results and shows how the relative importance of topics was calculated. It shows, for instance, that topic *20* was assigned 30 Hs, 5 Ms, no Ls and was thus included in the high-importance topic range. By contrast, topic *1* was assigned no Hs, 7 Ms and 28 Ls and was included in the low-importance topic-range.

Fig. 6. Calculation[4] of the *H-/M-/L-importance* feature assigned to 45 Greek
    TT article topics.

Topic importance range	High		Moderate		Low	
Topic Id. No	*20*	*7*	*23*	*41*	*2*	*1*
Total of assigned Hs	30	17	15	4	4	–
Ms	5	11	14	19	14	7
Ls per topic	-	6	6	21	16	28

Results showed   that, in the low-importance topic-range, authoritative opinions which were transferred *modified* (in the ways described, above) were *more* than those transferred intact. By contrast, in the high- and moderate-importance topic-ranges, the authoritative opinions which were modified in the target version were *less* than the ones transferred intact. In the low-importance topic-range 8 out of 16 articles had *more* modified expressions than intact, whereas in the moderate- and high-importance topic-ranges the ratio was 3/18 and 2/10, respectively.

Translator's intervention here is shown to be affected by cognitive parameters relating to the estimated importance of issues in a specific environment. The claim that language expresses perceived-and-experienced reality is shown here to explain preferences in the structure of argumentative discourse.

Similar cognitive considerations have been shown to affect the structure of discourse in monolingual research. Parameters like perception of sharing the

---

[4] High-importance topics were considered those which gathered a total of more than 30 Hs and Ms, Hs being more than 16 (see *Topic No 20* or *7*, Figure 6). Low-importance topics were considered those which gathered a total of more than 30 Ms and Ls, Ls being more than 16 (see *Topic No 2* or *1*, Figure 6). Moderate-importance topics were considered those which gathered a total of less than 30 Hs and Ms, and a total of 30 or less for Hs and Ls (see *Topic No 23* and *41*). A fragment of the questionnaire answered by the 35 university students appears in the Appendix.

majority or minority position on a topic affected the argumentation pattern adopted in discourse. In examining factual argumentation in private opinions about nuclear energy, Wegman (1994) showed that weakly involved people were *highly* factual in their statements on safety when they perceived the majority to be against nuclear energy, whereas they were *low* on factivity when they perceived the majority to be in favour of nuclear energy (ibid: 309).

The data may be showing that a *low-effort strategy* is applied in news translation: where the reader's interest/involvement in the topic is assumed to be *high*, the translator's intervention, as far as the above modifications are concerned, is kept to an acceptable minimum. By contrast, where the reader's involvement is assumed to be *low*, translator intervention adjusts the pattern by elaborating on the way authoritative statements are presented, to compensate for readership non-involvement. Thus, assumptions about readership interest/ involvement are shown to affect translator behaviour. The translator as mediator regulates his/her intervention on the basis of his/her own inferencing about public involvement and readership response in a particular social and political setting. Alternatively, the data may be showing that in high-importance topic cases, translators are affected by the seriousness of the situation described and value accuracy (and adherence to ST) higher than appropriateness. By contrast, in low-importance topics, translators were more concerned with appropriateness (rather than accuracy) and thus felt free to modify source discourse structures. Whatever the reason, translators' perception of reality has affected their behaviour in translation. Cognitive and cultural aspects of language use merge to identify the nature of the translator's mediation between the two cultural environments.

Mediator behaviour can be described in terms of the following *probabilistic* (Toury 1995) translation law: apart from ideological parameters which may affect translator interference patterns in the target version, the degree of interference is also likely to fluctuate on the basis of mediators' assumption about readership interest and involvement in the topic dealt with. The degree of inteference is likely to raise if readership interest in the topic is assumed to be low, whereas it is likely to run low if readership interest in the topic is assumed to be high.

The following section describes a similar phenomenon in translation behaviour, with respect to metaphor treatment in English-Greek news translation. A factor regulating translator interference in metaphor treatment, the assumed *psychological distance* of target reader from the topic dealt with, echoes the *relative importance* feature assigned to the news topic in the target environment, in the present testimonial discourse situation. Diversity in translator behaviour, in both cases, seems to be based on some *reevaluation* of the news item topic in the target environment, according to target cultural assumptions.

The fact that low- or high-effort strategies or ideological assumptions in translation may influence the intensity of linguistic tendencies inscribed in target discourses seems to contradict the claim that juxtaposition of source and target versions can yield reliable linguistic conclusions about a target language. However, even if measurement results fluctuate relative to such factors as the estimated importance of topics, tendencies are still inscribed in target discourses to point to preferred linguistic patterns and generic conventions in discourses. Besides, factors like the relative importance of topics can affect producer behaviour in original production, but measurement fluctuation would not decrease the validity of arguments in monolingual research.

SUMMARY OF 7 (I)
The section examined the treatment of testimonial material across source and target versions of news texts. The modifications traced in the present study echoed preference observed elsewhere in translation and in contrastive studies between English and Greek. The intensity of preferences inscribed in target versions fluctuated relative to mediator's evaluation of the significance of the topic in the target environment. Tendencies in original production may also be affected by such cognitive parameters. Translator or assumed audience involvement in the topic dealt with is a variable to be taken into consideration in the study of variation in linguistic identities through translation, as it is in original production.

8. Metaphoring in Press Translation

Cognitive scientists have focused attention on one of the major human cognitive abilities, imagination, the ability to project concepts onto other concepts. Imaginative devices like metaphor and metonymy have been studied extensively, in the literature. Lakoff and Johnson (1980) report that general principles of understanding "are often metaphoric in nature and involve understanding of one kind of experience in terms of another" (ibid: 116). Metaphors have been described both as a realization of a dynamic *cognitive* process but also of a *cultural* one (Mac Cormac 1985/1988).

As far as the cognitive aspect of the process is concerned, metaphors have been described as linguistic devices which mediate between the world of ordinary language (surface language) and cognition. At a deeper level of explanation, they are knowledge processes that through linguistic expressions manifest themselves in culture. The cognitive and cultural aspects of the nature of metaphor can be a central issue in the study of intercultural communication. As Lakoff and Jonhson (1980) claim, a metaphor is not a matter of words alone but of thought and action as well.

In discussing cognition and metaphor, Mey (1993) argues that

metaphors are essential for our understanding of how people communicate...a unique way of understanding the human cognitive capability and an indispensable tool when it comes to solving problems of language understanding.. (ibid: 301).

Projected upon translation practice, Mey's concern about investigating the 'use conditions' that hold in the context of each metaphorical wording, draws attention to (source and target) language contexts which are to determine whether or what metaphors are available cross-culturally.

Sweetser (1990: 45) studied conceptual metaphors through the vocabulary of physical perceptions and their systematic metaphorical connections with the vocabulary of internal self and internal sensations. She argued that metaphors may be fairly common cross-culturally, if not universal (e.g. the connection between vision and knowledge, as in *I see what you mean*), while others (e.g. the choice of the vital organ which is thought to be the seat of emotion) may vary between cultures. Examination of metaphorical link-ups understood differently across cultures may constitute extremely interesting studies of cultural variation with respect to patterns of national thinking.

Even when the same metaphor is used across cultures, the type of metaphoric representation may be different, bearing consequences for negotiation and bond construction between cultures. Thornborrow (1993:100), in examining the different types of metaphoric representation in

French and English, within the metaphorical domain of security and defense, claims that even though these metaphors occur in both languages, there are some marked differences in the way security and Europe are conceptualized metaphorically in the two languages.

Transferring a metaphor from one language system to another is likely to differentiate the set of implicatures generated and, have unintended effects on target readerships. In political communication, metaphorical language has a central role to play (Wilson, 1990:104). Metaphors may be used for connotative or emotional purposes or for making complex political arguments simpler. They have a strong persuasive force in the news reporting business and are, thus, extensively used in this genre. In fact, political metaphors carrying particular ideological implications abound in this type of genre and need to be focused in translation, because metaphors (Chilton and Ilying, 1993: 27) are not transferred with fixed meanings, but are processed in accordance with local languages, local discourse formations and local political interests.

8.1. Metaphorical Expressions in English (source) and Greek (target) Press News

A 38.300-word sample of translated 1997 Greek press news material was contrasted to its source version, in the English press, with respect to the types of modifications metaphors undergo when crossing the intercultural filter. There were metaphors which were transferred intact in the Greek version, others which were modified in various ways, created from scratch or completely abandoned. The following figure summarizes types of modifications in the 38.300-word sample of the Greek (target) version and indicates frequency of occurrence.

Fig. 7. Types and occurrence of modifications in a 1997 38.300-word sample of Greek (target) news material, with respect to the treatment of metaphorical expressions in translation

Transferred INTACT	CREATED	ABANDONED	Transferred MODIFIED
> 147	41	28	138

Metaphorical mappings are often transferred intact in target versions of texts. One such example appears below. This is Toury's (1995: 82) category 1 in the metaphor translation treatment scheme, namely, an instance of a metaphor turned *into 'same' metaphor* in the target text. This is the most common pattern in the sample examined. Politics is paralleled to a *turbulent sea* with *more trouble beneath the surface.* The metaphor serves some explanatory function (Goatly 1993), since it is used to account for the fairly abstract concept of political instability.

ST   *...on the turbulent sea of regional politics*, more trouble can lurk beneath the surface of the Turkish Straits than on the waves.
('The Dire Straits', *Time*, March 24, 1997)

TT   *...in the turbulent sea of regional politics*, dangers are many and usually hide beneath the surface. [my translation]
('The Vosporous Key', *I Kathimerini*, March 23, 1997)

...στην ταραγμένη θάλασσα της περιφεριακής πολιτικής οι κίνδυνοι είναι πολλοί και κρύβονται συνήθως κάτω απο την επιφάνεια.
('Το Κλειδί του Βοσπόρου', Η Καθημερινή, 23.3.97)

A second common device employed by translators is neutralizing metaphorical expressions in favour of simplicity and informativity. As shown in Fig. 7, avoiding metaphorical language in the target text is the least common type of intervention, in cases where the target language does allow some equivalent metaphorical structures. Modifications are rather due to assumed unfamiliarity with source cultural elements. This is Toury's (1995: 82) category 4, in the metaphor treatment scheme, namely, an instance of a metaphor turned *into 0*, a complete omission, leaving no trace in the target text.

A relatively more common device is introducing conventional/root metaphors in the target text to enrich its emotional texture. In the target version, below, Hitler's character is implied to be a stone chiseled by traumatic experiences, whereas Mozart's innate talent is metaphorically seen as a living organism which grew on fertile soil.

In Toury's metaphor treatment scheme, the present modification falls into category 5, namely, turning *a non-metaphor into metaphor.* The functional variety these target metaphors fall into is that of *reconceptualization* (Goatly 1993): they invite readerships to view experience "from a different perspective by categorizing it with unconventional terms" (ibid:124).

A fourth device employed in the sample data is modifying the original metaphor in various ways. The modifications range from instances of

- modifying the source metaphor –to various degrees– or replacing the source metaphor by another target metaphor (Toury's category 2 of the metaphor treatment scheme: *turning a metaphor into a 'different' metaphor*) to
- rendering the source metaphor in terms of its ground (Toury's category 3 of the metaphor treatment scheme: turning *a metaphor into non-metaphor*).

ST   In 'The Boys from Brazil', the 94 boys made from one of Hitler's cells were exposed to the same traumatic and other *formative* experiences as Hitler, for the fictional plotters knew that genes alone would not guarantee Fuhrers II through VC. ...
'A Mozart born into a primitive tribe in Papua New Guinea would never have written a symphony,' says neurologist ... But because Mozart's father was a composer and his older sister took piano lessons, whatever innate talent little Wolfgang possessed *could be realized.*
('Little Lamb Who Made Thee?', *Newsweek*, March 10, 1997)

TT   ...in the film 'The Boys from Brazil' the 94 people who were made from Hitler's cells were exposed to the same traumatic experiences which *chiseled* the character of the Third Reich leader. ...
'If Mozart were born into a primitive African tribe, most probably we would not have enjoyed his symphonies,' ... However in a family in which the father was a composer and the older sister took piano lessons, the young composer's talent *found fertile soil to be developed* [my translation]
('After the ship, the shepherd', *To Via*, March 9, 1997)

...στην ταινία «The boys from Brazil», τα 94 άτομα που φιάχνονται απο κύτταρα του Χίτλερ υπόκεινται στις ίδιες τραυματικές εμπειρίες που λάξευσαν τον χαρακτήρα του αρχηγού του Τρίτου Ράιχ. ...
Αν ο Μότσαρντ είχε γεννηθεί σε μια πρωτόγονη αφρικανική φυλή, μάλλον δεν θα είχαμε απολαύσει τις συμφωνίες του. Σε μια οικογένεια όμως όπου ο πατέρας ήταν συνθέτης και η μεγάλη αδελφή έπαιρνε μαθήματα πιάνου, το ταλέντο του νεαρού συνθέτη βρήκε πρόσφορο έδαφος για να αναπτυχθεί.
('Μετά το πρόβατο ο τσοπάνος;', Το Βήμα, 9.3.97).

The following examples illustrate more types of diversity. The analogies are modified in the target version to accord with culturally preferred metaphorical connections, for conventionality to be ensured. Had the source metaphorical mappings been transferred in the Greek TT, they would have been new, non-conventional metaphors creating a foreignnizing effect.

STa   Is it the *relabeling* of the policy... or does it mark a genuine shift
       toward attempting to reconcile perceptions...?
  b   Jordan has its *hands full* with its own security
       concerns...
  c   Once a legal system is established and a measure for predictability
       introduced, the *economy should recover* as well.
       ('A World we have not known', *Newsweek*, January 27, 1997)

TTa   Is it policy *rechewing*...or is it a genuine attempt to reconcile
       views and perceptions...?
  b   Jordan is *too busy* with the problems its geographical position
       causes to its safety...
  c   Once the Russians manage to establish a reliable legal system
       allowing predictions, to some extent, they'll be able to *restructure
       their economy.* [my translation]
       ('A World we did not Know', *To Vima*, January 26, 1997)

  a   *Πρόκειται άραγε για αναμάσημα της πολιτικής...ή πρόκειται για
       ειλικρινή προσπάθεια σύγκλισης απόψεων και αντιλήψεων;...*
  b   *Η Ιορδανία είναι πολύ απασχολημένη με τα προβλήματα που
       δημιουργεί στην ασφάλειά της η γεωγραφική της θέση....*
  c   *Μόλις κατορθώσουν οι Ρώσοι να δημιουργήσουν ένα σοβαρό νομικό
       σύστημα, που θα επιτρέπει τις προβλέψεις, σε κάποιο μέτρο, θα
       μπορέσουν να ανασυγκροτήσουν την οικονομία τους.
       ('Ένας κόσμος που δεν ξέραμε', Το Βήμα, 26.1.97)*

The idea of the state as a living organism is maintained and what is modified
is the bodily function referred to (*relabeling* in (a) is rendered as *rechewing*).
The *full hands of the state of Jordan* expression is turned into non-metaphor:
(Jordan being) too busy with security concerns in (b). By contrast, in (c),
economy is implied to be a construction rather than a living organism (ST
economy should recover, in (c), is turned into TT *restructuring their
economy*). This type of modification has been anticipated in Marmaridou
(1994). In her examination of conceptual metaphors in Greek financial
discourse, she observed that in the "Greek cultural experience, it is less
tolerated to view financial entities as living organisms and on a par with
humans than it is in the Anglo-Saxon cultural experience" (ibid: 251).

The personification of economic organizations, below, is maintained
while the choice of the vital organ involved in the fighting is modified. This
is another instance of cross-cultural variation in the metaphorical link-ups,
referred to in Sweetser (1990: 45), which are understood differently across
cultures.

ST ... the two titans that will *go nose to nose*...
('Hilton has room for ITT', *Time*, February 10, 1997)

TT ...like titans who will fight *chest to chest*... [my translation]
('Additions to the Hilton Hotels Chain', *I Kathimerini*, February 9, 1997)

... ως «τιτάνες που θα πολεμήσουν στήθος με στήθος»...
(*'Προσθήκες στην αλυσίδα της Hilton Hotels'*, *Η Καθημερινή*, 9.2.97)

Evidently, one of the functions of metaphor is to reinforce intimacy and a sense of community in the target environment. Cultivating intimacy is one of the common functions of metaphorical expressions (Goatly, 1993:127), achieved through activating knowledge shared among people.

A fifth type of modification is transferring a metaphorical expression by rendering its *ground-term* (=the similarity or analogy involved) in the target text. This is a relatively common type of interference, because disregard for figurative language and abstraction –in favour of informativity– has been observed in the translation of political articles in press news translation rather extensively.

ST The decision has *kept the oil and gas pumping*...
('In Algeria Oil and Islam Make a Volatile Mixture', *The New York Times*, Dec. 28, 1996)

TT The decision has on the one hand ensured... *continuation of enterprises*... [my translation]
('The Volatile Mixture', *To Vima*, January 12, 1997)

Η απόφαση έχει μεν εξασφαλίσει... τη συνέχιση των
επιχειρήσεων...(*'Το Εκρηκτικό Μείγμα'*, *Το Βήμα*, 12.1.97)

Although the types of metaphors focused upon in intercultural studies are the conventional ones, unconventional metaphors may also occur in news reporting and may undergo modifications. In English 'hyperinflation *threatens*'..., in Greek it seems to *ambush* (*ενεδρεύει*).

News reporting favours *conventional/inactive/dead/root* metaphors. Hyperbolic, cliché and mixed metaphors are also particularly distinctive in this genre (Goatly 1993). In the English-Greek translation situation, these features are usually transferred intact and are, thus, not problematic. Otherwise metaphorical mappings are either

---

ST   ...hyperinflation *threatened...*
('Thoughts of Russia's shock therapist', *Financial Times*, April 3, 1997)

TT   ...hyperinflation *ambushed...* [my translation]
('The Inspirator of the Shock-therapy accuses the Communist Heritage', *Naftemporiki*, April 14, 1997)

...ο πληθωρισμός ενέδρευε...
("Ο εμπνευστής της θεραπείας-σόκ κατηγορεί την κομμουνιστική κληρονομιά", Η Ναυτεμπορική, 4.4.97)

- maintained as metaphors (in which case, they have a rather limited set of functions: they are explanatory, they help readers conceptualize, adjust emotion etc.) or
- neutralized (in which case, they are reduced to the analogy they imply).

8.2. Local Constraints on Metaphor Treatment

The question arises as to what it is that determines whether a metaphor is to be maintained (and possibly enriched/reinforced) in the target version, or whether it it is to be downgraded to its ground. Another question is what local constraints can possibly be regulating metaphor treatment in news reporting in Greek. Evidently, this is to be investigated in cases where the target language HAS an equivalent metaphor, which however is neutralized in the target text for some reason.

The data show that there seems to be a correlation between the topic dealt with in the article and the treatment of the source metaphor in the target text. The present data suggest that, if the topic dealt with in the relevant fragment of the article is considered a 'hot' issue in the target environment, the metaphors are likely to be reduced to their ground-terms, in the target version. By contrast, if the article refers to some less alarming situation, metaphors are more likely to retain their metaphorical status and be rendered by a metaphor in the target version.

Psychological research on metaphor (Paivio [1979], in Wilson, 1990:108) suggests that metaphors may in part be employed to allow us talk about experiences that cannot be literally described. This is called the *inexpressibility thesis*. In the present context, Paivio's inexpressibility thesis could be replaced by one related to the psychological distance of the target reader from the topic of the article. It could be called the *psychological remoteness thesis*: when the target reader is assumed (or intended) to be psychologically remote, metaphors retain their metaphorical status in the target version; by contrast, psychological immediacy to the topic dealt with filters the metaphorical status of the expression out, in the target version.

Fig. 8 presents two lists of topics dealt with in ten sample source-and-target-article pairs. Psychologically remote topics (left column) allowed for metaphors to survive the intercultural filter. By contrast, psychologically immediate topics (right column) filtered metaphorical expressions out leaving the ground-term to appear in the target version.

Fig. 8. Psychologically remote vs. psychologically immediate topics dealt with in a set of target sample articles in which metaphor treatment varies

+ REMOTENESS	+ IMMEDIACY
Film making about Adolf Hitler	US scandals (probably associated with Clinton)
Russian army giving up a fight	
	Oil economy & Islam making a 'volatile mixture'
Russia reappearing on political stage	
	Human cloning
Forthcoming combination of Hilton Hotels with ITT	
	Mad cows
Thoughts of Russia's shock-Therapist	US war games

This variation in mediator behaviour with respect to the treatment of metaphors may be due to more than one reason. The tendency may be

(a) a realization of a low-effort translation strategy in the rendition of metaphors in high interest topics. The low-effort strategy is justified on the basis that high-interest topics attract readers' attention and thus no extra effort is needed on the part of the mediator to boost that interest by creating intimacy between text and reader. Similarly, low-interest topics may be assumed to require some extra effort in order for readership attention and interest to be ensured.

Alternatively, it may be

(b) a realization of a normative constraint which disallows the use of metaphorical language in the translation of articles dealing with crucial political/national issues. In the latter case, my understanding as a member of the Greek readership is that certain issues are too 'hot' to be part of a language game employing metaphors. Communication, in these cases, has to be clear and specific, it cannot be left to the responsibility of the hearer to infer metaphorical entailments, and thus, analogies have to be described rather than implied by a metaphor. Abstaining from treating a phenomenon in translation may itself be an instance of normative behaviour. For instance, Zabalbeascoa (1996), in examining translating jokes for dubbed television comedies, claims that "it may even make sense not to translate the jokes at all, …if the norms of the target audience exclude using humour for the sake of rhetorical purposes in similar conditions" (ibid: 244).

or

(c) a realization of a general (sub/conscious) mediator tendency to suppress expression of linguistic identities in target discourses, in which accuracy is more important than appropriateness. Such a tendency was observed in political news articles which dealt with the breakout of the war in Iraq (2003), in contrast to news articles which dealt with less ideologically significant issues, like popular science, health and nutritional issues etc. Translators' perception of their role modified their translation behaviour (Sidiropoulou 2004b).

The next section elaborates on the second reason.

8.3. Conceptual Variation in Viewing the World

As Mey (1993) argues, metaphors are ways of wording the world, but

…this wording, in order to obtain the true pragmatic significance that it is usually assigned should include and respect its own context: after all, it is the context of our lives which determines what metaphors are available and what our wordings are going to be. (ibid: 302)

National styles can be distinguished on the basis of choices with respect to the use of metaphors (Chilton and Ilyin, 1993: 28), and thus, filtering metaphors out could be seen as an instance of a varying cultural style. Metaphors can be culture-specific (Lakoff and Johnson, 1980: 5) and where metaphors are to be used can be a realization of a *normative* behaviour. The filtering strategy adopted in the Greek version with respect to the treatment of metaphors, echoes Levinson's (1987) *minimization maxim* applying to the sequential structure of conversation: "produce the minimal linguistic clues sufficient to achieve your ends" (ibid: 168-169).

The maxim could be adapted to the present situation as follows: produce the minimal metaphorical clues sufficient to achieve your ends, when dealing with crucial issues, as audiences may not be psychologically prepared to enjoy linguistic 'games'.

Even if all reasons seem plausible in accounting for metaphor treatment in the present target material, it is suggested that the second one has a fair share in accounting for the phenomenon. This is partly because a similar tendency has been reflected in the target version of English-Greek translation. In one of the following sections it will be shown that a similar phenomenon is observed in romantic poetry translation: in text fragments displaying some realism or cynicism, a grounding strategy is preferred over metaphor preservation. Fuertes-Olivera and Pizarro-Sánchez (2002) examined similarity-creating metaphors in specialized texts and pointed to metaphor as a cognitive tool and an aesthetic device. In the present context, the aesthetic function is cancelled in hot-issue news items together with the metaphor (ibid: 63), while it survives with psychologically remote political (or other) issues and lyrical descriptions (see romantic poetry translation, 3III).

The psychological remoteness thesis, which encourages metaphorical language in low-interest topics in Greek target news articles, contributes to the following theoretical points. The treatment of metaphors, in English-Greek news translation, IS ideologically constrained, in that estimating psychological remoteness is an ideological issue. The ideological significance of metaphors has been stressed in Lakoff and Johnson (1980). They claim that "political and economic ideologies are framed in metaphorical terms" and that "like all other metaphors, political and economic metaphors can hide aspects of reality" (ibid: 236).

The fact that notions like *psychological distance* may affect metaphor treatment, in translation, is another point suggesting that metaphors are pragmatic/cognitive phenomena, as there is information conveyed above and beyond the surface form of what is been said. Variation in metaphor treatment in translation, on the basis of such regulating factors (e.g. the reader's psychological distance from the topic discussed) allows an understanding of how cultures 'mean' with respect to metaphoring. As anticipated in Mey (1993),

a pragmatic view of 'metaphoring' can serve to point the way to a better understanding of our fellow humans, in particular of *what other groups in society, other classes, other nations attach weight to in their daily interaction* with themselves, the others (including us) and the environment (ibid: 304, emphasis added)

The fact that translators subconsciously estimate the psychological distance between intended reader and the issue discussed (in order to en-/dis-courage metaphorical wording in the target version) points to the cognitively reverse directionality of translation process. In studying directionality in translation process from a cognitive point of view, Marmaridou (1996) has argued that translation itself is an instance of conceptual metaphor, "whereby conceptual structures of the target language are mapped onto the source text in order to make it understood by the TL reader" (ibid: 49). Translators calculate target psychological distance between text and readership, conceptualize the appropriate target structures available in their mind and map them on the source structures.

The translation of metaphors is shown here to conform to language-specific generic conventions, in the target version. Norm variation is an issue rooted in cultural tradition and has to be investigated as it promotes intercultural understanding. As Bassnett points out (1997)

...many European societies are having to look long and hard at their cultural traditions...because in the 1990s old questions about national identity and national culture are once again being raised (ibid: xvii).

Results in this section are in accordance with Toury's (1995) claim that translation is a norm-governed activity. The treatment of metaphors (and of testimonial material) in translation, are shown to manifest norm-governed instances of behaviour which involve varying cultural assumptions.

In testimonial material, the normative behaviour was manifested on the basis of *assumed readership non-/involvement*. Inferencing about readership involvement was performed with reference to target ideological and cultural assumptions. In metaphor treatment, the normative behaviour was manifested on the basis of *assumed psychological distance* between intended (target) readership and topic dealt with in the news item. Inferencing about the psychological distance was also performed on the basis of target ideological/cultural presuppositions.

Results in this section echo some interactionist view of cognition, one which argues that concepts can organize the world differently. Research in this area advocates that our concepts "do indeed construct our world view and are not reflections of pre-existing, mind-independent structures in the world, and yet that this construction is not arbitrary" (Indurkhya, 1947/1992: 94). One of the hypotheses is that the same environment, or the same sense data can be organized in different conceptual ways. The same data set is organized in different conceptual ways across cultures and is assigned different features in each cognitive representation.

This normative behaviour is on a par with other findings in the cognitive framework. Within the interactionist framework, the psychologist Luria studied the effects of cultural background on individual perception and cognition and concluded that "we do not always 'see' what is in front of the eye, but fabricate the object of perception and cognition" (Indurkhya, 1947/

1992: 100-101). Similarly, Lakoff and Johnson (1980) claim that it is not only the body that structures our concepts; "rather *every* experience takes place within a vast background of cultural presuppositions" (ibid: 57).

Apart from the cultural presuppositions involved in determining target norms, the mediators' cognitive mechanism is involved in drawing norm-related inferences for appropriateness to be met in target versions. In one of the following sections, metaphor treatment is observed in another genre, in romantic poetry translation.

SUMMARY OF 8 (I)
The section explored normative preferences in the rendition of metaphorical mappings in Greek target versions of news reporting data with a view to examining whether they can be assumed to be contributing to linguistic identity awareness. Cognitive parameters like the estimated psychological remoteness of readers from the topic dealt with in the articles regulated normative behaviour in the rendition of metaphors. Metaphors were encouraged in articles which dealt with topics psychologically remote from target readerships. This may be assumed to be due to a low-effort strategy manifested in articles dealing with high-interest topics. Priority, in this section, is given to the psychological remoteness thesis rather than the a low-effort strategy in items dealing with high-importance topics. A similar constraint operating in romantic poetry translation is to be presented in one of the following sections. The psychological remoteness thesis postulated in this section echoes an interactionist view of cognition and enforces the idea that the study of linguistic identities through translation is a feasible project.

9. Linguistic Identities through Ideological Assumptions

Linguistic identities in news reporting are assumed here to be constructed through ideological assumptions prevalent in source and target versions of texts and reflected in discourses through linguistic realizations generating the assumptions.

Constructing ideologies is a phenomenon that arises from the use of particular expressions in context, for instance, through internalisation of presuppositions following from expressions. Such expressions create, maintain or challenge the interlocutors' views of reality, while assigning the speaker the power to do so (Marmaridou 2000). In cognitive approaches to language, presupposition triggers (words or constructions) are analysed as framing scenes of experience corresponding to idealised cognitive models (ICMs) which construct ideologies. Likewise, target versions are constructed around culturally compatible/ preferred cognitive models. In translation, ICMs may need to be modified to conform to target cultural preferences and generic conventions. It is as if they carry the genetic codes that allow different identity profiles across languages. The present research draws attention to varied ICM constructions through translation.

As Simpson (1993) argues, ideologies may be constructed in terms of cultural assumptions, political beliefs or institutional practices

... language use cannot be rendered as neutral, value-free or exempt from at least one 'angle of telling'. Rather, it is shaped by a mosaic of *cultural assumptions*, *political beliefs* and *institutional practices* – in other words ideologies (ibid: 176, emphasis added).

The translational phenomena examined, in this part, instantiate Simpson's "mosaic of cultural assumptions" that shapes the "angle of telling" in discourse: for instance,

- the intensification intention in transferring time adverbials in press news, encodes a *political belief* pertaining in the target environment,
- the open-endedness tendency in time specification encodes a preferred *cultural assumption* about time, whereas
- the inconsitency in the translator's behaviour in advertisement translation has been attributed to gender-sensitive *institutional practices* operating in target situations.

From a Critical Linguistics (CL) and Critical Discourse Analysis (CDA) perspective, linguistic choices in discourse have been shown to reflect political beliefs and institutional practices. As Fowler (1996) claims, CL insists that all representation is "mediated by the value-systems that are ingrained in the medium (language in this case) used for representation" (ibid: 6).

From a translation perspective, the benefit from a CDA approach to discourse can be immense in that issues of misrepresentation and discrimination in public discourses may be identified to be handled accordingly in target versions. Topics may include aspects of Simpson's mosaic: political beliefs, for instance, reproduced in discourse may involve assumptions of political elites about ethnic or racial dominance (van Djk, 1993: 59). Issues like racism, sexism, inequality in education, employment, the courts etc. concerning minority groups are foregrounded for defamiliarization in CDA. This consciousness-raising goal (Fowler, 1996: 5) of CL promotes translator awareness that language is a medium of representation where culture-specific norms combine to produce an appropriate result. For instance, van Leeuwen's (1996) concern about the representation of social actors in discourse (not only in terms of how they are realized linguistically but also in terms of the sociological and critical relevance of categories (ibid: 33)) points to directions that contribute to enhancing translators' awareness of the ideological significance of certain choices. The consciousness-raising goal of CL could be extended to include linguistic-identity awareness with a view to linguistic/cultural identity formation and preservation.

Prospective goals of CL and CDA like the one below, described in Kress (1996), can provide valuable tools for translation theory and practice. In fact, the present book is inteded as a contribution towards the goal set up by Kress:

One essential and urgent task in a multicultural society is to conduct an ethnography of representational resourses across all major identifiable groups in a society. This ethnography would include descriptions of social valuations which attach to the representational resources used by various groups (ibid:18).

Describing linguistic identities through translation is moving towards conducting an ethnography of representational resources across major identifiable groups of society.

From an educational perspective, the goal is awareness of the interdependence between linguistic realizations in press news to the underlying principles that govern these choices. Valiouli (1996) argues, in her discussion of syllabus designing in the School of Journalism and Mass Media, that we should expect students to "realize the close relationship between the various principles, criteria and values that underlie the selection and presentation of news…, on the one hand, and their linguistic realization, on the other" (ibid: 92). Valiouli also stresses the role of writers' *empathy* in news discourse construction, which is associated to an assumed *ideological* model. Students, she notes, are given instruction for the construction of the so-called summary or straight-news lead paragraph, in learning how to write news stories for print. One of these instructions focuses on the ordering of facts in the lead and, in particular, on the choice of the focal point, which the student is urged to place first. Its selection, however, among a number of equally important facts is dependent on the "writer's empathy" (ibid: 96).

In translation courses, students should be made aware of and sensitive to the potential of source and target language structures to carry the intended ideological message across and at the same time reflect audience profiles. Modifying the linguistic potential of target texts to comply with local preferences and ideologies is among the translators' tasks which the consciousness-raising intention of this book seeks to facilitate.

PART II
Readership Identities through EU Discourse Diversity

1. EU Discourse Texture

A fundamental aim in the EU is asserting a European identity internationally and a basic principle in establishing this identity is multilingualism. Language is part of one's identity and, thus, multilingualism raises the issue of how and to what extent identities along with the cultural characteristics they assume can be reflected in texts rendered in the official languages. Does the institutional setting in the EU promote or understate intercultural differences reflected in discourse? The political significance of multilingualism and the 'equal rights for all official languages' principle entail a strong concern in the EU for avoiding the imposition of some sort of an artificial Euro-identity, which suppresses diverse cultural characteristics.

Yet, institutional practice cannot prevent Greek versions of European discourse from echoing linguistic preferences of English or French. EU texts create an illusion of identity (Koskinen 2000). EU translators tend to create some EU register which differs from the actual use of Greek both in structure and style (Babiniotis, 1991: 6). Trosborg (1997: 152) refers to a "kind of Union legalese" developed by the institutional bodies, which displays own preferences in discourse construction. Standardization in the EU context promotes simplification and rationalization to such an extent that there seems to be a lingua franca emerging in the EU to fulfill the communicative needs of member states, despite the Union's policy. Evidently, concern for values like sameness and uniformity in EU institutions allow discourses which deviate from preferences dictated by specific linguistic backgrounds. I assume that one of the reasons for the reflection of foreign identities in domestic texts is that before some EU documents are adopted at a meeting of the Commission, they are provided in the so-called procedural languages (English, French, German). The rest non-procedural language versions "must be produced, but for a later deadline, usually 48 hours after the meeting" (Wagner, Bech & Martínez, 2002: 10).

The new EU drafting guidelines, the 'fight the fog' campaign[1], the editing or 're-writing' services for authors and the linguistic revision carried out for EU translators show the EU's concern for the problem. EU texts are rather non-reliable sources for data collection for an additional reason: the pressing deadlines authors and translators are often faced with. In the EU discourse genre, the most reliable direction of document flow, for data collection, seems to be the outgoing one, i.e. translating for readers outside the EU institutions. Outgoing texts are more likely to allow intercultural difference to be reflected between official language versions because they address specific cultural readerships, whose demands and expectations can be more easily assumed. Incoming and internal documents may be assumed to qualify less as candidate sources. Incoming texts, for instance, are translated into a lingua franca and may address readers who do not have this lingua franca as mother tongue. Outgoing documents are

texts written inside the institutions, usually in English or French, and translated into the other languages for readers in the Member States – and the target readers may range from top-notch specialists to school-children… In the EU institutions, most of the translators… spend most of their time translating outgoing documents. Much of their output will be published in the Official Journal, in glossy publications or on the Internet. Translators of outgoing documents face the most demanding readers, and the problem of "translating a different reality"' (ibid: 68).

The following sections attempt to explore diversity in English – Greek versions of outgoing EU texts with a view to identifying systematic preferences that may constitute part of an identity.

2.   Across Language Barriers: EU 'Outsailing Vessels'

In the previous quotation 'a different reality' refers, as the authors explain, to culture-specific terms and notions conceptualized differently across language barriers. In what follows, two Greek versions of a text fragment from a 1991 EU brochure are contrasted to the English version, with a view to illustrating potential types of diversity between official language text versions. One of the Greek versions was produced by a student in a translation class (1993) and, since then, this unofficial version has often been assessed and edited by other translation students, before it was finally contrasted to the official English version. The students' comments about the Greek unofficial version, below, have been rather favourable. They have never thought that there is something particularly unacceptable about this text, although they have

---

[1] Advice to EU translators to avoid to create foggy texts.

always preferred the official Greek version presented to them afterwards. The text describes patterns of lifestyles the European Community expected its young people to have.

Juxtaposing official English and Greek versions, in the classroom context, was intended to raise awareness of what type of diversity would make a text more appealing to a general Greek readership, thus betraying a distinct linguistic profile. The diversity between the two official versions amounts to tightening TT cohesion through enforcing:

- logical connection

For instance, the Greek equivalent for *entail* (*συνεπάγεται*) assumes a stronger cause-and-effect relation between connected text fragments than *means* does in the official English version. See also recurrence of *entail* and insertion of another *also* occurrence in the Greek official version

- collocational patterns

See pro-form expansion, in terms of English *This* vs. the Greek *participation in it (Η συμμετοχή σε αυτήν)*.

- nominalizations

See *information* (*πληροφόρηση*), *exploitation* (*εκμετάλλευση*), *familiarization* (*εξοικείωση*), *search* (*αναζήτηση*) in place of English verbal constructions. Tightening cohesion is also enforced through

- lexical item selection

Lexical item selection establishes culturally compatible metaphorical mappings: English *shape tomorrow's community* vs. Greek *build* (*οικοδομώ*) *tomorrow's community* allowing implications in accordance with the intended, in the EU context, optimistic view about the future of Europe. It also establishes appropriate tenor levels. See (a) the Greek passive *are called to shape* (*καλούνται να*) vs. the active construction in English and (b) raising formality in the Greek official version through nominalizing.

Instead, the Greek unofficial version, although grammatically correct, is closer to the English version, in that

- it does not establish what may be assumed to be culturally compatible metaphors (it opts for *shape tomorrow's community* rather than the *build* option),
- preserves tenor levels of the English version by retaining verbal constructions (rather than turning them to nominalizations),
- avoids recurrence of *entails* (*συνεπάγεται*), which would have facilitated processing and would register the Greek preference for signalling cause-and-effect relations in discourse.

It appears that, even within the range of what may be called 'Greek EU generic conventions', there are types of preference in professionally translated EU texts which are *readily recognizable as superior* to linguistic choices suggested by Greek translator-trainees. This implies that a linguistic identity can be traced in outgoing EU texts, despite suggestions that EU translated texts may echo linguistic preferences of other official EU versions.

In what follows attention is directed to a systematic preference in the Greek version of EU outgoing texts to thematize certain elements of sentence structure in search of a communicatively equivalent discourse structure.

ENGLISH OFFICIAL VERSION
These 130 million young people will shape tomorrow's community, which will be their Community. This presupposes, firstly, that they are well-informed and, secondly, that thy are capable of seizing the opportunities on offer. Europe expects its young people to be mobile, that is to say, prepared to move around, learn other people's languages and get to know their neighbours. Being mobile also means taking a broader view, being open to new technologies seeking co-operation whenever opportunity presents itself. In short, it means behaving quite differently from previous generations.
('A Young People's Europe', *Europe on the Move*, Brussels, 1991, p. 2)

GREEK OFFICIAL VERSION
These 130 million young people *are called to build* the European Community, which will be their Community. *Participation in it*, firstly, presupposes *information* and, secondly, *exploitation* of new opportunities. Europe expects *mobility* from its young people, that is to say, for them to be ready to move around, learn foreign languages and get to know their neighbours. Mobility also entails taking a broader view. *It also entails familiarisation* with the new technologies, *search* for co-operation every time such a possibility presents itself. *Indeed,* it entails a different behaviour from the one often followed by previous generations.
[my translation]

Αυτοί οι 130 εκατομμύρια νέων καλούνται να οικοδομήσουν την Ευρωπαϊκή Κοινότητα που θα αποτελέσει την Κοινότητά τους. Η συμμετοχή σ' αυτήν συνεπάγεται κατα πρώτο λόγο ενημέρωση και κατα δεύτερο λόγο ανασκούμπωμα και αξιοποίηση των νέων ευκαιριών. Η Ευρώπη περιμένει από τους νέους κινητικότητα, δηλαδή να είναι έτοιμοι να μετακινηθούν, να μάθουν ξένες γλώσσες, να γνωρίσουν τους γείτονές τους. Η κινητικότητα συνεπάγεται επίσης μεγαλύτερη ευρύτητα σκέψης. Συνεπάγεται επίσης εξοικείωση με τις νέες τεχνολογίες και αναζήτηση της συνεργασίας κάθε φορά που παρουσιάζεται παρόμοια δυνατότητα. Συνεπάγεται στην ουσία, διαφορετική συμπεριφορά από αυτήν που ακολουθούσαν πολύ συχνά οι προηγούμενες γενιές
('Η Ευρώπη των Νέων', Η Ευρώπη σε Εξέλιξη, Βρυξέλλες 1991).

GREEK UNOFFICIAL VERSION
These 130 million young people will shape tomorrow's community, which will be their Community. This presupposes, firstly, that they will be well-informed and, secondly, they will be capable of seizing the opportunities on offer. Europe expects its young people to be mobile, that is to say, that they will be prepared to move around, learn other people's languages and get to know their neighbours. Being mobile also means that you adopt a broader view of things, are open to new technologies, and are co-operative whenever an opportunity presents itself. In short, it means behaving quite differently from previous generations. [my translation]

Αυτοί οι 130 εκατομμύρια νέοι θα διαμορφώσουν την αυριανή Κοινότητα η οποία θα είναι η δική τους Κοινότητα. Αυτό προϋποθέτει, πρώτα απ' όλα, ότι θα είναι καλά πληροφορημένοι και, δεύτερον, ότι θα είναι ικανοί να εκμεταλλευτούν τις ευκαιρίες που τους προσφέρονται. Η Ευρώπη περιμένει από τους νέους της να είναι κινητικοί, δηλαδή να είναι προετοιμασμένοι να μετακινούνται, να μάθουν ξένες γλώσσες και τους γείτονές τους. Το να είναι κινητικός επίσης σημαίνει να υιοθετείς μια ευρεία άποψη για τα πράγματα, να είσαι ανοικτός σε νέα τεχνολογικά επιτεύγματα και να είσαι συνεργάσιμος όπου σου παρουσιαστεί μια ευκαιρία. Εν ολίγοις, σημαίνει ότι θα συμπεριφέρονται εντελώς διαφορετικά από τις προηγούμενες γενιές.

3. Theme-Rheme, Old-New, Topic-Comment

'Theme' is the constituent in a clause which is assigned first position in the sequence by the speaker. It is the Hallidayan distinction concerning the organization of the message in a clause, the "point of departure for the message" (Halliday in Kress, 1976: 180). Thematic elements are context-dependent and consequently of lesser communicative importance than rhematic elements.

The *theme-rheme* distincion has often been associated to *old* and *new* information in the clause. Theme-rheme is a speaker-oriented distinction; it signals the speaker's starting point. The old-new distinction is a reader-oriented one, in that it reflects what the speaker assumes the status of the information is in the mind of the hearer. Given/old-new is a discourse feature, theme-rheme is not. Information (the given-new distinction) "structures the item in such a way as to relate it to the preceding discourse, while thematization structures it in a way that is independent of what has gone before" (ibid).

The English – Greek samples of the EU texts examined for the purposes of the present research did not differ considerably in clause organization due to the uniformity principle in the EU translation context. A few differences in the treatment of the theme-rheme distinction appear in "equative clauses" (Halliday in Kress, 1976: 182). In the following example, *peace* has a thematic position in English and a rhematic position in Greek.

The topic-comment distincion has often been associated to the theme-rheme one. Topicalization frequency, contrastive analysis between English and Greek suggests (King [1990] in Baker, 1992: 192) can be a point of intercultural difference. Topicalization expressions like 'as for' or 'with regards to' are more frequent in Greek than in English (see *oson afora, oso gia, os pros* in Greek) and thus Greek learners tend to overuse this structure and create unintended markedness effects. The topic is assumed to suggest some kind of framework within which conversation develops, e.g. some kind of a temporal framework, spatial or other.

ENGLISH VERSION
Young Peoples' Attachment to European Values
Peace is the 'European value' ranked highest by young Europeans in the 15 to 24 age bracket...
('A Young People's Europe', *Europe on the Move*, Brussels, 1991, p. 5)

GREEK VERSION
Young Peoples' Devotion to European Values
The 'European value' to which young Europeans in the age of 15 to 24 are
devoted is *peace*…[my translation]

Προσήλωση των Νέων στις Ευρωπαϊκές Αξίες
Η ευρωπαϊκή αξία' στην οποία είναι περισσότερο προσηλωμένοι οι νέοι
Ευρωπαίοι ηλικίας 15 έως 24 ετών είναι η ειρήνη…
('Η Ευρώπη των Νέων', Η Ευρώπη σε Εξέλιξη, Βρυξέλλες 1991).

ENGLISH VERSION
Europeans got no respite when the fighting ended. The Second World
War was hardly over and the threat of a third…was soon to loom on the
horizon… The moment of truth came *in the spring of 1950*…
('Europe – A Fresh Start', *European Documentaion Periodical 3*,
Luxembourg, 1990, p. 9)

GREEK VERSION
The Historical Background
Europeans got no respite that should follow the end of the fighting.
Immediately after the end of he Second World War the threat of a
third…was not late to show up… *In the spring of 1950*, the moment of
truth came ... [my translation]

Το Ιστορικό Πλαίσιο
Οι Ευρωπαίοι δεν γνώρισαν την ανάπαυλα που έπρεπε να ακολουθήσει τον
τερματισμό των εχθροπραξιών. Αμέσως μετά την λήξη του Δευτέρου
Παγκοσμίου πολέμου, δεν άργησε να φανεί η απειλή ενός τρίτου πολέμου…
Την άνοιξη του 1950 σήμανε η ώρα της αλήθειας…
('Μια Νέα Ιδέα για την Ευρώπη', Ευρωπαϊκά Κείμενα Περιοδική Έκδοση
3, Λουξεμβούργο, 1990).

The example comes from a text providing an EU historical background and
assumes a temporal framework: in the third clause the temporal adjunct is
topicalized in Greek (*In the spring of 1950,*…)

Knowles claims that the trigger for inversion to signal old-new information
should be felt "as a psychological rather than logical focus but the quest for
stylistic adornment is also part of this" (1998: 109). Translators' highest
priority, he argues, is to resolve what is old vs. what is new in discourses.

In the following section, the psychological focus, or else, the framework in terms of which reality is conceptualized implies stronger spatial and temporal awareness in the Greek version of the data. The preference seems to be exceeding the EU convention system. A systematic preference for spatial an temporal deictic specificity was also traced in the context of E>G literary translation, i.e. in the context of rendering Virginia Woolf's *The Mark on the Wall* into Greek.

The claim was that in the target receivers' mental representation of the universe of discourse, temporal and spatial entities had to become more "accessible" and thus translators "were tempted to deictically specify them" in the Greek TT (Sidiropoulou, 2003: 90).

3.1 Adjunct, Conjunct, Disjunct Rendering

The treatment of the wide category of adverbials (adjuncts, disjuncts, conjuncts) as described in Quirk *et al* (1992) shows some variation in the Greek data.

Adverbial position in the clause is often preserved, but some *place* and *time* adjuncts are placed at initial position in Greek, whereas in the English version they do not appear sentence-initially. About half of the adjuncts in the data have been placed at initial position in the Greek official version. The following example shows a fronting transformation of a place and a time adjunct (emphasis added).

ENGLISH VERSION
The richest region *in the European Community* is six times richer than the poorest region. When Spain and Portugal joined the Community *in 1986*, the number of people doubled...
('Working with the Regions', *Europe on the Move*, Brussels, 1991, p. 1)

GREEK VERSION
In the European Community, the richest region is six times richer than the poorest. *In 1986*, the last enlargement of the Community, with Spain and Portugal , doubled the number of inhabitants... [my translation]

Στην Ευρωπαϊκή Κοινότητα, η πιό πλούσια περιφέρεια είναι έξι φορές πιο πλούσια από την πιό φτωχή. Το 1986, η τελευταία διεύρυνση της κοινότητας, με την ένταξη της Ισπανίας και της Πορτογαλίας, διπλασίασε τον αριθμό των κατοίκων....
('Στην Υπηρεσία των Περιφερειών'', Η Ευρώπη σε Εξέλιξη, Βρυξέλλες 1991).

ENGLISH VERSION
Major, potentially Community-wide disasters can be averted *in this way*. ('Consumer Policy in the Single Market', *European Documentaion*, Luxembourg, 1991, p. 16)

GREEK VERSION
In this way, it is possible for major, large-scale disasters to be averted that can ...harm the Community. [my translation]

Με αυτόν τον τρόπο, είναι δυνατό να αποφεύγονται μεγαλύτερων διαστάσεων καταστροφές που, στη χειρότερη περίπτωση, μπορούν να πλήξουν ολόκληρη την Κοινότητα.
('Η Πολιτική για τους Καταναλωτές στην Εσωτερική Αγορά', Ευρωπαϊκά Κείμενα, Λουξεμβούργο, 1991).

Conjunct connectives (result and adversative ones) are also placed at initial position in the Greek official version. Less than half of the conjuncts which in the English version are not sentence-initial are thematized in Greek. The following text provides a good example of the fronting mechanism.

ENGLISH VERSION
...Italy, *by contrast*, abandoned this wider margin of fluctuation at the beginning of 1990. ('What is the EMS?', Europe on the Move, Brussels, 1991, p. 6)
GREEK VERSION
... *By contrast*, Italy abandoned this wider margin of fluctuation at the beginning of 1990. [my translation]

...Αντίθετα, η Ιταλία εγκατέλειψε το ερύτερο περιθώριο διακύμανσης στις αρχές του 1990.
('Στην Υπηρεσία των Περιφερειών'', Η Ευρώπη σε Εξέλιξη, Βρυξέλλες 1991).

Some time adverbials appear modified in the Greek official version in terms of evaluative particles. The following example shows an instance of both adverbial preposing and evaluation.

ENGLISH VERSION
An examination is to be made *before 1997* as to whether...
... ('What is the EMS?', Europe on the Move, Brussels, 1991, p. 6)

GREEK VERSION
Already before 1997, an examination will be set up as to whether...

Ήδη από το 1997, θα εξεταστεί κατα πόσο...
('Στην Υπηρεσία των Περιφερειών', Η Ευρώπη σε Εξέλιξη, Βρυξέλλες 1991).

The following are some of the changes in the data. In addition to preposing adjuncts, either intact or modified by an evaluative item, disjuncts (e.g. *indeed*) and conjuncts (*so*) are often added to the Greek official version. Diversity echoes the rise in the level of cohesive explicitness discussed in the news part of this book.

English Version:	x, *in 1975* *in April 1968*, x	Greek Version:	*Since 1975*, x *Already in April 1968*, x
	x. y x. y		x. *Indeed* y x. *So* y

Languages differ in thematization preferences, with respect to particular genres: detective novels tend to thematize time adverbials whereas travel brochures thematize locational adverbials (Brown and Yule, 1983: 132). In the Greek conceptualization of the EU framework, both temporal and spatial dimensions tend to have priority over others. Although part of the diversity in the present data may be due to the explicitation tendency in translation, EU translation data may be assumed to provide evidence that, in the English-Greek paradigm, the persuasion strategy on the Greek side favours conceptualizations of EU reality which exhibit higher degree of specificity in terms of time and space. The fact that the preference for deictic specificity with respect to time and space overruns genres (see also news reporting (Part I) and literary translation (Part III) makes it a better candidate for being part of Greek cultural heritage.

3.2. An Adverbializing Tendency

Another type of diversity is concern for adverbialization in the Greek official version. In the following example, whole sentence parts have been adverbialized, three times in a text fragment which does not exceed a single page. Parts of the sentences have become 'topical' in the Greek official version (emphasis added).

The pragmatics of discourse and the functions associated with the topic-comment distinction have often attracted the attention of theorists. Van Dijk (1981) argues that 'topical' function is assigned to those phrases of a sentence (or components of the underlying proposition) which are assumed to be 'presupposed'. The topic, van Dijk argues, can be associated with cognitive notions such as 'actualization'. The topic has the function to indicate the concepts which are actualized in working memory, due to previous information. A third function van Dijk assigns to sentential topic is that it "determines the way in which a sentence is connected with established informational structure" (ibid: 121).

ENGLISH VERSION
The growing volume of trade between Community countries made concerted action increasingly necessary: on the one hand, in order to remove bureaucratic impediments...
The general directive on additives authorized for use in foodstuffs stipulates that additives may be used in foods only if ...
This transposal has to secure the objectives and content of the Community provisions...
('Consumer Policy in the Single Market', *European Documentaion*, Luxembourg, 1991, p. 13)

GREEK VERSION
With the increase in trade exchange among EEC Member States, necessity for concerted action was becoming more and more intense: on the one hand, for removal of bureaucratic impediments...
According to the general directive on additives authorized for use in foodstuffs, the use of these substances is permitted only if...
Through this transposal, the objectives and content of Community provisions... [my translation]

Με την αύξηση των εμπορικών συναλλαγών, μεταξύ των κρατών της ΕΟΚ, γινόταν ολοένα επιτακτικότερη η ανάγκη κοινών πρωτοβουλιών: αφενός, για την κατάργηση γραφειοκρατικών εμποδίων...
Σύμφωνα με την 'Οδηγία–πλαίσιο για τα επιτρεπόμενα στα είδη διατροφής πρόσθετα τροφίμων' η χρήση των ουσιών αυτών επιτρέπεται μόνον όταν...
Με την ενσωμάτωση αυτή, πρέπει να υλοποιούνται οι στόχοι και το περιεχόμενο των κοινοτικών διατάξεων...
('Η Πολιτική για τους Καταναλωτές στην Εσωτερική Αγορά', Ευρωπαϊκά Κείμενα, Λουξεμβούργο, 1991).

In terms of the hierarchical design of sentence content, subordinating part of the sentence (as the case is in adverbializing) is downgrading the sentence part by presenting it as background knowledge. The items that are assigned topical function as presupposed, in these examples, were downgraded even further by adverbialization.

The Greek text producer is very much concerned with givenness and actualization of concepts in working memory and, thus, allows levels of communicative importance to increase the communicative potential of text for an intended readership. Concern for concept actualizing is verified by frequent pro-form expansion and recurrence in the Greek official version. The following example shows an instance of pro-form expansion: English pro-form *this* is expanded as Greek *these results* (τα αποτελέσματα αυτά). Recurrence has been shown above.

ENGLISH VERSION
…40% of those questioned put peace top of the list ahead of democracy (37%), culture (36%), lifestyle (30%), quality of life (28%) and standard of living (25%). *This* emerges from a survey conducted…
('Young People's Europe', *Europe on the Move*, Brussels 1991, p. 5)

GREEK VERSION
Indeed, …40% of the young who were questioned put peace top of the list of the topics they were concerned with, ahead of democracy (37%), culture (36%), lifestyle (30%), quality of life (28%) and standard of living (25%). *These results* emerged from a survey conducted…[my translation]

…Πράγματι, το 40% των νέων που ρωτήθηκαν τοποθέτησαν την ειρήνη στην πρώτη θέση των θεμάτων που τους απασχολούν, μπροστά από την δημοκρατία (37%), τον πολιτισμό (36%)…και το επίπεδο ζωής (25%). Τα αποτελέσματα αυτά προέκυψαν απο σφυγμομέτρηση που πραγματοποι-ήθηκε…
('Η Ευρώπη των Νέων', Η Ευρώπη σε Εξέλιξη, Βρυξέλλες, 1991)

3.3. Adjusting Tenor

Sixteen instances of adjuncts moved to initial position in a 4000-word data set. Some adjuncts were placed clause initially, others at a later point in clause structure but earlier than the corresponding position in the English version. Instances of adjunct *post*posing in Greek hardly appear in the data.

The question arises as to what the effect is of this diversity in the interpretation of the message by receivers. In examining the level of formality assumed in left-branching (LB, hereafter), centre-branching (CB) and right-branching (RB) sentences in English, Levin and Garrett (1990) argued that English readers judged LB sentences to be more formal than RB ones and that CB ones were even more clearly judged more formal than LB ones. If the same holds for Greek, the tendency in the Greek official version for preposing adverbials may be attributed to a preference for a higher level of formality in this genre, which triggers adverbial preposing.

Evidence that LB sentences are more formal than RB ones in Greek comes from an experiment conducted in class. Fifty university students, all native speakers of Greek, were given six sentences in Greek with adverbials of the type most frequently encountered in the present data, i.e. time, place, and purpose ones. Each sentence appeared in LB, CB and RB versions and students were asked to identify which sentences they would use to address a formal (professor/employer) or an informal (parent, sibling, close friend) listener. They had to identify the most formal and most informal choice according to intuition, leaving one choice unspecified.

Results showed that RB sentences were identifiable as informal choices by the majority, whereas LB sentences were judged as formal, except for sentence 2 (see increased percentages in bold, relevant column, Fig. 9). Fig. 9 indicates that e.g. the LB version of sentence 1 on the 'Test on Tenor' was judged as formal by 48% and informal by 20%. By contrast, the RB version of sentence 1 was judged as formal by 12% and informal by 68%.

Fig. 9. Tenor measurement in Greek LB, CB and RB sentences

Sentence No	LB F-----I % %		CB F-----I % %		RB F-----I % %	
1.	**48**	20	**42**	12	12	**68**
2.	32	**41**	**32**	16	32	**46**
3.	**74**	8	18	**20**	8	**74**
4.	**46**	22	26	**30**	26	**48**
5.	**70**	16	14	**20**	18	**62**
6.	**86**	14	-	-	14	**86**

The preference for raising the level of formality in the official Greek version of the data can be assumed to be part of its identity. Persuasion strategy in the Greek version is assumed to be more effective when the level of formality is raised thus, revealing a distinct readership profile, which would not have been easily identified except in juxtaposition with other official versions.

A TEST ON TENOR:
LB, CB AND RB[2] SENTENCES in GREEK

1. [*Today*] the inequalities that exist [] are less significant []
LB: Σήμερα, οι ανισότητες που υπάρχουν είναι μικρότερες
CB: Οι ανισότητες που υπάρχουν σήμερα είναι μικρότερες
RB: Οι ανισότητες που υπάρχουν είναι μικρότερες σήμερα

2. [for immediate communication] Services [] had a teleprinter []
CB: Οι υπηρεσίες για άμεση επικοινωνία είχαν τηλέτυπο
LB: Για άμεση επικοινωνία, οι υπηρεσίες είχαν τηλέτυπο
RB: Οι υπηρεσίες είχαν τηλέτυπο για άμεση επικοινωνία

3. [In this way] we'll avoid [] disasters []
CB: Θα αποφύγουμε με τον τρόπο αυτό καταστροφές
LB: Με τον τρόπο αυτό θα αποφύγουμε καταστροφές
RB: Θα αποφύγουμε καταστροφές με τον τρόπο αυτό.

4. [For big disasters] they get [] a good compensation []
LB: Για μεγάλες καταστροφές παίρνουν μεγάλη αποζημίωση
RB: Παίρνουν μεγάλη αποζημίωση για μεγάλες καταστροφές
CB: Παίρνουν για μεγάλες καταστροφές μεγάλη αποζημίωση

5. [By 1993] in transports [] there will be free competition []
LB: Μέχρι το 1993, στις μεταφορές θα υπάρχει ελεύθερος ανταγωνισμός
CB: Στις μεταφορές, μέχρι το 1993, θα υπάρχει ελεύθερος ανταγωνισμός
RB: Στις μεταφορές θα υπάρχει ελεύθερος ανταγωνισμός μέχρι το 1993

6. [Due to overbooking] they do not go on the trip []
LB: Δεν πραγματοποιούν το ταξίδι τους, λόγω υπεράριθμων κρατήσεων
RB: Λόγω υπεράριθμων κρατήσεων, δεν πραγματοποιούν το ταξίδι τους

---

[2] LB sentence: adverbial placed sentence initially, CB sentence: adverbial placed in the middle, RB sentence: adverbial placed sentence finally.

3.4. Distinct Readership Profiles

The two tendencies in Greek EU discourses, the preference for adverbialisation and adjunct preposing point to culture-specific types of preference in the Greek context.

Emphasis on actualization processes and the preference for givenness, in the Greek version, assume that text producers are concerned about whether addressees are following the thread of argument in discourse. It reflects readership profile in that it implies that reasoning and logical thinking (facilitated by levels of communicative importance) is highly valued in the mind of text receivers. In fact, reason giving is itself part of a positively polite behaviour which Greeks tend to prefer (Sifianou 1992).

Raising the level of formality is a preference to be connected to generic conventions. The EU discourse genre in Greek requires longer interpersonal distance between interlocutors for the communicative event to be effective. Increasing interpersonal distance between interlocutors is a negative politeness preference, which seems to run contrary to the effect the adverbializing tendency has had on the EU discourse. Conflicting tendencies in discourses is a frequent phenomenon establishing balance in the use of communicative devices. In the present context, it is as if this latter preference is employed to create a culturally-specific balance between preferred linguistic choices in order to increase the communicative potential of Greek EU discourse versions.

Linguistic preferences may be identified even in the form of norm *clash*. Tirkkonen-Condit (1995) reports that two different rhetorical norms may clash, in the context of EU project proposals by Finnish individual applicants or international consortia. The Finnish applicant or the Finnish translator may produce an English text which is grammatically correct but rhetorically deviant. In the Anglo-American scientific rhetoric, Tirkkonen-Condit claims,

the style is assertive and straight to the point. It does not hide the merits of the applicants. The text is reader-friendly in that it uses metatext and other structural signals to guide the reader. The Finnish rhetorical tradition is different. It is more implicit and impersonal. It starts from a background and tends to leave it to the reader to infer the aims of the project as well as the merits of the researchers. Praising oneself is felt to be impolite, and metatext is frowned upon as a sign of underestimating the reader's intelligence. The 'point' of the text tends to be left towards the end of the text. (ibid: 331)

The question arises as to whether the explicitation tendency often manifested in translation can blur the reflection of this culture-specific combination of normative features (or features of norm clash), thus diminishing the validity of translational data as a source for the study of identity. Instead of being assumed as an impediment to valid conclusions about linguistic identities through translation, the explicitation tendency in translation could be taken to contribute invaluable insights to the study of linguistic identities. It is a process which reveals the 'truth of the subconscious', the mental reality in the mind of translator which is assumed to have some stronger communicative potential in the intended environment. Even if it foregrounds 'invented' (target) material or discourse configurations and is simply triggered by excessive concern for establishing communication with an intended readership, it still reveals a communicative preference which is part of the intended readership's collective identity. In this book, the claim is that the explicitation tendency can be a tool contributing to the study of linguistic identities.

SUMMARY OF 3 (II)
Section 3 explores the potential of drawing conclusions about linguistic identities from English and Greek official versions of EU texts. It is claimed that although EU texts is not the most eligible genre for linguistic diversity observation, certain variables like topic-comment organization and information structure can function as analytic tools for deciphering preferred patterns that reveal varied conceptualizations of reality. The explicitation tendency which is said to blur linguistic conclusions in a target version is claimed to be capable of contributing (rather than blurring) linguistic identity awareness. It is argued to be revealing the 'truth of the subconscious', as it were, a highly probable alternative discourse structure, if not the most appropriate one, that corresponds to preferred conceptualized discourse realities in TTs.

4. Analytical Tools for Identities

Theme, like other features of discourse organization, is a variable sensitive to cultural and generic contexts. Hatim (1997: 88) claims that the theme-transition-rheme (together with cohesion and information structure) is a "variety-sensitive variable of texture" which corresponds to specific text structures and specific contextual directives. It is an analytic tool for the study of texts which can respond to textual conditions to reflect identities, once these conditions are specified.

Another metaphor for theme progression in discourse -apart from the "framework in which discourse develops" and the "psychological focus" metaphor (Knowles 1998) mentioned earlier- comes from interpretation. Torsello (1997) considers theme the "interpreter's path indicator through the unfolding discourse" (ibid: 181).

EU is not the most promising text type for the study of identities, because of the uniformity pursued across official versions of documents. However, investigation into phenomena which can function as analytic tools for the study of texts can uncover patterns of diversity across language versions, as evidence for the operation of such variables in specific genres and on specific contextual conditions. As Schäffner and Herting (1992) maintain, "even with Europe coming closer together, and, as a consequence, knowledge and ideas becoming mutual, the concept of culture-specificity should be reflected upon anew" for nations, languages and cultures do not totally coincide (ibid: 35).

Pragmatically oriented translation research has suggested notions as tools, along which diversity can be explored in translational contexts or 'parallel' text contexts. Fawcett (1998) looks into the notion of presupposition as a tool for identifying diversity in translation. Schäffner (1998) searches into the English-German language pair along the axis of hedges in political texts: "hedges are linked to presuppositions and implicatures" and call for a pragmatic explanation because they activate background knowledge, which is often culture-specific (ibid: 199-200).

Varying deictic perspectives among languages can be another point in focus. Richardson (1998) looks into the English-Spanish language paradigm to identify meaningful diversity in the treatment of deictic perspective of utterances in translation. He concludes that stylistic considerations are often "a significant factor in the translation of demonstratives and anaphoric referents, as they are in the deployment of metaphors for spatial representation and the representation of movement" in the mind of the mediator (ibid: 140). Zlateva (1998) explores the "mechanism of substitution" of whole utterances in English, Bulgarian and Russian to cater for inadequacies observed in translations (ibid: 167).

Text politeness is associated to the Hallidayan interpersonal function and comprises another pragmatic variable along which intercultural diversity presents itself in translational contexts. Politeness is a discoursal perspective tackled in both translational and non-translational contexts. Deference and formality of register, for instance, have been assumed to reveal varying preferences across language barriers (Hatim, 1998: 85). House (1998: 70) demonstrates how equivalence of politeness is achieved and assessed in English-German translational contexts. The contrast between the negative politeness behaviour preferred in English (Levinson 1987) vs. the positive politeness patterns favoured in Greek (Sifianou 1992) has numerous manifestations in translational contexts (see modification of politeness patterns in various Pinter play translations for the Greek stage, Sidiropoulou 2002).

EU official versions of discourses, like all genres, are eligible for the investigation of a specific, probably restricted, set of diversity types. A small-scale research project conducted in class has revealed that among the most common sources of variation in the EU context have been the manipulation of logical relations, thematization preferences, reference patterns, collocational patterns. Lexical item selection was manipulated to allow aspects of meaning in tune with intended, in the EU context, prevailing ideological assumptions. By contrast, in a literary translation context, the range of diversity types was found to be considerably wider. In the next part, the potential of drawing conclusions about linguistic identities in the English-Greek translational paradigm will be explored in the literary and theatre genres.

PART III
Intercultural Variation
in Literature and Theatre Translation

1. On Cognition and Translation

This part expands on the potential of target literary and theatre production to contribute to the study of linguistic identities. It examines intercultural variation between ST and TT versions in English-Greek and Greek-English literary translation situations. Results indicate that there are readily identifiable tendencies in the translation of these genres that allow conclusions to be drawn about intercultural preferences in message construction. Translation practice is shown to provide data that can contribute to the study of linguistic identities, with a view to linguistic identity awareness, preservation or formation, in a world in which globalization has a fair share. Section 3 in this Part explores the treatment of metaphor & metonymy in romantic poetry translation, against the background of cognitive linguistics. The goal is identifying target normative behaviour in metaphor use that can be claimed to (a) contribute to linguistic identity awareness and (b) shed light on issues that fall within the area and interests of cognitive linguistics. Section 4 explores how Venuti's minoritizing translation, within a cultural studies approach, can contribute insights into drawing linguistic conclusions about intercultural preference. Section 5 focuses on the treatment of connectives in E>G and G>E theatre translation to suggest that translation for the stage (rather than for the page) can allow more accurate conclusions about linguistic preferences.

Cognition is reframing the study of language, literature and mind. In cognitive linguistics, the semantic content of a linguistic expression is considered to crucially involve the way we choose to mentally construe it. Adopting this subjective view of meaning, linguists focus on different mental construals that languages adopt in order to portray what is basically the same situation.

In its multidisciplinary perspective, cognition affects more areas than linguistics alone. Literary studies have borrowed the conceptual apparatus from cognitive science to analyse poetry. Karagiannidou and Kitis (1997) analyse Anne Sexton's poem *Buying the Whore* using a cognitive framework. They further employ it to define the notion of literariness. The claim is that a high degree of literariness has traditionally been assigned to texts "which project textual worlds which deviate from our conceptual schemata" (ibid:128), exerting a subversive, distorting function on them. Indurkhya (1992) discusses three versions of the interaction view of cognition in different fields of research: Goodman's [1978] worldmaking in philosophy, Piaget's [1936-1983] constructivism in psychology and Lakoff and Johnson's [1980] experiential account in linguistics.

Lakoff and Johnson's account intends to show that reality can be conceptualized in alternate ways but not in an arbitrary manner. This view of cognition intends to bring about a balance between the objectivist and the subjectivist view of the world (ibid: 124). On the one hand, there is some objective pre-existing ontology and structure of the world, and our concepts reflect this ontology and structure, while on the other, there is no external constraint on meaning and experience, and concepts can arbitrarily organise our experience. As Lakoff and Johnson (1980) maintain, a single motivation behind these views is a concern for understanding. Experientialism can offer a perspective in which both external and internal aspects of understanding can meet:

We see a single human motivation behind the myths of both objectivism and subjectivism, namely, a concern for understanding. The myth of objectivism reflects the human need to understand the *external* world in order to be able to function successfully in it. The myth of subjectivism is focused on *internal* aspects of understanding- what the individual finds meaningful and what makes his life worth living (ibid: 229, italics in original).

These internal aspects of understanding allow for alternative conceptualizations of the world by different people (let alone different cultures) and for the fact that the same environment can be conceptualized in "radically different fashions" (Indurkhya, 1992:127). The *external aspects* of understanding allow for the non-arbitrariness feature.

The cognitive interest in linguistics has been extended to translation studies. Alexieva (1993) suggests a cognitive approach to translation equivalence. She notes that language is not just a means of communication but also a reflection of the way we experience and know the world in terms of "universal experiential and cognitive models, as members of the human species, and in terms of a specific application of those models, as members of a linguistic and cultural community" (ibid: 105). She also claims that

the reason why, translators find it difficult to achieve greater similarity in the effect that source and target texts have on source and target receivers respectively is that *experiential and cognitive models are often used differently in the different linguistic and cultural communities* with respect to area, scope and time of operation and, most importantly, choice of the domain for comparison (ibid: 107, my emphasis)

An example she provides to elaborate on the difference between English and Bulgarian in metaphorical mappings is the case of the 'arguments are like constructs' metaphor. The mapping, she observes, is similar but the specific constructs themselves are not the same: In Bulgarian, the construct is reduced to ashes or dust, (ibid:107)

> She reduced his arguments to fluff and dust
> [=*Tya napravi dovodite mou na puh I pra*]

Likewise, in Russian, Alexieva notes (ibid: 104), the presence of a fly on the ceiling would normally be described in terms of

> A fly sits of the ceiling [=*Na potolke sidit muha*]

whereas in Bulgarian, in terms of

> On the ceiling a fly has perched [=*Na tavana e kaznala muha*]

In discussing culture-specific metaphorical mappings in humourous translations, Nilsen (1989) reports on pairs of situations and culture-specific mental representations. In German, if people are tough, they are said to

> have hairs on the teeth [=*Haare auf den Zänen haben*],

whereas, if they have big plans, they

> have raisins in the head [=*rosinen im kopf haben*].

Similarly, in Iranian, if a situation is complicated, it is

> like raisins stuck together [=*oza esh keshmeshiy*],

whereas, if something is difficult,

> the rug is being pulled out of the water [=*galim as ad birun keshidan*].

Such alternative conceptualizations across languages are numerous. Marmaridou (1994), in her study of conceptual metaphor in Greek financial discourse, points to a difference in the mappings employed with respect to financial entities. She claims that, in the Greek cultural experience, "it is less tolerated to view financial entities as living organisms and on a par with humans than it is in the Anglo-Saxon cultural experience" (ibid: 251). Thus, in translation, Alexieva concludes, we can establish the relationship between the 'real' situation and its 'language/culture-specific' mental picture through the use of cognitive and experiential modes.

Translation has been viewed as a process of mapping conceptual structures of one language onto those of another. It involves considerations about what alternative conceptualizations of the world might be relevant to the source and target cultures and in what ways these conceptualizations are constrained. The translator, as a cognitive agent, apprehends reality in one language through his/her perceptual apparatus and projects it onto another language.

Indurkhya (1992), in describing operations of cognitive models, discusses the mechanism of projection as a process involving an attempt to group the 'sensorimotor data set' to a structure which already exists and comes from the concept network being projected. The following extract from Indurkhya has been modified below to account for the fact that translation has been viewed as a process of mapping conceptual structures of one language onto another with a view to identifying culture specific constraints in metaphor use that can be part of a linguistic identity.

...One already has a structure that comes from the concept network being projected. The problem now is with coming up with a grouping of the sensorimotor data set that respects this structure. Since the sensorimotor data set has an autonomous structure, it limits the possible ways in which it can be grouped so as to reflect the structure of the concept network. The cognitive agent selects one such grouping, though this selection process might also be constrained by the physical or biological structure of the cognitive agent. (ibid:167)

The analogy between metaphorical mapping and translation process could be elaborated by 'rewriting' the above fragment as follows[1]:

...The translator already has a target structure that comes from the concept network being projected. The problem now for the translator is with coming up with a grouping of the source data that respects this target structure. Since the source data set has an autonomous structure it limits the possible ways in which it can be grouped so as to reflect the structure of the concept network. The translator as a cognitive agent selects one such grouping, though this selection process might also be constrained by physical or biological structure (level of biculturalism, cultural presuppositions etc.) of the cognitive agent.

In the translation situation described in Section 3, the translator maps internal aspects of target structure understanding on those represented in the source

---

[1] Additions to and modifications of the original fragment appear underlined.

version of a romantic poem. He, finally, comes up with a 'version' of the source data (that respects this target structure understanding by selecting an appropriate option). Section 3 observes the mapping of a system of poetic metaphors from one language onto that of another.

Alternative conceptualisations of the world, internal aspects of understanding, may thus be depicted in the process of translation, where the translator, as a cognitive agent, selects an appropriate grouping. Figure 10a is an adaptation of Indurkhya's figure 5.15 showing a perspective on projection (1992:177). Figure 10b presents an analogous figure showing a type of projection involved in translation.

2. Metaphorical Thinking in Cognitive Science and Poetry

Through metaphors, human beings understand new areas of experience in terms of others. Metaphor and metonymy have attracted cognitive scientists' attention because they have been considered basic cognitive mechanisms involved in understanding. Nikiforidou (1998), for instance, in her analysis of the concept of silence through metaphor, notes that although many dictionaries define silence negatively as absence of speech or noise etc., through metaphor we can gain direct and positive access to its meaning. As Barcelona (1998) argues, metaphors

...make it possible for human beings to understand new areas or domains of experience, or old domains of experience which are relatively difficult to apprehend conceptually, through domains that are more comprehensible because they are constituted by more direct experiences: for instance the abstract notion of life is typically understood as a journey (*He's at a crossroads in life*). (ibid: 45, emphasis in original)

Metonymy also involves a similar mechanism of projection of one domain onto another. We understand a whole concept in terms of its parts, a part in terms of the whole or a part in terms of another part. Barcelona claims that metonymy

...reflects our ability to perspectivise and to understand one domain of experience in terms of just one of its 'parts' ('hands' for 'people', as in *He's a good hand at fencing*), a part in terms of the whole domain (*'The Times' is here*, to refer to one of its reporters) or one part in terms of another part of the same domain (saying *He's a good pen*, where the instrument stands for the action) (ibid, emphasis in original).

Metaphors are relevant to translation process in two ways. As mentioned above, one perspective that makes metaphor (and possibly metonymy) relevant to translation is that translation itself is seen as an instance of metaphorical mapping from one language domain to another.

Another perspective relates to the culture-specificity of metaphorical expression which is to be reflected in translation. Metaphors and conditions on their use are culture specific because the domains of experience may differ from culture to culture, and therefore some equivalence between the varying domains of experience has to be calculated in translation.

The type of metaphors cognitive scientists are mainly focusing on is the unconscious, conventional, similarity-based type of metaphor that can be traced in dictionaries. By contrast, novel, creative, conscious, unconventional, similarity-creating metaphors (very common in poetry) seem

Fig. 10a/b. The *Projection* mechanism involved in cognition and translation: an Analogy

10a.
Adaptation of Indurkhya's Figure 5.15 (1992: 177) showing a perspective on *projection* involved in mapping

10b.

Analogy of *projection* involved in translation process

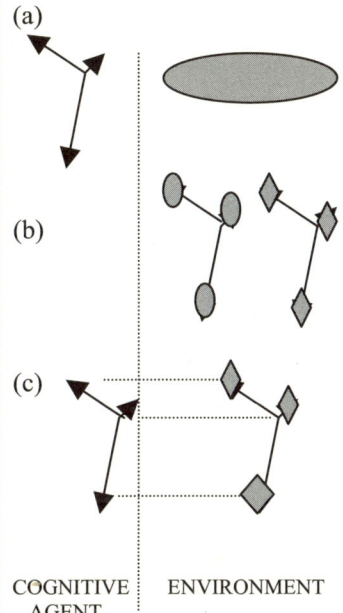

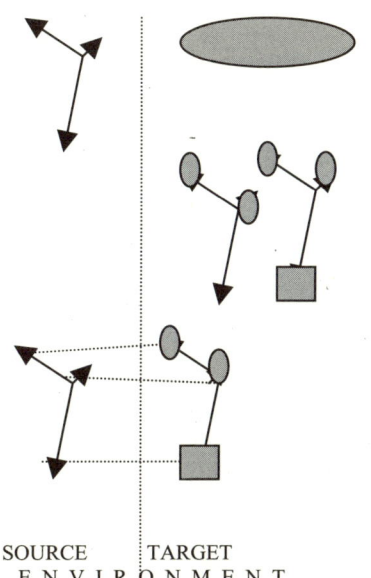

(a)

(b)

(c)

COGNITIVE ENVIRONMENT
AGENT

SOURCE TARGET
E N V I R O N M E N T

In (a), the cognitive agent selects a concept network with an autonomous structure. In (b), the environment, based on its autonomous structure,determines the possible groupings that respect the structure of the concept network. In (c), the cognitive agent, in instantiating cognition, chooses one such grouping.

In (a), the translator selects a concept network with an autonomous structure. In (b), the possible groupings are determined that respect the structure of the concept network according to what is considered appropriate in the target environment. In (c), the translator, in instantiating cognition, chooses one such grouping .

to be outside the cognitive scientist's focus, although some argue (Indurkhya, 1992:40) that similarity-creating metaphors "are quite real and play an important role in cognition".

The following section examines the treatment of metaphorical expressions in the translation of English romantic poetry into Greek, and draws conclusions about parameters that affect translator behaviour. The focus is on both types of metaphorical thinking, namely, unconscious, unoriginal, conventional metaphoring (e.g. *life is a journey*, as in the example from Lord Byron, below),

---

ST   Alas ! such is our nature! All but aim
At the same end by pathways not the same;
(*The Island* or *Christian and his Comrades*,
Canto A/6, pp.38-39, ll.115-116, transl. M. B. Raizis)[2]

TT   Man's nature has it, unfortunately, for people
to try to reach the same end from different pathways [my translation]

Φύση του ανθρώπου τόχει, δυστυχώς, να προσπαθούμε
Απο κάθε είδους δρόμους σ'ένα τέρμα να βρεθούμε
(Το Νησί ή Ο Κρίστιαν και οι Σύντροφοί του)

---

and the non-conventional, original metaphoring, the creation of similarity in the conscious mind of a cognitive agent.

The non-/conventionality features need not be associated with different metaphors. They may be aspects of a single metaphor. One single metaphor may be intended as a non-/conventional contribution, whereas the degree of non-/conventionality may be calculated in particular contexts. Unoriginal, conventional metaphors may become the basis for literary invention. As Turner (1991) points out, a reading of a poetic metaphor may be simply inheriting "prefabricated satisfactions of constraints from conventionalized metaphoric understandings" (ibid: 56), while leaving the possibilities for metaphoric construal open in any directions. In demonstrating how an *original* aspect of invention can be "constituted as an exploitation of an *unoriginal* constraint in metaphoric invention", Turner (1991: 51-67) examines the treatment of the unoriginal conventional understanding of *life is a journey* in three literary contexts. These are (a) John Bunyan's *The Pilgrim's Progress*, (b) the Fourth Gospel and (c) John Ashbery's *At North Farm*. The non-/conventionality aspects of the particular metaphor were

---

[2] Hereafter: A/6, 38-39,115-116)

treated differently in the three contexts. While the *Pilgrim's Progress* simply "inherited the conventional and unoriginal...metaphoric understanding of life as a journey", the Fourth Gospel asked the reader to do some original work in order to satisfy an unoriginal constraint. Furthermore, Ashbery's poem moved out along this gradient: although one recognizes the conventional metaphoric understanding of life experiences as journeys, possibilities for metaphoric construal, beyond that, are open in any direction. A correspondence may be assumed of apparent physical capacities of the traveller to personal capacities of the person with the goal, or a correspondence of physical relentlessness of the traveller to the psychological or social relentlessness of the person with the goal etc. (ibid: 63).

In a translation context, a translator is expected to decide in what direction possibilities for metaphoric construal are open with respect to a particular metaphor and which correspondences will be allowed in the target version.

3. Metaphors in Romantic Poetry Translation

The data in this section come from Lord Byron's narrative poem *The Island, or Christian and his Comrades* (1823) translated into Greek by Marios-Byron Raizis (1987) as

'To nisi' or *'O Kristian ke i Syntrofi tou'*
'Το Νησί' or *'Ο Κρίστιαν και οι Σύντροφοί του'*.

The sample comes from the first Canto of the poem, although attention is occasionally drawn to other parts of the poem. Metaphors employed in the source version are contrasted to their rendition in the target text and the emerging pattern of translator behaviour is discussed.

The Island is a story of "love with life, eros and freedom" (Raizis, 1987:12). It is about the mutinous Christian who, although destined for something extraordinary because of his parentage, skill and experience, "pursued his exceptional quality in the wrong way, under the urges of his instinct and idiosyncracy" (ibid: 20). He sought something nearly impossible: total freedom, love and happiness, which the official justice of his country punished him for.

As Bassnett (1980) argues, "the greatest problem when translating a text from a period remote in time is not only that the poet and his contemporaries are dead, but the *significance of the poem* in it's context is dead too" (ibid: 83, my emphasis). Byron's narrative is not dead in the present context, but a reevaluation of the significance of the poem might be one reason why the three motion pictures based on *The Island* have adopted varying points of view in the dramatization. As Raizis (1987) points out,

...completely different issues challenged the producers of films titled "Mutiny on the *Bounty*". Hollywood dramatized the injustice, tyranny and cruel treatment of crews by the naval establishment, and, naturally, justified the bold attempt of the victims against their oppressor and the institutions that supported him. The romantic poet, though, gave priority to the urges and demands of youth – to the dream of return to the Eden they had known some time (ibid: 28).

Thus, Byron did *not* justify mutiny; he only

...attributed the rebellion...to the overwhelming attraction of an existing Eden in contrast to the dire reality of the ship's "microcosm", or to the miserable life in their impoverished villages in Britain (ibid: 22).

The ideological shift in the dramatized versions reflects Hollywood's attempt to secure present day audience response. The translator - being in a similar position – has to reevaluate 'the significance of the poem in its context' and decide which aspects of the target readership's preferences are to be accommodated in the target version. The treatment of metaphors in the target version of *The Island* reflects the translator's awareness of varying constraints operating along the axes of realism, lyricism, (the poet's) philosophical awareness etc.

The types of strategies employed in transferring metaphorical expressions from source to target version, are metaphor preservation, metaphor modification and metaphor grounding. Metaphors are

- *preserved* in the target version, or are
- *modified* by either being
  - *enforced* in Greek,
  - rendered by a *different* (conventional or unconventional) target metaphor,

or, alternatively, the metaphorical status of an expression is somehow
  - *reduced* in the target version.

- Metaphor *grounding*, on the other hand, is rendering a metaphor by a non-metaphor in the target version.

Instances of intact rendition of metaphorical expressions are not extremely frequent because of non-equivalence of linguistic categories between the two languages but also because of the translator's rhyming considerations, as described in the introduction of the book:

The rhyming couplet suits 'The Island' very well because the many and colourful descriptions of the natural setting by Byron…are articulated with epigrammatic completeness and perfection in this metrical form. These artistic qualities of the text must not be ignored in a translation that would render *only the meaning* exactly. A poem is *a form with meaning*. Therefore, I rendered Byron's couplets **into Greek fifteen-syllable rhyming couplets** which respect the form, meaning and spirit of the original. **The language material has been transferred without substantial loss in most couplets;** while some were rendered more freely, and very few were recast in terms of diction and length but remained faithful to the style, technique and overall spirit of the poem (1987: 28, italics in original, bold added).

With respect to whether these rhyming condsiderations have substantially restricted translator's freedom in rendering metaphorical expressions in the target version, I would suggest that no such assumption is plausible. Given the ease and inventiveness with which the translator handles the Greek verse, I would not consider his rhyming considerations a considerable obstacle for metaphor rendering in the target version. Instead, I would attribute the observed modifications to other factors.

3.1. Patterns in Translating Lord Byron Metaphors

The example below is an instance of metaphor preservation. The type of modification the source metaphor undergoes in the target version appears in square brackets.

[English ST: *Unwilling feet* → Greek TT: *feet without willingness*]

ST   Alas! His deck was trod by *unwilling feet*,
And wilder hands would hold the vessel's sheet;
(A/2, 32-33, 25-26)

TT   *Πόδια πόστο που πατούνε, πανω, δίχως προθυμία,*
Χέρια τα πανιά κρατούνε με αγριότερη μανία

I would also consider instances of metaphor preservation cases in which
- minimal loss is observed (as, for instance, in the following example – the missing item appears in bold in the source version),

---

[English ST: *nor mercy clouds* → Greek TT: *no more clouds at*
          *rebellion's daw*n →   *rebellion's dawn*]

ST   But soon observed, this guardian was withdrawn,
Nor further ***mercy*** clouds rebellion's dawn.
(A/8, 40-41, 150-151)

TT   *μόλις όμως τον προσέξαν, τον τραβήξανε μακρυά,*
στην αυγή της ανταρσίας οχι άλλη συννεφιά.

---

or cases in which
- the source metaphor is implicitly preserved through a related lexical item (e.g. the *duty is a path* metaphor is implicitly preserved below in terms of the TT *deviation (εκτροπή)* lexical item.

[English ST: *desperate escape* → Greek TT: *desperate deviation from*
          from duty's path   *its mission*]

ST   The savage spirit which would lull by wrath
Its desperate escape from *duty's path*,
(A/3, 34-35, 59-60)

> TT τ'άγριο θάρρος τούτο είναι που γλυκαίνει την οργή του
> εκτροπή απελπισμένη απο την αποστολή του

The translator's intention to preserve the metaphorical status of expressions in the target version is also reflected in that he very often employs target conventional or non-conventional metaphors in rendering a source metaphor. As non-/conventionality of metaphors in a particular culture is rather a matter of degree, target metaphors may be placed on a continuum, with some mappings placed closer to the conventional end of the continuum and others closer to the non-conventional end. The FEAR IS A SEED metaphor (*sowing fear*) is conventional in the target language.

> [English ST: *armadas shake the world,* Greek TT: *armadas sow fear, yet*
>   *yet crumble in the wind* →   *tremble at the northern*
>   *winds*]
>
> ST And triumph's o'er the armadas of mankind,
>   Which *shake the world*, yet *crumble* in the wind
>   (A/7,40-41,139-140)
>
> TT κι υπερνικάει εύκολα ανθρώπινες αρμάδες,
>   τρόμο που σπέρνουνε παντού, μα τρέμουν τους βοριάδες)

By contrast, the rendering of the following metaphor should be placed towards the non-conventional end of the continuum.

> [English ST: *passion returns to* → Greek TT*: reason throws them to reefs*]
>   *reason's shoal*
>
> ST And raise it in his followers –'Ho! The bowl!'
>   *Lest passion should return to reason's shoal.*
>   (A/6, 38-39, 99-100)
>
> TT και στους οπαδούς σηκώνει το ποτήρι της χαράς,
>   μήπως λογική τους ρίξει στους υφάλους της ξηράς!)

The translator is making use of a similar metaphorical universe but produces a different metaphor: in ST, *passion is a ship to return to reason's shoal*, whereas in TT *reason can be a wind throwing passionate people to a reef.*

Using a TL equivalent metaphor, as in the last two examples, implies restricting or widening the set of metaphorical domains to be involved in the mapping, following culture-specific preferences. In the STs below, the wind is a bird that *flutters,* has *wings,* or *springs up.* By contrast, in the TTs, the translator felt the *flying* metaphor need not occur twice, and that the breeze does not *sink* (it is *reduced* (έπεσε)), nor has it *wings*; instead it has *breath* (πνοές). The metaphoricity range allowed for the *wind/breeze* is widened, in the target version, to include culture-specific preferences with respect to mapping domains.

[English ST: *the breeze sank,* → Greek TT: *the breeze fell,*
            had wings →   *had breath*]

ST   The arctic sun rose broad above the wave;
      The breeze now *sank,* now whisper'd from his cave;
      As on the Aeolian harp, his fitful *wings*
      Now *swell'd,* now *flutter'd* o'er his ocean strings.
      (A/9, 42-43, 169-172)

TT   *Ήλιος στο κύμα αρκτικός έριξε τη ματιά του*
      Η αύρα τώρα έπεσε, ψίθυρος στη σπηλιά του
      σ' άρπα καθώς Αιολική, οι άστατες πνοές της
      μιά τέντωναν, μιά πάλλονταν, σ'ωκεανού χορδές της.

[English ST: *the breeze springs up* → Greek TT: *the wind strengthened*]

ST   The breeze *springs up*; the lately flapping sail
      Extends its arch before the growing gale;
      (A/10, 46-47, 225-226)

TT   *Εδυνάμωσε τ'αγέρι. Τα πανιά που 'χαν κρεμάσει,*
      φούσκωσαν καμπυλωμένα, καταιγίδα πριν ξεσπάσει

Another modification, in metaphor treatment, is enforcing the metaphorical status of some metaphorical expressions. In the following TT, the human character of dolphins is enforced by the translator's introducing an additional item implying a [+ desire] human quality e.g. *yearned* (λαχταρούσαν). ST <u>*not*</u>

unconscious of the day implies a [+ awareness/ knowledge] feature which is rendered by the *their knowledge* item (τη γνώση τους) in TT. Similarly, ST *eager of the coming ray* implies a [+willingness] feature rendered by the expression *full of eagerness* (όλο ζήλο) in TT. Enforcing the original metaphor here is realized in terms of the [+desire] feature attributed to dolphins in the target version.

[English ST: Greek TT:
dolphins swam not unconscious of x → *dolphins swam with willingness*
dolphins were eager of x   → *dolphins yearned* x]

ST   The dolphins, *not unconscious of* the day,
         Swam high, as *eager of* the coming ray;
         (A/1, 32-33, 9-10)

TT   *με τη γνώση τους δελφίνια όλο ζήλο κολυμπούσαν*
        ήλιου ερχομό και μέρας στον αφρό τους λαχταρούσαν

Enforcing the human qualities of natural environment appears elsewhere, as well, in terms of showing nature to be involved in more active processes than those described in the source version. One instance of this appears on page 120: in the target version the sun *glanced at* the wave ('*έριξε τη ματιά του*'), while, in the source, it just *rose* above the wave. Similarly, TT benefactor (*ευεργέτης*) implies more active human involvement than ST *soul* does below

---

[English ST: *navigation's soul*   →   Greek TT: *navigation's benefactor*]

ST   And last, that trembling vassal of the Pole –
        The feeling compass – Navigation's *soul.*
        (A/5, 38-39, 95-96)

TT   *και τέλος, ο τρεμάμενος του Πόλου υπηρέτης –*
        η ευαίσθητη πυξίδα – Ναυτιλίας ευεργέτης)

Among others, another elaborative, lyrical intention on the part of the mediator is observed in rendering the movement of the ship.

Grounding (turning a metaphor into a non-metaphor) is another strategy employed in the rendition of metaphors in Lord Byron's *The Island.* In TT below, *where rests the warrior's head* is turned into its ground (*were buried*), while *death's promise* is grounded in terms of *killing.*

[English ST: Greek TT:
where rests the warriors head   →   *where brave men were buried*]

ST   We'll cull the flowers that grow above the dead,
      For these most bloom *where rests* the warrior's *head*;
      (B/1, 48-49, 7-8)

TT   *θα μαζέψουμε λουλούδια που στα μνήματα φυτρώνουν*
      όπου θάφτηκαν γενναίοι άνθη πάντα μεγαλώνουν

[English ST: Greek TT:
their hands deny death promises   →   *they did not kill you*]

ST   Her only cargo such a scant supply
      As *promises death* their hands deny;
      (A/5, 36-37, 87-88)

TT   *τόσα λιγοστά εφόδια το μοναδικό της βάρος*
      δε σε σκότωσαν εκείνοι, μα σε καρτερεί ο Χάρος)

3.2. Metaphor Treatment against Author Disposition

The question now arises as to what alternative conceptualizations might be relevant to the source and target culture and in what ways these conceptualizations are constrained in practice. A suggestion comes from considering the author intention prevalent in text fragments.

In the narrative, the chronological presentation of events is interrupted by many digressions allowing the poet to reveal his "inner cosmos, his thoughts and moods" (Raizis, 1987:10). These digressions are assumed to be contributing to decoding a pattern followed by the translator in the rendition of metaphorical expressions into the Greek TT. Digressions are of various kinds:

Some [digressions] express an **intensely romantic temper**, with **dissappointment** or **bitterness** over eternally unrealised ideals. For instance
       The wish – which ages have not subdued
       In man - to have no master save his mood;
Others show **realism**, or even cynicism, no matter whether they agree with common sense, or advocate diametrically opposing views, such as:

> *But vainly wolves and lions seek their den*
> *And still more vainly men escape from men.*

Others rhetorically reiforce the articulation of themes, as they contain **historical, geographical, philosophical** etc. details from the Poet's cultural awareness… (ibid:10, italics in original, bold added)

If the treatment of metaphors in TT is observed against the digressions these metaphors are connected to (along with the lyrical descriptions of tropical landscapes and the ocean[3]), it is observed that particular translation strategies relate to certain digressions and not to others. Grounding is the dominant technique along the realism axis, whereas preserving the metaphorical status of expressions mainly relates to the rest of the digressions. Figure 11 groups source metaphorical expressions under particular digressions and indicates the correlation between the strategy employed in TT per digression. It is shown that modifications in the translation strategy employed result from the translator's attempt to *be tuned to* appropriate modes of expression. He is concerned with creating culturally appropriate combinations of speaker attitudes (realistic, philosophical, lyrical etc.) and patterns of linguistic expression. The translator is, thus, projecting patterns of one language onto those of another.

In Fig. 11, there is some overlapping between the digressions associated with particular metaphors (e.g. philosophical attitude might be traced in examples presented under 'lyrical descriptions') and, therefore, the distinction between the first two digressions should not be considered absolute. Wherever the distinction might be placed, however, between the first two digressions, Fig. 11 clearly shows that the grounding strategy is employed when a realistic attitude is being expressed or, partially, for the expression of disappointment and bitterness. The realistic digression is central in the poem with reference to the destructive vitrues each 'Byronic Hero' possesses, hence the translator's focus on that. As Raizis (1987) claims, Christian

…was not motivated by the positive power of love which would have turned him towards life. The *negative spectre of death had never ceased to haunt him* (ibid: 24, my emphasis).

Expressing a realistic point of view, in the Greek TT, seems to be triggering a grounding strategy in metaphor translation, rather than a metaphor preservation strategy. This works on a par with the psychological

---

[3] The translator points out that Byron's *strong point* is the exquisite *lyrical description* of tropical landscapes, the ocean and the beautiful girl Neuha (ibid:12), the "personification of the spirit of love" (ibid: 26).

remoteness thesis postulated in Part I, where metaphor treatment was examined in press news translation.

Fig 11. Digressions vs. translation strategies in Byronic translation with respect to metaphor treatment.

DIGRESSIONS	Source metaphorical expressions	STRATEGY Preserv. Enforc.		TL equiv. Ground.	
		Preserv.	Enforc.	TL equiv.	Ground.
Lyrical descriptions	Wind *fluttered*	+			
	Shake the world			+	
	Crumble in the wind			+	
	Argo *plough'ed*..foam			+	
	The tide *yield reluctant* to the strong			+	
	Breeze *sank/wings flutter'd*			+	
	Breeze *springs up*			+	
	Dolphins..*not unconscious of*		+		
	Dolphins..*eager of*		+		
	Sun *rose* ..above the wave		+		
	Nature *owns* a nation		+		
	Made her liquid *way*		+		
Historical, Philosophical Awareness	The *raven fled the ark*	+			
	To *nestle with the dove*	+			
	Feeling *ceased*			+	
	Dip souls in blood			+	
Disappointment/ Bitterness over eternally unrealized ideals	*Mercy clouds rebellion's dawn*	+			
	Passion..return to reason's shoal			+	
	Have no master save mood				+
Realism	Where *rests the..head*				+
	The *deadly rest*				+
	As promises death				+
	The *sensation* of his crime				+

At that point, psychologically immediate topics (i.e. those considered to endanger our well-being: US scandals and war games, oil economy, human cloning, mad cows) disallowed metaphors into target texts, whereas psychologically remote topics (e.g. film making about Adolf Hitler, Russian army giving up a fight, Russia reappearing on political stage, forthcoming combination of Hilton Hotels with ITT, etc.) posed no such barrier.

It is as if Greek, does not tolerate use of metaphors along the axis of realism, with the same ease, as English does. In the present poetic paradigm, death-related metaphors ARE allowed in the target version but here, too, the prevailing strategy is that of grounding. In terms of representation, this grounding preference along the axis of realism may be implicitly represented by the 'square' option along the third axis in Fig. 10b (b), above. The translator, in instantiating cognition, comes up with a grouping of the target data that conforms to target structure preferences.

3.3. What about Metonymy?

Although the instances of metonymies in the present sample data are limited and conclusions cannot be drawn from the work of just one translator or one type of poetry, observation may suggest some aspects of difference with respect to the metaphor-metonymy pair and translator behaviour. The present data indicate that metaphors and metonymies are treated differently with reference to particular prevailing attitudes (philosophical, realistic, lyrical or other) in the text fragments. The present data show that, in contrast to metaphors, metonymies can be grounded both with lyrical descriptions and philosophical attitudes. They are employed to enforce a dramatic effect in support of a realistic or a disappointed point of view, unless in the context of metaphor grounding areas or in the context of other metonymies or metaphors.

In the present set of data, metonymies –most of which involve mapping within the body domain– are preserved or even created (by metonymic translation) in text fragments involving bayonets and cruel behaviour to enforce a dramatic effect (ST *throat* > TT *caratid,* ST *eye of death* > TT *death's face* and ST *breast* > TT *heart*).

[English ST: *thy throat* → Greek TT: *your naked caratid*]

ST   Full in thine eyes is waved the glittering blade,
        Close to *thy throat* the pointed bayonet laid.
        (A/4, 36-37, 71-72)

> TT   Μπρος στα μάτια σου σαλεύει η γιαλιστερή λεπίδα,
> λόγχης άκρο σημαδεύει τη γυμνή σου καρωτίδα.

In contrast to metaphors, metonymies tend to be grounded with philosophical hints and lyrical descriptions.

> [English ST: *equal land* → Greek TT: *all of them equal*]
>
> ST   The field o'er which promiscuous Plenty pour'd
> Her horn; the *equal land* without a lord;
> (A/2, 34-35, 35-36)
>
> TT   κτήμα όπου Αφθονία άδειαζε χωρίς ντροπή
> κέρας της – χωρίς αφέντη, όλοι ίσοι τους εκεί.

Instances of metonymic grounding may appear in the context of metaphor grounding areas, where metaphoring is discouraged in the target version (e.g. ST *their hands* < TT *they* and ST *thy breast* < TT *your body*).

> [English ST: *their hands* → Greek TT: *they*]
>
> ST   Her only cargo such a scant supply
> As *promises death* their hands deny;
> (A/5, 36-37, 87-88)
>
> TT   τόσα λιγοστά εφόδια το μοναδικό της βάρος
> δε σε σκότωσαν εκείνοι, μα σε καρτερεί ο Χάρος

> [English STs: *thy breast* → Greek TTs: *your heart*
>   *the hands* →   *the sailors*
>
> ST   Thy limbs are bound, the bayonet at *thy breast;*
> *The hands,* which trembled at thy voice arrest;
> (A/3, 34-35, 55-56)
>
> TT   Χειροπόδαρα σε δένουν, λόγχη πιέζει την καρδιά σου
> σε συλλάβανε οι ναύτες πού 'τρεμαν προστάγματά σου

Some instances of metonymic grounding appear in contexts in which the translator has introduced another metaphor or metonymy: the example above shows an instance of metonymic grounding (ST *hands* < TT *sailor*) in the context of metonymic translation (:metonymy introduction in the target version – *breast* > *heart*).

Fig. 12 shows the complementary distribution between metaphors and metonymies in target lyrical and philosophical text fragments. The reason probably is that metonymies are weaker figurative devices than metaphors and often demand less processing effort, since they involve mapping within a single domain (Barcelona, 1998: 47 and Goosens, 1995: 16), in contrast to metaphors, which involve mapping two discrete domains. Goosens (ibid: 201), focusing on metonymy in diachronic perspective, reports that metonymy is an important strategy to extend the meaning of symbolic units "probably even more pervasive than metaphor". In examining metonymic extentions associated with the symbolic item 'mouth' in Ælfric, Chaucer and Shakespeare, Goosens argues that there is a *literal-metonymy-metaphor* continuum exhibiting various patterns of interpenetration between metonymy and metaphor (ibid).

In the present context, they are complementary devices used for creating a particular effect. Being relatively weaker devices, metonymies

- need not be employed for lyrical descriptions and philosophical attitudes
  - where the prevailing figurative device is metaphor,

and

- are more heavily constrained by context (e.g. they may be constrained by the appearance of another metonymy/metaphor or by the prevailing grounding preference occuring in realistic text fragments).

It is as if there is some redundancy created: co-occurrence of metaphoric and metonymic devices raises metaphoricity to some intolerable level in the target language, which the translator (consciously or subconsciously) attempts to regulate by ruling out the weaker device.

Fig. 12. Distribution of metaphor and metonymy in romantic poetry translation into Greek.

DIGRESSIONS	METAPHOR	METONYMY
Lyrical descriptions	+	-
Philosophical attitude	+	-
Disappointment or Bitterness	±	±
Realism	±	±

The restricted set of data examined here does not allow for accurate conclusions to be drawn about the constraints operating in Greek with respect to the use of metaphors and metonymies. Whatever the constraints with reference to translation of a particular poet, a period, a genre or with reference to a particular translator, the point remains that there are (culture-) specific structures in the mind of translators, which they project onto those of the source language in search of a structure ('an appropriate grouping') which respects the structure they have in mind. Cognition and the process of understanding as viewed by cognitive scientists account for mechanisms in the mind of translator, in search of an appropriate option.

In what follows, it is shown that the apparatus employed to account for metaphorical mappings, in cognitive linguistics, can account for instances of translator behaviour, thus enlightening the issue of drawing conclusions about linguistic identities through translation.

3.4. Cognitive Linguistics and Translator Behaviour

The aim of this section is to indicate that exploration into the nature of conceptual processes involved in metaphorical and metonymic extentions –as generally understood in cognitive linguistics– goes a long way towards explaining instances of translator behaviour.

It can account for instances of deviation from the expected/ normative behaviour described above. The translator of *The Island* allows certain mappings but crosses out others which would normally be expected to be retained in the Greek TT. It is claimed that such deviations can be accounted for in terms of a donor-domain evaluation approach (Simon-Vandenbergen 1995). The unexpected translator behaviour occurs in

---

[English ST: *the stars creep* → Greek TT: *the stars move away*]
                 the stars lift their eyelids →   *the stars move their eyelids*

ST   The stars from broader beams began *to creep,*
        And lift their shining eyelids from the deep;
        (A/1, 32-33, 11-12)

TT   *Άρχισαν να ξεμακραίνουν τ' άστρα απο τις αχτίδες,*
        Κι απ' το κύμα να σηκώνουν τις λαμπρές τους βλεφαρίδες

The part of the poem, the extract comes from, is a lyrical description. As claimed previously, the strategies for metaphor translation in lyrical descriptions of the poem are expected to be those of preservation, TL equivalence, enforcing the metaphorical status etc., but not grounding. In other words, translator would be expected to exploit the metaphoricity of the text fragment and not let it go.

In the source version, there are two source/donor domains (reptiles -*creep* & body parts -*eyelids*, respectively) mapped on the target domain (stars) in the metaphorical mapping. In the translation, the reptile domain (represented in terms of *creep*) does not survive, it is grounded (*move away*). The question arises as to why it is only the body part domain that survived the intercultural filter and not the reptile domain. Not preserving this latter source domain does not seem to be an ad hoc choice, because it occurs elsewhere in the data.

An answer to this question comes from empirical investigation into the conceptualization of the domain of linguistic action in English, with a focus on figurative extensions into that domain. Simon-Vandenbergen (1995), in examining to what extent conventionalized metaphors reflect positive or negative *evaluations* of certain aspects of linguistic behaviour, shows that the expression of value judgements is a rule and that most of the time they are negative. She also deals with the contribution of specific donor domains to the expression of value judgements. A value judgement, she claims, may be transferred from the source domain directly or may come in only after extension to a specific aspect of the target domain. She also comments on the context-dependency of certain value judgements associated with metaphorical mappings in view of varying sub-cultural or individual values and attitudes:

> … it appears that sub-**cultural** as well as individual **values** and attitudes play a role in judgements. The same expression may evoke contexts which by one group/ individual are evaluated in a positive way and by another one in a negative way. For instance, self-control and refinement are obviously not always valued positively by everybody. The association of types of behaviour with particular evaluations **depend on one's broader value system**. (See e.g. the discussion of *keep a stiff upper lip…*) (1995:111, italics in original, bold added)

If the expression of value judgements can be extended to poetic, non-conventional metaphor[4] and if –as claimed above– subcultural and individual value systems affect the value judgements associated with particular metaphorical mappings, it goes without saying that there are specific evaluations associated with source/donor domains (e.g. reptiles) which are reflected in non-conventionalized metaphors as well. Such evaluation differences may be specific to cultures, individuals etc (see also the Lakoff and Johnson extract below), but also specific to temporal periods. Pauwels (1995: 129) shows how historical change may cause a change in salience of

---

[4] Indurkhya (1992:40) argues that similarity-creating (non-conventional) metaphors are "are quite real and play an important role in cognition".

certain conceptual domains. Value judgements may change as time passes and, thus, translators would have to adjust metaphorical mappings, in the target version, in order to secure an appropriate (positive/negative) value. In the example above, a negative value attributed to the source/donor domain (*reptiles*) is discouraging the translator from allowing it to cross the intercultural filter, in a context in which only positive judgements are being expected (e.g. in a lyrical description of the ocean). By contrast, the body-parts donor domain (*shining eyelids*) does not create such an incompatibility.

A second issue to be tackled with a view to showing that the theoretical apparatus, in cognitive linguistics can go a long way towards accounting for instances of translator behaviour, is the translator's modifying the donor domain in the target version to meet culture-specific preferences. This instance of translation behaviour can be accounted for in terms of the image-schematic approach adopted in empirical investigation of conceptual mappings. Image-schemata are universal physical notions which seem to be at the root of our abstract concepts (Barcelona, 1998: 46) used in metaphorical mapping. The nature of metaphorical mapping is partial: the source domain does not necessarily project upon all its semantic structure onto the target domain, because there is often some incompatibility between source and target domain.

The compatibility between particular source and target domains in metaphorical mapping seems to be a matter of degree across cultures. As Lakoff and Johnson (1980) maintain,

…there are cartoon conventions where mountains become animate and their peaks become heads. The point, here, is that there are metaphors, like A MOUNTAIN IS A PERSON, that are *marginal in our culture and our language*; their used part may consist of only one conventionally fixed expression in the language, and they do not systematically interact with other metaphorical concepts because so little of them is used. This makes them relatively uninteresting for our purposes but not necessarily so, since they can be extended to their unused part in coining *novel metaphorical expressions*, making jokes etc. (ibid: 54-55, capitalization in original, italics added)

In the example below, there is a difference with respect to the compatibility of the *target*/recipient (*billow*) and *source*/donor (*flash* -light domain) image-schemata between the source (English) and the target version (Greek), whatever reasons (diachronic or not) there might exist.

The assumption is that the translator is discouraged from allowing the image-schematic structure of the donor domain (*light*) to be projected on that of the target domain (*billow*) in Greek, because the *light-billow* schematic structures in Greek are incompatible in conventional use. Translator behaviour here is accounted for in terms of the theoretical apparatus employed in cognitive linguistics to explore the conceptual processes involved in metaphorical mapping.

[English ST: *the billow flashed* → Greek TT: *the billow sprang up*]

ST   The cloven billow *flash'd* from off her prow
In furrows form'd by that majestic plough;
(A/1, 32-33, 3-4)

TT   *πίσω χωρισμένο κύμα απ'την πρύμη ξεπετιόταν*
σ' αύλακες απο της πλώρης την αιχμή καθώς κοβόταν

In this section, metaphorical extensions, as understood in cognitive linguistics, are shown to provide tools accounting for translator behaviour in metaphor translation. The translation-as-a-metaphor-for-human-cognition claim is verified, through examination of metaphor treatment in the translation of romantic poetry.

Translators are mapping internal aspects of target structure understanding onto those of the source version of the poem. The emerging pattern of translator behaviour with respect to metaphor treatment in Byronic translation involves the selection of a (culturally) appropriate pattern of linguistic behaviour that respects the (target) pattern the translator has in mind. Focus is shifted to metonymy, which – in the present restricted set of data – is shown to be a device weaker than metaphor, almost in complementary distribution with it, in the target version.

Furthermore, instances of translator behaviour in Byronic metaphor translation are accounted for in terms of theoretical approaches and constructs employed in cognitive linguistics: the donor-domain evaluation approach (Simon-Vandenbergen 1995) and the image-schematic approach (Lakoff and Johnson 1980) go a long way towards explaining translator behaviour.

Within the cognitive framework, universality is stressed although peculiarities of cultures are also emphasized. As Delabastita (1997) points out, cognitive linguistics "assumes the existence of certain universal cognitive mechanisms, but also highlights the specificity of the way every community draws on its own experiences in shaping its knowledge of reality" (ibid:12). In the following section, emphasis will be on particularity rather than universality. Translators, like ethnographers (Valero-Garcés 1995), have to be both bilingual and bicultural in order to successfully act as 'interpreters of experience' between two cultures. They need to observe socio-economic and political conditions while manipulation of information is part of their task. Attention is drawn, in the following section, on aspects of less widely spoken (sourse) languages whose identities may be suppressed and assimilated by widely-spoken languages.

SUMMARY OF 3 (III)

Section 3 explores the treatment of metaphors in the context of English>Greek Byronic poetry translation. Metaphor and metonymy treatment in the target data shows some prevalent normative pattern, which is in accordance to preferred patterns of metaphor treatment in the news reporting translation examined in previous sections in this volume. Metaphorical mappings are treated differently in the present target version of the poem, relative to the digression type (lyrical, philosophical, realistic) prevalent in the relevant text fragments. A target language preference is manifested in that metaphors tend to be grounded along the axis of realism, but are transferred along the other digressions. Conclusions in this section are in accordance with the psychological remoteness thesis postulated with respect to the treatment of metaphors in news reporting translation. Translation production allows for preferred linguistic patterns to be retrieved that cut across genres and are, thus, better candidates for culturally preferred linguistc traits, which can constitute a linguistic identity.

4. The Cultural Orientation: Minoritizing Translation

This section considers domesticating (rather than foreignizing) moves in the rendition of a Greek novel into English to show that the domesticating intention of a translator may contribute useful insights into studying linguistic identities across languages. The English target data, in this section, show the reverse tendencies in the treatment of linguistic phenomena to those observed in the E>G direction studied in previous sections. This suggests that systematic types of interference in the target data may be considered a manifestation of a target linguistic identity rather than a reflection of translator explicitation tendency.

Within the literary and cultural studies orientation, an important issue is the power relations between translated and translating languages and cultures.

...assymetries, inequities, relations of domination and dependence exist in every act of translation of putting the translated in the service of the translating culture...
...In practice the fact of translation is erased by suppressing the linguistic and cultural differences of the foreign text, assimilating to dominant values in the target language culture, making it recognizable and therefore seemingly untranslated (Venuti, 1998: 4/31).

Translations should be written, read and evaluated with greater respect for linguistic and cultural differences. Major, hegemonic (target) languages may suppress cultural values reflected in texts from marginal (source) cultures by domesticating and assimilating foreign literary texts 'too forcefully to dominant values at home, erasing the sense of *foreignness* that was likely to have invited translation in the first place' (ibid: 5, my emphasis). As Venuti argues,

translating can never simply be communication between equals because it is fundamentally ethnocentric. Most literary projects are initiated in the domestic culture, where the foreign text is selected to satisfy different tastes from those that motivated its composition and reception in its native culture. And the very function of translation is assimilation, the inscription of a foreign text with domestic intelligibilities and interests. I follow Berman ... *in suspecting any literary translation that mystifies this inevitable domestication as an uncontrolled communicative act. Good translation is demystifying: it manifests in its own language the foreignness of the foreign text* .... (ibid: 11, my emphasis)

The issue is particularly relevant to Greek-English translation, as Greek is a less widely spoken language worldwide and runs the risk of being 'domesticated' too forcefully into English, and losing its 'heterogeneity' in translation.

Awareness of asymmetries in the transmission of foreign values and the need to protect heterogenious discourses from being too forcefully assimilated in the domestic culture lead to the notion of minoritizing translation. The heterogenious discourse of minoritizing translation "resists this assimilationist ethic by signaling the linguistic and cultural differences in the text – within the major language" (ibid: 12).

Translator training programmes need to take into account the issue of heterogeneity of language and the transmission of cultural and political values involved in the process of translation. This section focuses on the issue of heterogeneity of language in a Greek-English translation situation, namely, in the translation of Aris Alexandrou's *To Kivotio* (*Το κιβώτιο* 1974) translated by Robert Crist (*Mission Box*, 1996)[5].

Preserving the heterogeneity of a source (foreign) text in a target (domestic) version is a realization of a foreignizing intention in translation process, implying respect for cultural differences between languages and cultures. By contrast, assimilating relates to a domesticating intention on the part of translators which – if extensively applied – leads to suppression of foreign cultural values. The aim is to claim that although assimilationist or minoritizing considerations in translation primarily relate to cultural values rather than particular linguistic preferences, they presuppose awareness of preferred linguistic traits in source and target environments, thus enforcing the view that TTs may offer insights into the study of linguistic identities.

The foreignizing intention involves both the selection of the foreign text and the linguistic devices employed in the translation. As Venuti (1998) claims, the translator has to be 'strategic both in selecting foreign texts and in developing discourses to translate them (ibid:10). Similarly, Tahir-Gürçağlar (2003) discusses the strategic significance of selecting a repertoire according to practices of the Translation Bureau in Turkey between 1940-1966. Its products "came to be identified with the modernization and westernization project of early republican Turkey" (ibid: 113).

In identifying domesticating and foreignizing techniques in the translation of *Mission Box* attention is directed to the contribution of both variables to the study of linguistic identities.

---

[5] Alexandrou, Aris. 1996. *Mission Box*. Athens: Kedros. Translated by Robert Crist (Aris Alexandrou. 1974. *To Kivotio*. Athens: Kedros)

4.1. 'Selecting Foreign Texts'

A translator's interest in the novel is justified both on thematic and linguistic grounds. Scholars[6] have referred to some of the strengths of the novel. As Crist (1996) points out in the "Translator's Epilogue", in the English edition, the story in *Mission Box*

...clearly reflects both the nation's and the author's tragic experience [of the Greek civil war, 1946-1949]. The narrator, believing deeply in the humanity of the socialist struggle, devotes himself to political activism and armed resistence to oppression. A soldier in the army of liberation (ELAS), his commitment climaxes in his participation in Mission Box – a mission which, according to his superiors, will win the war and bring about the triumph of socialism in Greece, at the very time that defeat seems inevitable. The narrator alone survives the mission, yet he accomplishes the transport of the box to its destination. However, at the time he believes the goal has been achieved, he finds himself imprisoned by his own party, accused apparently, of treason to the cause. His narration of his actions and his search for the locus of guilt constitute the novel, which is composed in the narrator's cell and sent to a shadowy interrogator, who refuses to respond or enter into dialogue with the prisoner (ibid: 345).

The novel exhibits both intertextual affinities[7], which would facilitate recognition of domestic values on the part of domestic audiences, but also allows for the source cultural identity to be promoted in the English target context, involving values like a sense of duty, self-sacrifice, solidarity, betrayal, full submission to political hierarchies etc. in the context of the Greek civil war.

Cultural identity is a point of interest in cultural studies. As Inglis (1993/1994) claims, Cultural Studies in its solidarity, seriousness and commitment to spontaneity, makes much of the value of cultural identity. Furthermore, the story in *Mission Box (To Kivotio)* is interesting from a cultural studies perspective because, as Inglis notes, the "most useful life-stories are those which throw a light net over a historical moment, and reveal its essential contours on the historical map" (ibid: 235).

Raising issues like 'personal freedom' and 'national identity' in a novel is of basic interest to cultural studies. On a par, translating novels which raise

---

[6] D. Maronitis (*To Vima,* June 26, 1975), R. Crist (*Anti*, April 14, 19979), A. Kotzias (*I Kathimerini*, May 18, 1975), A. Argyriou (*Anti*, Nov. 15, 1975), N. Grigoriades (*Chroniko*, Sept./Aug. 1995). While Maronitis refers to Alexandrou's linguistic achievement, Crist, Kotzias, Argyriou and Grigoriades additionally expand on the treatment of particular themes and perspectives, in the novel.

[7] see Crist and Kotzias: Alexandrou's writing echoes Dostoyevsky's, Joyce's, Heminway's, Kafka's, Faukner's writing.

such issues is an enterprise of double significance. On the one hand, the translator promotes particular values as a part of a nation's identity. Translating *Mission Box (To Kivotio)* is strategic in that it promotes particular cultural values related to the socialist struggle: human suffering, self-sacrifice etc. These are shown to be part of the source Greek national identity in addition to or in place of the widespread view about a compound of touristic values widely associated with the source culture in the English target environment (wine, hospitality etc). On the other, being aware of the power relations between languages one can adjust translation strategies towards preserving national identity.

The translator is fully aware that *Mission Box* has some "mission to carry abroad" as stated in the 'Translator's Epilogue' in the English edition, alluding - among other things- to the 'strategic' significance of the novel in the domestic culture:

…With fond memories and gratitude to Aris and Katy, *To kivotio* is sent forth to carry its mission abroad.
Robert Crist, University of Athens, Nov. 1, 1995. ('Translator's Epilogue'. *Mission Box*. 1996. p.346)

In what follows, attention will be drawn to the other aspect of strategic significance anticipated in Venuti (1998), namely, *developing discourses* in minoritizing translation. A few domesticating and foreignizing devices consciously or subconsciously employed in the translation of *Mission Box* are identified below. The goal is showing that apart from cultural value considerations prevalent in translation, domesticating/foreignizing intentions may be manifested through linguistic preferences implicitly associated with particular languages, thus, enforcing the view that translation can contribute to the study of linguistic identities.

4.2. 'Developing the Discourses'

Venuti's concern about translators having to be strategic in developing discourses aims at avoiding repressing the heterogeneity of the foreign language in the domestic environment. Developing discourses in the *Mission Box*, involves a number of domesticating (:contributing to assimilating the foreign text in the domestic culture) and foreignizing modifications (:contributing to preserving the heterogeneity of the foreign text in the domestic culture (1998:10)). The intention here is to cater for domesticating rather than foreignizing moves, because the domesticating interventions are the ones that would shed light on linguistic identities through juxtaposition of Greek STs and English TTs. In this reverse translation direction (G>E), translators' subconscious behaviour can point to source preferences that are assumed to be part of the source linguistic identity and need to be modified in the English target version for communicative equivalence to be ensured.

Domesticating moves may be observed in (a) the treatment of conventional expressions, (b) the signalling of discourse intentions by the narrator and (c) some modification of the profile of the reader assumed by narrator in the novel.

The treatment of metaphors and fixed expressions ranges from employing a target language equivalent conventional expression to introducing conventional expressions in the target version. Omitting or grounding metaphors is rather rare.

ST	...inscribing all the changes, *with every n and every s,* without making a mistake anywhere; as regards that I'm sure... [my translation]
	...καταγράφοντας όλες τις αλλαγές με το νι και με το σίγμα, χωρίς να κάνω λάθος πουθενά, ως προς αυτό είμαι σίγουρος... (*To Kivotio*, 1974, p.282)
TT	...inscribing all the changes, *dotting every i and crossing every t,* without making a mistake anywhere; as regards that I'm sure... (*Mission Box*, 1996, p. 326, transl. Robert Crist)

Expressions like the ones above are evidently employed to enforce the communicative potential of the text[8].

---

[8] For more moves raising the communicative potential of the text, see

Greek STs [my tramslation]	English TTs
...only our own folks do *not talk* *μονάχα οι δικοί μας δε μιλάνε* (p.287)	...only our own don't *spill their guts* (p.332)
... all five of us *sat* in the jeep *...Καθήσαμε και οι πέντε στο τζιπ...*(p. 42)	The five of us *piled* into the jeep (p.47)
...beautiful *like cold water* *...όμορφη σαν τα κρύα νερά...*(p.283)	a...beauty, *fresh as a daizy...* (p.328).
...to take care of him *as they do of their eyes ....σαν τα μάτια τους...* (p.287)	...watch it *like hawks* (p.319)

Unconventional metaphoring is absent. As Raftopoulos (1996) points out, the narrator's discourse, in *To Kivotio,* is primarily denotative and the metaphors employed conventional.

Conventional expressions/metaphors are added, in the following examples to make dircourse appropriate in the receiving culture, by elaborating on a tendency which in English was observed to be prevalent even outside literary genres (see preference for metaphoring in English source press news items, Part I). In contrast to omitting metaphors, conventional expression or metaphor introduction is a frequently employed device in the data.

The metaphor introduction device, in this context, is far from random and arbitrary. The level of tolerance with respect to metaphoring was shown to vary between English and Greek, across genres. In English-Greek news translation, metaphorical expressions were filtered out, in the target version, when hot political issues were dealt with in the news article. In news headline translation, between English and Greek, translators also preferred to present the readership with factual information rather than create an artistic effect through metaphor introduction (Sidiropoulou, 1995a: 303). Similarly, in Lord Byron translation into Greek, the metaphorical status of expressions tended to be eliminated in the TT, in realistic text fragments (e.g. when the issue of *death* was involved).

ST   Indeed, late at the night on 11 July 1949, the trainer woke us, not
      with his shrill whistle, but by nudging us one by one. He whispered
      that we should *make no noise* and leave by the small side door in the
      basement to go to the Arbor Tavern. [my translation]

      Πράγματι, αργά το βράδυ της 11ης Ιουλίου 1949, ο προγυμναστής μας
      ξύπνησε, όχι με τη σφυρίχτρα, μα σκουντώντας μας έναν-έναν και
      λέγοντάς μας ψυθιριστά να μην κάνουμε θόρυβο, να κατέβουμε στο
      υπόγειο, να βγούμε απ'τη μικρή πλαϊνή πόρτα, και να πάμε στην
      ταβέρνα «Η κληματαριά» (To Kivotio, 1974, p. 31)

TT   Late in the night of 11 July 1949, the trainer woke us, not with his
      shrill whistle, but by nudging us one by one. He whispered that we
      should leave by the side door in the basement and go *quietly as*
      mice to the Arbor Tavern.
      (*Mission Box*, 1996, p. 35)

By contrast, in the present Greek-English translation situation, metaphorical expressions are encouraged in the target (English) version, even in cases in which *death* is dealt with. It is as if metaphoring is encouraged only under particular conditions in Greek, in contrast to English which somehow allows more frequent use of metaphoring in certain genres. Metaphor introduction into the English version is seen as a domesticating move, in the present context, as translation into English assumes enforcing metaphoricity, whereas translation into Greek assumes reduction of metaphoricity levels in some contexts.

ST   ...I did my best, though, not to be in the firing squad because I didn't want to be among those who *would kill* Capt. Nikitas, for he was a faithful fighter, a Leninist and a man of integrity. [my translation]

...*προσπάθησα ωστόσο να μην πάρω μέρος στο απόσπασμα, γιατι δεν τόθελα καθόλου να σκοτώσω τον λοχαγό Νικήτα, που ήταν τίμιος αγωνιστής, λενινιστής και ντόμπρος χαρακτήρας . (To Kivotio, 1974, p.38)*

TT   ...I did my best not to be in the firing squad because I didn't want to be among those who *had* Capt. Nikitas's *blood on their hands*, for he was a faithful fighter, a Leninist and a man of integrity. (*Mission Box*, 1996, p. 43)

Another domesticating move is crossing discourse intentions and illocutionary force of utterances out of the English TT. The narrator in *To Kivotio*, in order to facilitate the receiver (the Comrade Interrogator) with processing, has occasionally signalled discourse intentions. These are omitted in the English TT. A similar intention was observed in English-Greek headline translation (Sidiropoulou, 1995a: 301) in which translators were shown to restructure the Greek (target) headline in order to include schematic (in addition to thematic) information. Schematic information relates to van Dijk's (1985) schematic structures in news discourse (as opposed to content), in the representation of the overall form of the discourse. Offering schematic information is letting addressees know what the speaker's intention in discourse is, thus saving them some processing effort. In news headline translation, translators have included such a type of information in the Greek versions of headlines. Greek seems to encourage stating discourse intentions for attracting attention or saving the addressee some processing effort. Omitting discourse intentions in an English target version, as shown in the following example, is a domesticating move, which allows a Greek source linguistic preference to stand out.

ST   ...I accuse the Acting Commander of undermining security precautions). *I'm coming back to the adjutant's office.* Indeed, the soldier took me to the school's basement. He led me through arched passageways...[my translation]

> *...Κατηγορώ τον αντισυνταγματάρχη Βελισσάριο για παράβαση συνωμοτικών κανόνων). Επανέρχομαι στο υπασπιστήριο. Ο φαντάρος με οδήγησε πράγματι στο υπόγειο. Μπροστά εκείνος, πίσω εγώ, περάσαμε απο θολωτούς διαδρόμους...*
> *(To Kivotio, 1974, p.16)*
>
> TT ...I accuse the Acting Commander of undermining security precautions). [] From the office of the aid-de-camp a soldier took me to the school's basement. He led me through arched passageways...(*Mission Box*, 1996, p. 17/18)

Similarly, making the illocutionary force of utterances explicit was a device preferred in the Greek target version of news headline translation, whereas in the English source headline versions, the illocutionary potential of these headlines was left to be inferred by readers.   In the present translation situation, the illocutionary force of utterances is occasionally omitted echoing the explicitating-the-illocutionary-force-in-Greek preference observed in news headline.

Omitting the trait from the present English TT suggests that making the illocutionary force of utterances explicit in the Greek target news headline situation (E>G) was not a mere explicitation tendency. It was more than that. It was rather a preference intrinsic to the linguistic profile of Greek, evidently, associated with the positively polite linguistic behaviour preferred in the Greek cultural context. If it had been a mere manifestation of an explicitation tendency, the feature would not have been omitted from the English TT, it would have been enforced. It is omitted because it creates a foreignizing gloss. When preference stays on the same language side, no matter the directionality of translation (e.g. E>G or G>E) it is reasonable, I guess, to assume that the feature is a linguistic preference of that language rather than a mere manifestation of an explicitation tendency.

> ST ...however, *one might argue* that I did fulfill a special function in the battalion. *This may be supported by the fact that* upon my promotion to first sergeant, they made me political coordinator of the second Battalion, and *I can boast that* I did very well or if I *want to be absolutely objective* this *was* a post for which I was particularly suited because of my university studies. They would not find anyone with my background as a second-year law school attendant? [my translation]

> *...ωστόσο, απο μία άποψη, θα έλεγε κανείς οτι είμουνα απαραίτητος. Απόδειξη πως ενώ με είχανε προβιβάσει σε επιλοχία, τα χρέη μου τα εκτελούσε ένας λοχίας κι εμένα με αποσπάσανε στη διαφώτιση του τάγματος και μπορώ να καυχηθώ οτι τα κατάφερνα πολύ καλά, ή για να είμαι απολύτως αντικειμενικός, δεν μπορούσανε να βρούν καλύτερον απο μένα, γιατι δεν υπήρχε άλλος επιλοχίας που να έχει τελειώσει το δεύτερο έτος της Νομικής.* (*To Kivotio*, 1974, p.11)
>
> TT   ...but [] I did fulfill a special function in the battalion. [] Upon my promotion to first sergeant, they made me political coordinator of the second Battalion, [] a post for which I was particularly suited because of my university studies. Following my transfer, where would they find someone with my background as a second-year law school attendant? (*Mission Box*, 1996, p. 11)

A third domesticating device employed in the English target version of *To Kivotio* is that the narrator often presupposes a positive attitude on the part of the addressee (in this case, of the Comrade Interrogator). By contrast, in the Greek source version, it is a negative attitude which is presupposed of the Comrade Interrogator. The term 'positive' here has nothing to do with the positively polite behaviour which is claimed (Sifianou 1992) to be preferred in Greek. 'Negative attitude' rather assumes a preference in the Greek source version to promote structures which allow negative presuppositions with respect to how easily the addressee is expected to be convinced about the truth of the arguments put forward. *There is absolutely no doubt about this* (*όσο γι'αυτό δεν χωράει καμμια αμφιβολία*) assumes an addressee expected to doubt the truth of the proposition. Similarly, *who could he be afraid of?* (*ποιόν είχε να φοβηθεί*) assumes a denier attitude on the part of addressees and attempts to anticipate it by providing more reassurance.

ST   He was executed at dawn on 13 July 1949. *There is absolutely no
      doubt about this*, unfortunately, I can verify that, and it's also a fact
      that the lot fell to me -... [my translation]

      *Εκτελέστηκε τα χαράματα της 13ης Ιουλίου 1949, όσο γι αυτό δε
      χωράει καμμιά απολύτως αμφιβολία, είμαι δυστυχώς απολύτως
      σίγουρος, μου έπεσε κι εμένα ο κλήρος,...* (*To Kivotio*,1974, p.38)

TT   He was executed at dawn of 13 July 1949. [] Unfortunately, I can
      verify that, and it's also a fact that the last moment the lot fell to me -
      ... (*Mission Box*, 1996, p.43)

ST   We arrived at the former Gymnasium burdened with those heavy tree
      trunks and I was thinking that if the writer had wanted to complete
      the slogan on the board ("Death to Fascism"), he should have been
      able to do so in his own good time – *who could he be afraid of?* [my
      translation]

      *Γυρίσαμε στο πρώην γυμνάσιο φορτωμένοι με κορμούς κι εγώ
      σκεφτόμουνα πως αν ήθελε κάποιος να γράψει «Θάνατος στο
      φασισμό», θα συμπλήρωνε βέβαια το σύνθημα μ'όλη την ησυχία του –
      ποιόν είχε να φοβηθεί;* (*To Kivotio*, 1974, p.21)

TT   We arrived at the former Gymnasium burdened with those heavy tree
      trunks and I was thinking that if the writer had wanted to complete
      the slogan on the board ("Death to Fascism"), he should have been
      able to do so in his own good time. [] (*Mission Box*, 1996, p. 23/24)

In the examples above the source negative presupposition is simply deleted
from the English TT (a '[]' sign in the target version is used as a trace of the
omitted item).

In the following examples the negative options (*without x, y would have
sunk*) is replaced by positive ones in the English TT (*x alone would have
saved y*), while the Greek ST modifier *without any logical gaps* (*δίχως
διανοητικά χάσματα*) has disappeared in the English TT.

ST   All these days (and don't think I'm impatient – I know you have countless crucial duties; I realize that *without vigilance* the Party *would have been sunk* long ago; I assure you I'm not complaining) – ...I spelled out my testimony in my mind, and the words fell readily into place, forming a complete, accurate picture *without any logical gaps.* [my translation]

Ολες αυτές τις μέρες *(και μη νομίζετε οτι δυσανασχετώ, ξέρω πως έχετε πολλές και σπουδαίες ασχολίες, ξέρω πως χωρίς την επαγρύπνηση το Κόμμα θα είχε καταποντιστεί προ πολλού, σας βεβαιώ δεν παραπονιέμαι) ...κατέστρωνα νοερά την κατάθεσή μου και οι λέξεις μπαίνανε απο μόνες τους στη θέση τους και σχημάτιζαν φράσεις εναργείς, σύντομες, περιεκτικές, δίχως διανοητικά χάσματα. (To Kivotio, 1974, p.10)*

TT   All these days (don't think I'm impatient – I know you have countless crucial duties; I realize *that vigilance alone has saved the Party*; I assure you I'm not complaining) ...I spelled out my testimony in my mind, and everything fell readily into place, forming a complete, accurate picture []. (*Mission Box*, 1996, p.10)

Similarly, Greek ST *not late* is rendered in terms of English TT *soon,*

ST   Fortunately, I *was not late* to assure myself that my suspicions were groundless... [my translation]

Ευτυχώς, δεν άργησα να βεβαιωθώ οτι οι φόβοι μου είτανε αβάσιμοι...(To Kivotio, 1974, p.11)

TT   Fortunately, I *soon* had proof, as follows, that these suspicions were groundless... (*Mission Box*, 1996, p. 12)

and reassurance is sought for in the Greek ST in terms of *is it not true?*, while in the English TT in terms of *right?*

ST   ...to refuse to obey the orders of my superiors (for certainly they remained my superiors, *is it not true?*) ... [my translation]
...να αρνηθώ να εκτελέσω διαταγή των ανωτέρων μου (γιατι βέβαια εξακολουθούσαν να είναι ανώτεροί μου, ψέμματα;) και...
(To Kivotio, 1974, p. 38)

> TT   ...to refuse to obey the orders of my superiors (for certainly they remained my superiors, *right?*) and...
> (*Mission Box*, 1996, p. 43)

Constructing discourses as if expecting a negative reaction on the part of the addressee manifests a negative politeness orientation. Following theories of text and context in ancient Arabic rhetoric in this book, it has been argued that the way contrastive shifts are constructed, in the Greek target version of news reporting material, presupposed a Greek reader who is more of a denier (rather than an open-minded person). I'm not sure if 'open-mindedness' is the appropriate term here, as it may attribute negative qualities (such as 'narrow-mindedness') across the intercultural filter. My understanding is that reasoning is rather highly valued and, thus, speakers are concerned about addressees' potential objections. Erasing negative presuppositions from the English target version of the *Mission Box*, is a domesticating move because it echoes addressing an 'open-minded', less concerned, better-disposed audience.

In this section, domesticating moves were identified in developing target discourses in *Mission Box* with a view to showing the potential of a domestication tendency in translation to contribute to the study of linguistic identities in target versions of texts. The domesticating modifications referred to above were

- raising the level of metaphoricity in English TT,
- erasing narrator's discourse intentions from English TT and
- 'positivising' narrator assumption about audience disposition throughout the novel.

There have been foreignizing moves, as well, in the English TT, like

- raising the level of evaluativeness,
- explicitating-contrasts (both at the level of values and at discoursal level) in argumentation. The following example shows a contrast-creating intention (insertion of *while* and *but* connectors) and evaluation (insertion of *simply*)

> ST   ...(we were standing facing one another, at a distance of two or three steps, [] we had sat down in the beginning, politely somehow, [] like old friends, with sufficient reserve on my part since she had consented though silently to Aleko's verdict, "You may go now", so which of us first moved toward to the other I didn't know, [] then we rushed into each other's arms... [my translation]

> *(...είμασταν όρθιοι, ο ένας απέναντι στον άλλον, σε απόσταση δύο-τριών βημάτων, [] είχαμε κάτσει στην άκρη, κάπως τυπικά [] σαν παλιοί γνώριμοι, με αρκετή επιφύλαξη εκ μέρους μου, γιατι δεν είχα ξεχάσει πως μ' έδιωξε κ'εκείνη απ'το σπίτι του Αλέκου, εγκρίνοντας έστω και σιωπηρά την ετυμηγορία του, «Μπορείς να πηγαίνεις») δε θυμάμαι ποιός απ'τους δυό πλησίασε τον άλλον [] θα πρέπει να ορμήσαμε κ'οι δυό και να αγκαλιαστήκαμε...*
> (*To Kivotio*, 1974, p.259-260)

> TT ...(we were standing facing one another, at a distance of two or three steps, *while* we had sat down in the beginning, politely somehow, *simply* like old friends, with sufficient reserve on my part since she had consented though silently to Aleko's verdict, "You may go now", so which of us first moved toward to the other I didn't know, *but* then we rushed into each other's arms...
> (*Mission Box*, 1996, p. 299)

Other foreignizing devices have been

- allowing foreignizing stereotyping in the target version (see retaining a Greek ST conventional expression in the English TT, in the following example: *passing somebody through ten sieves*, and English TT *meandering* in place of a source lexical choice with carries religious connotations), and

- retaining Greek allusive proper names (*Nikitas, Polemitis*) in the body of the novel, while offering notes to make the allusive nature of the name clear. As Raftopoulos (1996) claims, names of places and villages carry some association of death in the novel. The allusive nature of these names is made clear in the translator's notes,

...Nikitas. Victor, *...Kriovrisi.* Cold Spring Village, *...Mavropetra.* Black Rock Village, *...Lefkopetra.* White Rock Village, *...Polemitis.* 'The War Disease', coined from the word *polemo* war, *...Likovrisi.* Wolf Springs Village, *...Kastro.* Village of the Fort, or Village of the Castle, *...Krania.* Scull Village... (ibid: 339-341)

allowing the domestic readership more foreign input. In discussing translation of naming puns in the Scriptures, de Vries and Verheij (1997) argue that the most common strategy is the use of footnotes as 'it allows the translator to preserve the established names in the main body of the text, while doing justice to the name's origin and meaning in the annotation' (ibid: 88). They claim that while translators may be keen on reproducing the function of the wordplay, these names are "so deeply rooted in sacred tradition as to suffer little manipulation" (ibid: 87). Similarly, Leppihalme (1997), in studying strategies in translating source-cultural allusions for readers in another culture, argues that preserving the source item in the target version may be possible for unfamiliar items where allusion works at the micro-level:

...the retention of an unfamiliar name as such may be a valid choice if the context can be thought to offer sufficient clues, or if the loss caused by the unfamiliarity is deemed not serious (as when the allusion works on the micro-level) (ibid: 91).

In the present translation situation, allusions to death function at a macro-level, rather than at a micro-level, while the text does provide sufficient clues. The whole Box-metaphor is to be read as a death-metaphor, as allusions to death, emptiness, decomposition prevail throughout the novel.

ST ...nor had he *passed through ten sieves* like the rest of us...
    [my translation]

    ... *ούτε πέρασε απο δέκα κόσκινα όπως όλοι εμείς οι άλλοι,*...
    (*To Kivotio*, 1974, p. 283)

TT ...nor had he *passed through ten sieves* like the rest of us...
    (*Mission Box*, 1996, p. 327)

ST ...the High Command decided finally to bring the *rotation* of
    the box to an end... [my translation]

    ...*το Γενικό Αρχηγείο αποφάσισε να τελειώσει πια η περιφορά*
    του κιβωτίου... (*To Kivotio*, 1974, p. 286)

TT ...the High Command decided finally to bring the *meandering*
    of the box to an end... (*Mission Box*, 1996, p. 330)

The first two foreignizing devices, enforcing evaluation and explicitating contrasts contribute to promoting a difference with respect to argumentation strategies employed in the target text. As argumentation strategies differ cross-culturally (Lakoff-Tolmack 1990, Tytler 1992), promoting a foreign (source) argumentation pattern would allow exposing domestic audiences to foreign preferences. Explicitating the contrastive network in *Mission Box* is opted for at the cost of implying a different mental state of the narrator: the discourse appears better-structured, more cohesive, loses spontaneity – which would be undesirable given the state of despair the narrator is moving towards in *Mission Box*.

The last two foreignizing devices, which allow foreign stereotypes and retain source allusive proper names, promote aspects of the source national culture, facilitate recognition and respect for national identity. Last but not least, national identity, in translating *To Kivotio* is preserved and enforced through promoting aspects of the foreign national history in domestic environments. Cultural translation theorists are concerned about whether ethnic, class (Simon 1996) and/or gender identities (von Flotow 1997) are being preserved in translation, and relate translation practice to the notion of solidarity. Venuti (1998), within the Cultural Materialist[9] version of Cultural Studies is interested in the implications of literary texts in history and questions the value of totality in favour of particularity and respect for differences.

4.3. Linguistic Identities and the Value of Solidarity

A cultural studies approach to translation presupposes interest in and respect for differences between languages and cultures on the basis of the solidarity value. As Inglis claims, "to stay with solidarity in a world as it is, is the plain duty of the intellectual…" (1994: 17). Studying linguistic identities through translation also questions the value of totality in favour of particularity and presupposes respect for language differences on the basis of solidarity. Linguistic identities may be studied along with the value of solidarity, which governs translator behaviour and has roots further back in history[10]. As the

---

[9] Easthope (1997), in tracing transformations that British Cultural Studies (BCS) has experienced, places Post-Structuralism and Cultural Materialism within Phase III of BCS, emerging (since 1980) from a post-modern rejection of totality… (ibid: 15).

[10] However urgent and relevant-to-present-day such approaches might be, they have roots further back in history, whereas the question of whether these solidarity-relevant purposes were being served was left open. Simon (1996) stresses this solidarity dimension in the 18th/19th century translation practice with respect to a cause by arguing that "translation was important to the networks of solidarity formed around progressive causes in the eighteenth and nineteenth centuries. One of the most important of the anti-slavery movement in which women played an important part… The translation of *Oroonoko* (published 1696) into French in 1745 by Pierre Antoine de la Place, for instance, had far-reaching consequences in French humanitarian thought…The translator, however…changes the tragic and melodramatic ending of the novel from Oroonoko's murder of wife and child (in order to prevent them from being bound in further slavery) to a long denouncement leading to a happy ending in Africa… Kadish argues that the omission of certain key passages…diminishes the power not only of the 'style' but also of the political clout of the text" (ibid: 58-60).

issue of solidarity is assumed to be the plain duty of the intellectual, the same holds for awareness of linguistic preferences that can function as a tool for creating target versions that respect the value of solidarity to a cause. Un/successful target versions with respect to a socio-political cause may be accounted for in terms of whether particular linguistic identities are adequately reflected in target versions of texts. von Flotow (1997: 45), for instance, in assessing translation of experiential feminist writing of the 1970s into German, argues that although these translations were undertaken in the name of feminist solidarity, "the problems posed by wordplay translation seem to jeopardize 'translational' goals of feminism as well as ideas about women's shared knowledge and experience"[11]. Ideas may be diffused and enriched in target cultures, while they may return to the source culture to enforce the local socio-political movement. This seemed to be the case with Simon de Beauvoir's *Le deusième sexe* (1949) which was translated into German, English and Greek (1958) and united feminists all over the world. No claim about the quality of translation has been made, but it can be assumed, I guess, that the solidarity value, as outlined in cultural studies, IS respected in the Greek TT, as the Greek version has been considered an invaluable contribution to the feminist cause. Awareness of linguistic identities reflected in TTs are, thus, assumed to be ensuring the value of solidarity in translation.

Venuti's concern about foreignizing techniques and minoritizing translation is an instance of applying the values of spontaneity, seriousness and solidarity in present day translation practice worldwide, the purpose being survival of cultural and national identities. The foreignizing devices employed in the target version can be seen as an attempt on the part of translators to avoid assimilating a foreign literary text too forcefully to domestic dominant values.

Juxtaposition of source and target versions of texts may provide useful insights into linguistic identities on the basis of the value of solidarity. On the one hand, foreignizing techniques in translation may straightforwardly point to linguistic preferences: they stand out in a target version as alienating elements which may 'disrupt' readers' participation monentarily (Venuti, 1998: 12). Domesticating techniques, on the other hand, allow researchers to identify preferences in source versions of texts through contrastive analysis of source and target versions.

The extent to which a foreignizing strategy should be applied is a matter of interpretation. On a par, the degree of domestication to be allowed in a TT is a decision to be made by translators. No matter the intention of translators,

---

[11] von Flotow focuses on wordplay translation in the German version of Mary Daly's American feminist classic 'Gyn/Ecology', where she looks in some detail at the German translator's options for wordplay translation and discusses their effects.

degrees of domestication in target versions of texts may be assessed for naturalness and appropriateness by target readerships for preferred linguistic patterns to be identified and degrees of preferences to be measured. In an experiment conducted in the context of a translation theory course (Univ. of Athens, 2002) domesticating tendencies were identified and measured with respect to the degree of appropiateness they exhibited. Subjects were given two Greek target versions of a short story, E.M. Foster's *The Road from Colonus*, which had been produced by postgrads in the 'Translation-Translatology' Postgraduate Programme of the University of Athens. The two target versions of the story exhibited varying degrees of foreignization/ domestication, at particular points, through linguistic options which created some alienation effect vs. others which made the text sound perfectly normal. Students were not given the source version because their appreciation of the original was expected to disturb their insight into their mother tongue.

The purpose of the experiment was to show (a) in what way domesticating and foreignizing moves in translation may crucially affect text reception and (b) that degrees of domestication and foreignization are identifiable and measurable. Among the preferences focused upon in the experiment, there are some which would particularly contribute to specifying a preferable target linguistic profile, in accordance to conclusions drawn in the context of monolingual research or in the context of contrastive linguistic studies. The experiment showed that

- active constructions were preferred over passive ones in TT, by 60.8%-89.1%
- higher level of certainty was preferred, by 55.9%-84.7%
- directness was preferred over indirectness, by 51%-91.3%
- introductory verbs were manipulated so that illocutionary force of utterances were made explicit (preferred by 57.6%-69.4%)
- expressiveness and intensification through lexical item selection was raised and preferred, by 64.4%-77.9%
- evaluation levels were raised and preferred,by 59.3%-79.6%
- contrastive shift markers were occasionally enforced and preferred by 62.7% and unexpectedness effects were created and preferred by 81.3%-95.6% (Sidiropoulou 2003).

Despite the explicitation tendency in translation which may distort the reflection of linguistic preferences, translation practice can provide insights into linguistic preferences across cultures with a view to broadening awareness of linguistic identities.

4.4. Assimilationist Translation and Endangered Linguistic Identities

Venuti (1995, 1998) draws back on postcolonial translation studies and issues dealt with in anthropology, ethnography and colonial history, especially on their interest in the clash of cultures. Postcolonial translation studies employed Gramsci's notion of 'hegemony' as the ruling political, social cultural, ideological and intellectual structures in a society and described its attitude as 'counter-hegemonic' (Robinson, 1997:13).

Beyond translation studies, the notion of hegemony has been employed to account for dominant practices in the construction of discourses. In her discussion of ideology and education in discourse in terms of Gramsci's notion of hegemony, Dendrinos (1992) notes that

Hegemony exists as a struggle to dominate subordinate groups because the social resistance of these groups constantly contradicts the roles that dominant ideology assigns for them in terms of themselves and of their social relations. (ibid: 84)

A Marxist viewpoint, Robinson (1997) claims, allowed the post-colonial scholar "not only to identify the power structures that oppress the subaltern but also to formulate a coherent 'identity politics' in opposition to oppressive political and ideological regimes" (ibid: 19). Thus, postcolonial scholars working to provincialize the West become increasingly interested in migrant border cultures.

Postcolonial translation thinking added considerations about the 'vast power differentials' (ibid: 28) between cultures in translation, rather than simply finding equivalents for phrases or registers between languages, or negotiating the norms of one culture in terms of the norms of another (not a trivial task, at all). Translation is, thus, seen as a channel of decolonization: English the language of the 'imperial centre', a *lingua franca*, because of a century and a half of first British and then American political, economic, military and cultural world dominance, is disseminated to the peripheries of the empire as the language of power and knowledge. Through foreignizing translation of an English text into the language of a dominated culture, control is extended over those who do not speak the language.

According to Jacquemond ([1992], in Robinson 1997: 34-35), translation practice has shown that hegemonic cultures typically select, for translation, works from the dominated culture that fit prevailing stereotypes (in the hegemonic culture) and often internalized by the dominated culture. Alternatively, authors in a dominated culture who dream of reaching a large audience will tend to write for translation into a hegemonic language and this "will require some degree of compliance with stereotypes" (ibid: 32)[12].

The hegemonic/dominated opposition works on a par with the domestic/foreign, self/other, assimilationist/nostalgic dualities. The idea behind all this is that assimilationist translation is a primary tool for empire encouraging stronger and hegemonic cultures. The issue of preserving cultural identities through translation concerns Greek cultural tradition, as Greek is among the less widely spoken languages worldwide. In drawing attention to the potential of translation as a tool for promoting Greek cultural values and national identity to United Europe and the rest of the world, Papaefthymiou-Lytra (1991) notes that foreign cultural values are imported in Greece through translation, while the reverse phenomenon is not observed. In his discussion about language and translation, Iliopoulos (1986) comments on the assimilationist danger in translation and points to Kourtovic[13] who argues that a text translated into Greek may sound alien because it reproduces associations incompatible with the Greek identity. Apostolou-Panara (1997), in her examination of the morphological integration of English loanwords in Modern Greek, touches upon translation and its role in leading to digressions from the norm of the target language. If not done properly, she argues, translation "may act as a Troyan horse, by instigating change either through introduction of new patterns, or by accelerating change through activation of latent possibilities" (ibid: 182). The questions Apostolou-Panara poses in her research on morphological change, namely,

- whether Greek is changing by moving towards a direction perhaps against its natural bent, or
- whether Greek is slowly becoming more analytical due to an interaction of internal or external forces,

are issues to be tackled in translation research bearing consequences for translation practice and instruction. A more optimistic view with respect to identity development through contact with foreign languages, suggests that linguistic identity is "dynamic and can absorb and recycle foreign elements into its own development" and translators may play a positive role in this process (Gile[14]).

---

[12] Hegemonic languages are also likely to be influenced in certain ways by languages in contact. A BBC World Service News Editor, Alan le Breton, reports that stories in the WS news room have to be written "clearly and concisely so they are easy to translate", which -I assume- will eventually affect hegemonic generic conventions.

[13] (*I Kathimerini*, 7.6.83).

[14] Daniel Gile, in the abstracts booklet of the "Choice and Difference in Translation" international conference, National Kapodistrian University of Athens, Athens 3-6 Dec. 2003, p. 12).

SUMMARY OF 4 (III)
Section 4 considers how the solidarity value in the Cultural Orientation Approach and Venuti's domesticating and foreignizing moves, in G>E prose translation, can contribute to linguistic identity awareness. Despite the explicitation tendency in translation which may distort the inscription of linguistic preferences in TTs, the section argues that linguistic identities may be reached at through juxtaposition of STs and TTs, on the grounds that when directionality in translation changes (e.g. from E>G to G>E) certain linguistic preferences remain on the same language side.

5. Theatre Translation and the Inscription of Identities

Theatre translation theorists underline cultural asymmetries between source and target cultures reflected in source and target versions of theatre texts. In a theatre context, translation usually struggles to defend the domestic against the foreign

Translated works provide valuable information about cultural asymmetries because texts never travel between cultures intact. They have existed in some form in another culture, but in order to survive in their new surroundings, they are recreated from within the receiving culture, using its own tools. Translation has a racist element in it, as it is always struggling to defend the domestic against the Foreign (Aaltonen, 2000: 114).

The aim of this section is to show that theatre texts provide valuable information about linguistic identities and about their potential in creating culturally appropriate and preferable discourse structures that can ensure audience response. Theatre translation requires for intercultural variation with respect to genre, social or age-based to be inscribed in discourses, in the most readily perceivable manner. Good speakers/writers and translators are distinguished from poor ones in that they are inventive in identifying appropriate linguistic options to reflect gender, social, age group identities compatible with a cultural context. The physical presence of an audience in the communicative situation is likely to trigger not only culturally compatible linguistic options in the domestic environment, but also highly preferable ones.

In a cultural studies orientation, domesticating interventions are often assumed at the level of values and bring about a cultural transformation of the foreign through production process in the receiving theatre system. Audience response presupposes, among others, culturally appropriate linguistic choices in target discourses for transmission of values. The purpose of theatre translation is to bring ST closer to target audience by transforming foreign cultural values to domestic ones, rather than bring the audience closer to the foreign situation. The latter would have allowed structures creating some alienating effect in TT at the linguistic or cultural level.

In what follows the treatment of connectives is examined in samples of E>G and G>E theatre translation data with a view to showing that performance translation data is an excellent resource for linguistic identity specification through translation.

5.1. Linguistic Preference on Page

Linguistic preference that can compose the collective identity of a target audience is imprinted on target versions in varying degrees according to translator intention. In the English-Greek paradigm explored in this book, a focus of interest has been, among others, establishing cohesion through connectives. In the news reporting genre, preference was shown for counter-argumentative formats in persuasion (rather than through-argumentative ones), while balance formats, a counter-argumentative subtype (i.e. contrasts), were shown to be preferred over lop-sided (i.e. concessive) ones.

The question arises as to whether such preferences can be a manifestation of a general target linguistic tendency or a mere manifestation of translators' effort to explain things for target audiences in order to ensure audience response. A suggestion would be for us to check whether the particular tendency is manifested in another genre, in the same translation direction. If the preference survives in that other genre, it could be a better candidate for constituting part of a linguistic identity. Another suggestion would be for researchers to check whether the tendency is reversed in the opposite translation direction. This would allow safer conclusions about linguistic preferences in intercultural environments.

In what follows attention is directed to the treatment of connective cohesive network in performance discourses. The goal is exploring whether the tendency for enriching the contrastive and causal network in E>G translation can be an instantiation of translator's agonizing effort to facilitate target readerships with processing or a sub/conscious effort to conform to culturally and linguistically preferred patterns of behaviour in the target context.

There have been considerable differences between two Greek versions of Shakespeare's *Twelfth Night* with respect to the rendition of the connective cohesive network in the play. Vasilis Rotas' (1960s) and Erikos Belies' (1997) Greek versions of *Twelfth Night* differ –among others- in that the former allows a comparable number of connectives in the ST and TT samples examined (Act I), while the latter opts for an enforced connective network (mainly contrastive). In the 1997 version, 9 out of the 16 contrastive connectives in the Greek TT sample were added rather than transferred. In the following example the two contrastive connectives inserted in TTb facilitate processing.

Translation interference in TTb is evidently justified on the basis of changing generic conventions and diachronic language change. Another reason for translator interference could be concern for explicitation. The question arises as to how these two forces, linguistic preference and translator explicitation tendency, can be distinguished and measured for reasonable conclusions to be drawn about linguistic identities.

English ST

VIOLA: And what should I do in Illyria? My brother he is in
         Elysium.
         Perchance he is not drown'd – what think you sailors?
CAPTAIN: It is perchance that you yourself were saved.
         (*Twelfth Night*, Act I, Scene II, l.3)

Greek TTa   Greek TTb

VIOLA: And what do I want in   VIOLA: And what shall I do in
         Illyria? My brother is in   Illyria? My brother is
         Elysium.   in Elysium.
         [] Is it possible that he   *However*, is it
         has not been   possible that he has
         drown'd ? What do you   not been drown'd ?
         think pals?   What do you think
                                              sailors?
CAPTAIN: [] ...   CAPTAIN: *But*, you were saved
                                              by chance as well.
[my translation]   [my translation]

*BIOΛA: Κι εγώ τί θέλω στην   *BIOΛA: Καί τί θά κάνω εγώ
         Ιλλυρία; Ο αδελφός μου   στην Ιλλυρία; Ο
         είναι στα Ηλύσια.*   αδελφός μου
                                              βρίσκεται στα Ηλύσια
                                              Πεδία.*
         *[]Μην τύχει και δεν   *Όμως, μήπως   κατά
         πνίγηκε; -   τύχη δεν πνίγηκε;
         Τί λέτε σείς, παιδιά;   Εσείς ναύτες τί λέτε;*
ΠΛΟΙΑΡΧΟΣ: - ...*   *ΠΛΟΙΑΡΧΟΣ:Μα, κατα τύχη
                                              σωθήκατε κι εσείς;*

(Transl. Vasilis Rotas, p. 19,   (Transl. Erikos Belies, p. 12,
1960s, Athens: Epikairotita)   1997, Athens: Kedros))

The assumption is that a preference in Greek for signalling logical relations between propositions has a cumulative effect on the explicitation tendency assumed in translation process, whatever the direction of translation. In the reverse translation direction (i.e. G>E), the explicitation tendency is expected to contradict the preference for an enforced logical network on the Greek side. In other words, in the reverse translation direction, there will be (a) connectives added to the English target text because of explicitation, and (b) others omitted from TT because of a subconscious tendency of translators to allow less connective cohesive links in the English TT as a manifestation of an internalized linguistic preference.

In fact, this is what the case is in the TTs of two Greek plays by Pavlos Matesis (1995 and 1997), translated by a different translator each: the ratio of added/omitted connectives in the target samples examined has been comparable. In *Roar* (*I Voui* [1997], transl. David Connolly, London: Arcadia Books, 2002), a comparable set of English TT connectives (*and*, *but*, *because*, *so*, *besides*) and evaluative items (*yet*, *even*, *all*, *at least*) have been added to the English TT to explain things for the audience, while a number of Greek ST connectives (*and*, *in order to*, *but*) and evaluative items (*indeed*) have been omitted from the English TT. In the same vein, in *Towards Eleusis* (*Pros Eleusina* [1995], transl. Fred A. Reed, ibid), comparable sets of added/omitted cohesive ties and evaluative items adjust connectivity levels to ensure a comparable effect on source and target audiences. In the text fragment below, two occurrences of ST *and* (*και*) have been omitted from the English TT in the translator's attempt to adjust connectivity to culturally/lingustically appropriate levels.

ST
MOTHER: (*looking down at them*) Look, how strange! *And* I never noticed before that there was sea around my bed. (*Announcing to her mother, who is somewhere backstage. Gleefully*) Ma! *And* the earth…has taste…
(*Pros Eleusina*, Pavlos Matesis, p. 34) [my translation]

ΜΗΤΕΡΑ, (*τους κοιτάζει*) Κοίτα θαύματα. Και δεν είχα προσέξει πώς γύρω απ' το κρεβάτι μου είχε θάλασσα.
(*Το ανακοινώνει στη μητέρα της, που είναι κάπου μέσα. Χαρούμενη*)
Μητέρα! Και το χώμα έχει …γεύση!
(*Προς Ελευσίνα*, Παύλος Μάτεσις, σ. 34)

TT
MOTHER: (*looking down at them*) Look, will wonders never cease! [] I never noticed before. The sea, it was all around my bed. (*Announcing to her mother, who is somewhere back stage. Gleefully*) Ma! [] The earth…has taste… (*Towards Eleusis*, transl. Fred Reed, p. 208)

By contrast, the following text fragment from Matesis (1997) shows an added evaluative item (*all*) and an added connective (*but*) to the English TT as an instantiation of translator explicitation tendency.

These two competing forces, the translator's tendency to conform to patterns of linguistically preferred behaviour in the TT and the explicitation tendency, have allowed a comparable set of omitted/added connectives in the English TT. The connectives that have been transferred intact have not been dealt with here, although they are also capable of inscribing a domesticating or foreignizing intention with respect to rendering connectivity levels.

In the present context, identifying linguistic preferences in a TT would be easier, if the explicitation tendency were somehow weakened so as not to blur results. The next section identifies a context in which translator concern for explicitation may be assumed to be weaker due to situational factors that do part of the explicitation job.

ST
CLYTEMNESTRA: I've no wish to bear any such titles – I've renounced them []! Forgotten them! Exorcized them...
ELECTRA: It's not you I feel sorry for, Mother. (*Groan from the* other one.) Your term is about to end. [] ME, how will I go on?
(*I Voui*, Pavlos Matesis, p.14) [my translation]

ΚΛΥΤΑΙΜΝΗΣΤΡΑ: Δεν επιθυμώ ν' ακούω τέτοια αξιώματα, τά 'χω ξεφορτωθεί! Λησμονήσει! Ξορκίσει...
ΗΛΕΚΤΡΑ: Εσένα δε σε κλαίω, μητέρα. (Μουγκρητό της άλλης.) Εσένα η θητεία σου κοντεύει να τελειώσει. ΕΓΩ πώς θα συνεχίσω...
(*Η Βουή*, Παύλος Μάτεσις, σ. 14)
TT
CLYTEMNESTRA: I've no wish to bear any such titles – I've renounced them *all*! Forgotten them! Exorcized them...
ELECTRA: It's not you I feel sorry for, Mother. (*Groan from* CLYTEMNESTRA.) Your term is about to end. *But* ME, how will I go on?
(*Roar*, transl. David Connolly, p. 136)

5.2. Linguistic Preference on Stage

Translator awareness of the presence of an audience is a significant variable in determining translator behaviour. Katan and Straniero-Sergio (2003) discuss how two main ideologies (consumer capitalism and popular television) mould an interpreter's performance on television. The media interpreter, they argue, foster – among other things – "a climate of comfort and hence the maintainance of the domestic environmental bubble" (ibid:144). Translation for the stage is expected to remould translator behaviour on the basis of different situational factors and variables.

In performance translation, the treatment of values and linguistic phenomena is claimed to vary due to the interaction of acoustic, visual and verbal codes in the communicative situation (Bassnett 1998, Aaltonen 2000). Translator concern about making aspects of meaning explicit for a target audience may be assumed to have decreased because target audiences are physically present and can retrieve meaning for themselves through the contribution of acoustic and visual codes. Linguistic phenomena are expected to be treated differently in performance translation, than they would have been, had they been tackled in theatre translation for the page. The assumption is verified through an examination of the treatment of connectives in G>E performance translation.

The treatment of the connective cohesive network in performance translation showed a different ratio of added/enforced to omitted connectives in the English target performance, than the one revealed in theatre translation for the page. The performance sample came from Dimitris Kehaidis/Eleni Haviara's play *With Power from Kifissia* (*Me Dynami apo tin Kifissia*), which was staged in London as *With Power from Shoreditch* (2001). Juxtaposition of the source Greek and the English target networks in the sample examined, reveals a ratio of 11 omitted vs. 3 added connectives: 11 source connectives were ignored in the English target version vs. 3 which were added and a few more which were simply enforced. Although there may be other factors which affect target discourse construction (as for instance translator background or source discourse texture), performance translation seems to be providing a clearer reflection of tendencies which may be part of a linguistic identity. The physical presence of an audience and the contribution of visual code and sound effects do part of the explicitation task and leave a more accurate imprint on target discourses. Stage translation is, thus, an invaluable resource for the study of linguistic identities through translation.

Value transformation may be pursued through adaptation, in addition to translation. Adaptation in a theatre context is more likely to enforce domestic values and preferences. As adaptation is more frequent on stage than on page, stage translation is an excellent candidate for the study of target domestic preferences.

Here, again, the choice of texts is based on the needs of the target system and the compatibility of ST discourse with values in the target culture. The adaptation, 'relocation' (Upton 2000) or 'acculturation' (Bassnett 1998) processes in theatre translation allow for creative reconstruction of target discourses which reflect the collective identity of intended audiences.

Tymoczko (2003) in a more linguistically oriented perception of ideological differences in translation claims that

the ideology of a translation will be an amalgam of the content of the source text and the various *speech acts* instantiated in the source text relevant to the source context, layered together with the representation of the content, its relevance to the receptor audience, and the various *speech acts* of the translation itself addressing the target context, as well as resonances and discrepancies between these two 'utterances'(ibid: 182, emphasis added).

Tymoczko traces the speech acts performed in Sophocles's *Antigone*[15] and those in Anouilh's staging of the play in 1994 Paris to analyze part of the relocation process in stage translation. If stage directors make such an effort to acculturate and relocate, would they attempt to do it in a foreignizing language?

The Foreign is manipulated either for the sake of the art or for the sake of the community. Whatever the reason for manipulation, the verbal medium (among the visual and acoustic ones) conveys a considerable portion of the receiving system's reaction to alterity, and allows linguistic preferences to be clearly imprinted on discourses.

---

[15] Tymoczko provides an example of varying speech acts in a performance translation of Sophocles's *Antigone*:
"A concrete example of the layering is found in the well known rewriting and staging of Sophocles's *Antigone* by Jean Anouilh, produced in Paris in 1944 during the Nazi occupation of France. Clearly Sophocles's text had its own ideological significance in its original context. Produced for the Great Dionysia festival held annually in Athens, as a *statement* about the dangers of tyranny and the importance of the heroic resistance to tyrants, *Antigone* implicitly *celebrated* Athenian democracy and *attempted to instill independence and moral responsibility* in its audience, as well *as pride in and allegiance to* the city-state of Athens itself, among other things. When Anouilh transposed Sophocles's play into French and staged it for his own time, however, those early ideological meanings were overwritten with contemporary meanings: he was implicitly commenting on the Nazi occupation in France, *inciting* his contemporaries and *encouraging resistance* against the Nazis, *calling for them to act out* against the Nazi usurpation. Here I've tried to emphasize the words associated with the illocutionary and perlocutionary dimensions of Sophocles's work and Anouilh's refraction, as well as to indicate briefly some of the relevant contextual dimensions that must be considered in determining the ideology of Anouilh's play" (ibid: 183, emphasis in original).

5.3. Degrees of Translator Interference in Performance Translation

The extent to which performance translators relocate or acculturate theatre texts in a target environment is a decision to be made by translators and stage-directors alike. Domesticating/target-oriented performance translation involves reflecting target linguistic preferences in message construction. Foreignizing/source-oriented performance translation involves retaining foreign preferences in target production. The very character (source-/target-oriented, Toury 1995) of a target performance version and degrees of translator interference may be defined in terms of the extent to which stage translators and directors have decided to acculturate. Performance translation is capable of reflecting domesticating and foreignizing tendencies in target versions through fluctuation in the treatment of linguistic phenomena.

A point of intercultural difference between source and target production is expected to be treated differently in domesticating and foreignizing approaches to theatre translation and thus, target versions for the stage can reflect linguistic preferences in various degrees of prominence which may well be measurable for research purposes. A point of intercultural difference between English and Greek is the politeness patterns preferred in interaction. English is a negatively polite language (Levinson 1987), while Greek prefers positively polite behaviour (Sifianou 1992).

Foreignizing and domesticating approaches to target versions of five plays by Harold Pinter, for the Greek stage, reveal considerable fluctuation in the inflow of positive politeness patterns into the Greek target versions. Fluctuation was manifested across target versions of different plays, due to translator/director intentions, but also within a single target version. The aim of translators was to reflect variation in the intensity of the conflict, imposition, insecurity, the struggle for power, in the subtext of Pinter's plays. There have been target versions in which the inflow of positive politeness devices has been steady throughout the target play text and others which show a decreasing inflow of politeness patterns according to assumed needs of the plot. Needless to say, that the presence of positive/negative politeness patterns in target performance versions of Pinter's plays affected students' value judgements as to which options may be more successfully rendering Pinter's word. Positive politeness patterns were overwhelmingly preferred even at the cost of losing intended stylistic effects (Sidiropoulou, 2002: 67-71).

Results show that there is a mutual benefit on both sides for studying inscription of linguistic identities in target versions of texts. Linguistic research benefits from studying inscription of linguistic identities in target versions of texts, in that it promotes awareness of linguistic identities through new methods and practices and explores their potential in achieving appropriateness in a target version. On the other hand, translation studies benefits from studying inscription of linguistic identities in TTs, in that it explores translator behaviour, the effect of target context in TT construction, the educational and computational consequences of inscribing identities in TTs etc.

5.4. Linguistic Identities in Literature and Theatre Translation

Malmkjaer (1998) claims that TTs of literary works can be an excellent source for drawing linguistic conclusions about target languages. Despite some objections that certain modifications between STs and TTs may be intended to create special artistic effects, rather than to promote conventionally preferred linguistic patterns, literary texts allow observation of situational factors relative to which situational appropriateness may be judged.

Another objection to drawing conclusions about linguistic identities from translational data might be that acceptability is an "evasive multifaceted" notion which may result in inaccurate measurement of linguistic preferences. For instance, in exploring acceptability in Finnish versions of children's books, Puurtinen (1992: 89) claims that it seems doubtful "whether an accurate definition of the evasive multifaceted concept of acceptability in translated children's books can ever be formed". The assumption in this book is that acceptability may be fairly safely defined in terms of cloze tests, readability tests and subjective value judgements of target readers (see subjective assessment test reported in 44 above).

Linguistic preference, in the construction of identities, is not meant as a static rule which regulates source or target production. It should rather be considered as a kind of "loaded expectation" (Hermans, 1995: 7) on either language side. It is an expectation that, in a particular situation, a (source) language speaker would react in one way, whereas a (target) language speaker would opt for a different linguistic reaction. Linguistic preference may be assumed to be something more than a probabilistic expectation, a convention, and perhaps less than a course of action generally accepted as 'correct' in given contexts. This evasiveness of what may be called a target linguistic preference in a TT is relevant to the precariousness with which translation is usually associated with. As Arrojo (1995) claims, while the original is generally associated with stability and authenticity through the presence of an author in the writing, "translation is often related to precariousness and the absence of what is unconditionally legitimate" (ibid: 21).

Yet, translation practice with all the systematic behaviour it exhibits in the preferred patterns across language barriers suggests otherwise. In discussing deictic features in translation, Richardson (1998) verifies that preferences in the use of deictic items may be attributed to specific cultural groups

...others [decisions made by the translator with regard to deictic features]... are quite subtle and affect precisely those quantities in the text which help *to give the text an identity as a 'Spanish' or 'English' text* (ibid: 138, emphasis added).

Investigation into the treatment of deictic markers in the target version of Virginia Woolf's *The Mark on the Wall*[16] has revealed a systematic preference for more accessible discourse entities in the target speakers' mental representation, the deictic idealized cognitive models (ICMs). This was manifested through a preference for deictic specificity, along a scale of intermediate degrees of impersonalization. In terms of pragmatics, the preference may be related to closer interpersonal distance favoured by positive politeness patterns in Greek contexts (Sidiropoulou, 2003: 87). A collective translation, in the present programme of postgraduate studies, is shown to subconsciously promote target linguistic preferences in a systematic manner, enforcing the claim that target versions of texts can be a reliable research source for the study of linguistic identities. Similarly, in examining the treatment of deixis in multiple translations of H. C. Andersen's stories, Malmkjaer (1998: 130) has argued that despite variance in the treatment of the phenomenon in the TT, quantitatively-oriented whole-text studies are expected to be more fruitful.

As language reflects society, changing realities are expected to be imprinted on target versions of texts to provide evidence for changing linguistic identities and normative preferences. Translation can, thus, cater for aspects of diachronic change in linguistic identities.

SUMMARY OF 5 (III)
In Section 5, focus on the treatment of connective cohesive ties in theatre translation is intended to show that the preference for specifying logical relations between propositions, in Greek target discourses of news reporting data, survives in target theatre versions. A sample of E>G theatre translation data reveals a strong concern for specifying discourse connection on the Greek side. This is claimed, on the one hand, to be a manifestation of an explicitation tendency in translation, and on the other, a manifestation of a cultural preference prevalent in the target environment, a trait that is assumed

---

[16] The TT was produced in a Seminar of the Translation-Translatology Postgraduate Programme, University of Athens.

to be part of the target linguistic identity. The tendency was checked in the reverse translation direction (G>E), in translation for the page and for the stage. Results showed that in the sample data *for the page*, the numbers of added/omitted (or enforced/weakened) cohesive ties were comparable, due to two competing forces affecting the construction of target discourse: a preference for strengthening the connective network in Greek (relative to English) and the explicitation tendency, which made logical relations explicit for target readership, no matter the translation direction. The sample of G>E translational data *for the stage* showed that the amount of the English target connectives was clearly reduced. This was assumed to be due to the physical presence of an audience and the contribution of the visual and acoustic codes in the interpretation of the message, which may do part of the explicitation job. In stage translation, the Greek ST exhibited stronger cohesive ties (as a manifestation of a linguistic preference) because the competing force, explicitation, which was expected to balance/neutralize the tendency, was in fact undertaken by parallel semiotic codes in the communicative situation, allowing a linguistic preference to prevail. Performance translation is claimed to be an invaluable resource for the study of linguistic identities. This is because the physical presence of an audience allows fairly accurate reflection of linguistic preferences in target discourses, while the situational factors that affect discourse construction may be specified in terms of the plot of the play and the social conditions in which the translation has occurred.

Identities in the English-Greek Translational Paradigm: Concluding Remarks

1. Three Genres

The book has explored the potential of translational data to contribute insights into the study of linguistic identities across cultures in contact. Variation is accounted within and across genres. It was examined within genres, because there are genre-specific situational factors that may affect translator behaviour. Variation is also accounted within a rather restricted time period, as social conditions are modified and the role of the translator is often reshaped. Katan and Straniero-Sergio (2003) report on a situation, in Italian media interpreting, in which changing conditions on TV reshape translator behaviour:

…as Italian TV becomes more globally oriented, and "the foreign" is brought into the Italian sitting room, so consumer capitalism is demanding a slicker media-professional and a more visible performer to maintain the comfort factor (ibid: 144).

The three genres in this book have been focused upon for their difference in 'culture-boundedness' (Schäffner, 1997: 120). EU discourses are the least culture bound texts and news reporting is at points less culture bound than literary and theatre texts. Difference in culture boundedness is a parameter expected to foreground varying layers of significance with respect to the reliability of the discourses as data for studying linguistic identities or with respect to the conditions on which linguistic preferences were reflected in discourses.

News reporting in a translational context serves as a window "onto ideologies…in the contemporary world" in the sense employed in Schäffner (2003), in her comparative analysis of the English and the German text of a Blair/Schröder paper. As Schäffner claims,

both the German text and the English text can thus serve as windows onto ideologies and political power relations in the contemporary world. Critical discourse analysis brings together the discursive with the textual, through a conjunction of analysis of both the text and its intertextual context (cf. Chouliaraki 2000: 297). A translation perspective to ideologically relevant discourse can add new ways of understanding politics and can thus make a substantial contribution to the study of cultures in contact (ibid: 41).

In this book, "a translation perspective to ideologically relevant discourses" can reveal ways of understanding linguistic behaviour across cultures and promote identity awareness.

EU discourses fall under the umbrella of political texts. EU discourse differs from news reporting in that the 'sameness' concern in the EU context acts as a heavy constraint on appropriateness and may be assumed to be blurring reflection of identities on discourses. Trosborg (1997), for instance, comments on the 'strangeness' of the so-called preambles which precede all legal documents in the Union, as follows: "In Danish ...[the separation of auxiliary and main verb] is contradictory to recommended Danish sentence formation and sounds very queer in Danish" (ibid: 153). This language which is often "blurred, complicated and hard to understand", she claims, "has been labelled *eurojargon*" (ibid).

Despite evidence that EU discourses are hardly 'native', the present book attempts to exploit EU legalese to reach linguistic identities through contrastive analysis of official language versions of texts. The attempt was made on the basis of the assumption that, given the difficulty of the native to understand such texts, the EU translator is particularly concerned with foregrounding 'native' linguistic preferences in discourse construction to compensate for the foggy nature of texts. The assumption is that the structures to be elicited by the EU translator's attempt to make the text contextually appropriate will be the most accessible ones in the repertoire of structures available in the mind of the translator, thereby revealing part of the native linguistic identity.

In literary translation, the study of linguistic identities results from the dynamic decision-making process referred to in Delabastita (1998). Much of the decision-making process, Delabastita claims,

depends on the *dynamic* interplay between what is technically possible (in linguistic-semiotic terms) and what is permissible and desirable (in terms of target-culture conventions and ideology). I cannot help feeling that somehow this interplay should be at the heart of any academic curriculum in translation, whether its primary objective is to train future translators or involve students in theoretical or historical research (ibid: 154).

What is linguistically possible combined with what is permissible and desirable in terms of target culture conventions and ideology have been assumed, in this book, to bring to light part of the set of manifestations that can comprise a linguistic identity.

In staged performances, various semiotic systems interact to promote culturally preferred conceptualization of realities. The spoken text, combined with bodily expression, the playing space and props, the lighting etc. allow for an interplay of semiotic systems (Bassnett, 1998: 99) which yield enlightening suggestions about target linguistic preferences. Mateo (1995) points to the mutual influence between translation strategies and the reception of drama which highlights the potential of theatre texts to reflect identities. The assumption in Part III of this book is that, because stage performance is live it has important consequences on translator decision-making that facilitate the study of linguistic identities.

2. The Linguistic Phenomena

A number of linguistic phenomena were tackled in E>G translation to provide examples of tendencies in translator behaviour in discourse construction. The preferred patterns inscribed in discourses, in translational contexts, reveal internalized, in the mind of the translator, preferred models of linguistic behaviour and promote awareness of linguistic identities, bearing ideological and educational consequences.

The news reporting part (Part I) examines the treatment of adversative and causal connectives in English ST and Greek TT versions of press news items. The tendency for explicit junction was assumed to be a manifestation of a linguistic preference in the Greek context and an explicitation tendency in translation. The preference was later verified in a E>G theatre translation context, in which explicit junction was preferred over implicit junction in the Greek TT. The point was whether this tendency is a manifestation of an explicitation tendency in translation or a manifestation of a language and culture specific tendency in discourse construction.

In the G>E translation direction, in which the explicitation tendency is expected to be manifested in the English target version, the ratio of omitted/added connectives was comparable. This was claimed to be a manifestation of the operation of two competing forces, that of explicitation (G→E) and that of a preference for explicit junction (G←E). The tension was resolved in the stage translation situation (G>E), in which the amount of English target connectives was clearly reduced. This was a manifestation of the explicit junction preference in Greek, as the need for explicitation was assumed to be undertaken, in the stage translation situation, by the contribution of the visual and acoustic codes. The following figure shows types of data that led to the conclusion that explicit junction is preferable in

Greek (bold indicates the version with the strongest preference for explicit junction).

DIRECTIONALITY of translation	TYPES OF DATA
E > **G**	Press news
E > **G**	Theatre
G > E	Theatre (transl. for the page)
G > E	Theatre (transl. for the stage)

The preference for explicit junction in Greek revealed a distinct reader/audience profile that appreciates logical thinking in persuasion strategy.

Examination of the treatment of temporal adverbials in E>G news reporting in translation contexts revealed a culture specific tendency in time reference in the news. On the one hand, the data revealed a tendency for intensification which was assumed to be enforcing the oppositional view of the world in the news. On the other, a tendency for open-endedness in time specification, in the news, foregrounds a culture-specific tendency.

In ad translating, variation in the treatment of target linguistic phenomena was attributed to translator intention to adjust persuasion strategies to gender-specific culturally preferred patterns, revealing an identity. Examination of testimonial material in E>G press news reveals variation in the target environment, along such cognitive parameters as assumed audience involvement (in the topic dealt with in the news item) thereby revealing part of the target identity.

Metaphoring in E>G news reporting was influenced by similar cognitive parameters such as psychological remoteness or proximity of the target audience to the topic dealt with in the press news item. A metaphor cancellation tendency was observed in the context of high importance topics, which was verified in the literature part, in E>G romantic poetry translation. The tendency revealed emphasis on the aesthetic function of metaphor on the Greek side, which was cancelled in realistic contexts.

In the EU context (Part II), samples of English and Greek official versions of texts were contrasted with a view to examining the treatment of thematization tendencies. EU texts are hybrid and hardly 'native' (Trosborg 1997) and, thus, variation is assumed to reveal – if nothing more – preferred discourse patterns readily available in the mind of the translator, intended to compensate for the foggy nature of texts and increase text processibility. Adverbializing is one such tendency and thematizing time and place adverbials is another, employed to signify layers of meaning, such as presupposed and new information. Pre-posing adverbials was shown to raise the level of formality in Greek, as it does in English, and thus part of the target readership's preferences in persuasive discourse construction may be revealed through juxtaposition of official versions in the EU context.

The literary and theatre data (Part III) verified the preference for explicit junction in Greek, that was previously traced in news reporting (Part I). It also foregrounded a tendency for metaphor grounding (cancellation) in realistic contexts in E>G Byronic poetry translation, which verified the tendency for metaphor grounding in news articles dealing with 'hot' political/ social issues.

Domesticating moves in G>E prose translation, in this part

- revealed positive politeness preferences in the Greek ST (which were abandoned in the English TT) for stating discourse intentions,
- kept metaphoricity to some reduced level relative to the English TT, as the whole novel is itself a death metaphor,
- omitted illocutionary force of utterances in the English TT (this tendency echoed the explicit junction preference attributed to Greek, in this book)
- presupposed a less 'denying' and 'contradiction' attitude on the part of addressees, verifying previously observed culture-specific traits.

Certain foreignizing intentions raised the level of evaluativeness at points and made contrasts explicit, but these tendencies were never extensive to function as counter examples. They were rather attributed to the explicitation tendency in translation. The theatre context supported the junction explicitness hypothesis in Greek through examination of stage translation data.

*

The flow of information and ideas has been from linguistics (in monolingual or contrastive studies) to translation studies. This book intends to show that translation studies can return the favour by contributing its own viewpoint to the study of linguistic issues, with a view to shared goals and expectations: intercultural understanding, linguistic identity awareness, formation and preservation.

The treatment of particular linguistic phenomena has been explored in English-Greek translational data and preferences have been identified across linguistic/cultural environments, towards identifying areas of intercultural difference. Results and conclusions about differences in preferred patterns of linguistic behaviour across cultures may overlap with findings in contrastive studies and monolingual research, but translational contrastive research can potentially identify more areas of intercultural difference, which may otherwise go unnoticed and point to new research directions.

The present study was initiated by the fact that long exposition to translational data leaves a strong impression of how outstandingly different languages are, in terms of their genericly/situationally preferred patterns of behaviour, that led to the conviction that the study of language difference should be given a chance through translational contexts, as well.

The benefit from such a project is considerable for its educational, computational and other applications. As mentioned above, the '*dynamic interplay*' between what is linguistically possible and what is conventionally permissible or desirable is highly valued in Delabastita (1998) for its educational potential. It should be, Delabastita claims, "at the heart of any academic curriculum in translation, whether its primary objective is to train future translators or involve students in theoretical or historical research" (ibid: 154). My impression is that juxtaposition of source and target versions of texts can enhance awareness of linguistic identities (both native and foreign) at secondary education levels by making the difference-in-linguistic-behaviour issue more tangible and prepare young learners for an encounter of the 'self' with the 'other' in multicultural societies.

References

Aaltonen, S. 2000. *Time-Sharing on Stage*. Clevedon: Multilingual Matters.

Abraham, E. 1991. 'Why "because"? The management of given/new information as a constraint of causal alternatives'. *Text*. 11 (3). 323-340.

Alexieva, B. 1993. 'Cognitive approach to translation equivalence' In Zlateva, P. (ed.) *Translation as Social Action –Russian and Bulgarian Perspectives*. 101-109. London: Routledge.

---. 1997. 'There Must Be Some System in this Madness – Metaphor, Polysemy, and Wordplay in a Cognitive Linguistics Framework'. In Delabastita, D. (ed) *Traductio – Essays on Punning and Translation*. 137 -154. Manchester: St. Jerome and Presses Universitaires de Namur.

Apostolou-Panara, A. M. 1997. *Language Change in Modern Greek –The Morphological Integration of English Loanwords*. Parousia 40. Athens.

Arrojo, A. 1995. 'The "death" of the author and the limits of the translator's visibility'. In Snell-Hornby M., Jettmarová Z. and K. Kaindl (eds) *Tranalation as Intercultural Communication*. 21-32. Amsterdam: John Benjamins.

Austin, J. 1962. *How to do Things with Words*. Oxford: Clarendon.

Babiniotis, G. 1991. [in Greek: Μπαμπινιώτης, Γ. 1991. 'Γλωσσική Επικοινωνία μεταξύ των Χωρών της Ευρωπαϊκής Κοινότητας: Μετάφραση – Διδασκαλία Γλωσσών', *Απάνθισμα Πρακτικών Προγράμματος Lingua*. *Γλωσσική Επικοινωνία και Ελληνική Γλώσσα στην Ευρωπαϊκή Κοινότητα*. Αθήνα, Ζάππειο]

Baker, M. 1992. *In Other Words*. London: Routledge.

Barcelona, A. 1998. 'The State of the Art in the Cognitive Theory of Metaphor and Metonymy and its Application to English Studies'. *The European English Messenger*. 7 (2). 45-50.

Bassnett, S. (ed).1997. *Studying British Cultures*. London: Routledge.

---. 1998a. 'Still Trapped in the Labyrinth: Further Reflections on Translation and Theatre'. In Bassnet, S and A. Lefevere (Eds). *Constructing Cultures*. 90-108. Clevedon: Multilingual Matters.

---. 1998b. 'Researching Translation Studies'. In Bush, P. and K. Malmkjaer (eds). *Rimbaud's Rainbow*. 105-118. Amsterdam: John Benjamins.

Bassnett-McGuire, S. 1980/1987/1988. *Translation Studies –An Integrated Approach*. London: Routledge.

Bassnett, S. and H. Trivedi. 1999. *Post-Colonial Translation*. London: Routledge.

Bell, R. 1991. *Translation and Translating*. London: Longman.

Bolton, K. and C. Hutton. 1995. 'Bad and banned language: Triad secret societies, the censorship of the Cantonese vernacular, and colonial language policy in Hong Kong'. *Language in Society*. 24. 159-186.

Brown, G and G. Yule. 1983. *Discourse Analysis*. Cambridge: CUP.

Brown, P. and S. Levinson. 1978/1987. *Politeness- Some universals in Language Usage*. Cambridge: CUP.

Cameron, D. 1985. *Feminism and Linguistic Theory*. Houndsmill, Basingstone, Hamshire: Macmillan.

Catford, J. K. 1965. *A Linguistic Theory of Translation*. Oxford: OUP.

Chilton, P. and M. Ilying. 1993. 'Metaphor in political discourse: the case of the 'common European house''. *Discourse & Society* 4 (1). 7-31.

Corbett, E.P.J. 1965/1971/1990. *Classical Rhetoric for the Modern Student*. Oxford: OUP.

Delabastita, D. 1994. 'Focus on the Pun: Wordplay as a Special problem in Translation Studies'. *Target.* 6 (2). 223-243.

---. 1997. 'Introduction'. In Delabastita, D. (ed) *Traductio – Essays on Punning and Translation*. 1-22. Manchester: St. Jerome and Presses Universitaires de Namur.

---. 1998. ' "I Will Something Affect the Letter" Shakespeare's Letter-Puns and the Translator'. In Bush P. and K. Malmkjaer (Eds). *Rimbaud's Rainbow*. 145-156. Amsterdam: John Benjamins.

Dendrinos, B. 1992. *The EFL Textbook and Ideology*. Athens: N.C. Grivas.

Dendrinos, B. and E. Pedro-Ribeiro. 1997. 'Giving Street Directions: The Silent Role of Women'. In Jaworski, A. (ed). *Silence: Interdisciplinary Perspectives*. 339-349.

Drossou, M. 1997. *Advertising as Manipulative Discourse*. Unpublished Doctoral Thesis. English Department. School of Philosophy. University of Athens.

de Vries, A. and A. Verheij. 1997. 'A Portion of Slippery Stones – Wordplay in Four Twentieth-Century Translations of the Hebrew Bible'. In Delabastita, D. (ed) *Traductio – Essays on Punning and Translation*. 67-94. Manchester: St. Jerome and Presses Universitaires de Namur.

Easthope, A. 1997. 'But what *is* Cultural Studies?'. In Bassnett, S. (Ed) *Studying British Cultures*. 3-18. London: Routledge.

Edwards, D. 1997. *Discourse and Cognition*. London: Sage Publications.

Eco, U. 1981. *The Role of the Reader*. London: Hutchinson.

Fairclough, N. 1989. *Language and Power*. London: Longman.

---. 1995. *Media Discourse*. London: Arnold.

Farghal, M. 1993. 'Arab Fatalism and Translation from Arabic into English'. *Target.* 5 (1). 43-53.

Fawcett, P. 1998. 'Presupposition and Translation'. . In Hickey, L. (Ed) *The Pragmatics of Translation*. 114-123. Clevedon: Multilingual Matters.

Fowler, R. 1996. 'On Critical Linguistics'. In Caldas-Coulthard, C.R. and M. Coulthard (eds). *Texts and Practices – Readings in Critical Discourse Analysis*. 3-14. London: Routledge.

Fowles, J. 1996. *Advertising and Popular Culture*. London: Sage.

Fuertes, P.A. and I. Pizarro. 2002. 'Translation and Similarity-creating Metaphors in Specialized Language'. *Target* 14 (1). 43-73.

Goatly, A. 1993. 'Species of metaphor in written and spoken varieties'. In Ghadessy, M. (ed.) *Register Analysis*. 110-147. London: Pinter Publishers.

Goosens, L. 1995. 'From Three Respectable Horses' Mouths – Metonymy and Conventionalization in a Diachronically Differentiated Data Base". In Goossens, L. *et al* (eds). *By Word of Mouth – Metaphor, Metonymy and Linguistic Action in a Cognitive Perspective*. 175-204. Amsterdam: John Benjamins.

Halliday, M.A.K. and R. Hasan. 1976. *Cohesion in English*. London: Longman.

Halliday, M.A.K. 1978/1990. *Language as Social Semiotic*. London: Edward Arnold.

---. 1985. *An Introduction to Functional Grammar*. Harlow: Longman.

Hartley, J. and M. Montgomery. 1985. 'Representations and Relations: Ideology and Power in Press and TV news'. In van Dijk, T. (ed). *Discourse and Communication*. 233-269. Berlin: Walter de Gruyter.

Harvey, K. 2003. "Events' and 'Horizons' – Reading Ideology in 'Bindings' of Translations'. in Calzada Pérez, M. (ed.), *Apropos of Ideology*. 43-69. Manchester: StJerome.

Hatim, B. 1991. 'The Pragmatics of Argumentation in Arabic'. *Text*. 11 (2). 189-199.

Hatim, B. 1998. 'Text Politeness: A Semiotic Regime for a More Interactive Pragmatics'. In Hickey, L. (ed.) *The Pragmatics of Translation*. 72-102. Clevedon: Multilingual Matters.

Hatim, B. and I. Mason. 1990. *Discourse and the Translator*. London: Longman.

Hatim, B. and I. Mason. 1997. *The Translator as Communicator*. London: Routledge.

Hermans, Th. 1995. 'Translation as Institution'. In Snell-Hornby M., Jettmarová Z. and K. Kaindl (eds) *Tranalation as Intercultural Communication*. 3-20. Amsterdam: John Benjamins.

Hodge, R. and G. Kress. 1979/1993. *Language as Ideology*. London: Routledge.

House, J. 1998. 'Politeness and Translation'. In Hickey, L. (ed.) *The Pragmatics of Translation*. 54-71. Clevedon: Multilingual Matters.

Indurkhya, B. 1947/1992. *Metaphor and Cognition*. Dordrecht: Kluwer Academic Publishers.

Iliopoulos, S. J. 1986. [In Greek: Ηλιόπουλος, Σ. 1986. 'Γλώσσα και Μετάφραση ή Πώς Φαμπρικάρεται το Σύνδρομο του Χορτοπηδηχτή'. *Δέντρο*. 27. 226-233]

Inglis, F. 1993/1994. *Cultural Studies*. Oxford: Blackwell.

Karagiannidou, A. and E. Kitis. 1997. 'A Frame-Theoretic Interpretation of Anne Sexton's Poem "Buying the Whore"'. In Efstathiadis, S. and A. Tangalidis (Eds). *Proceedings, 11th International Symposium on Theoretical & Applied Linguistics*. School of English. Department of Theoretical and Applied Linguistics. Aristotle University of Thessaloniki. 121-130.

Katan, D. and F. Straniero-Sergio. 2003. 'Submerged Ideologies in Media Interpreting'. in Calzada Pérez, M. (ed.), *Apropos of Ideology*. 131-144. Manchester: StJerome.

Kinneavy, J. L. 1990. 'Contemporary Rhetoric'. In Horner, W.B. (Ed). *The Present State of Scholarship in Historical and Contemporary Rhetoric*. Columbia: University of Missouri Press.

Kitis, E. 2000. 'Specific and General Remarks on Subordinating Connectives of Modern Greek'. *Studies in Greek Linguistics* 20. 222-233.

Khairullin, V. 1993. 'Time Reference in Different Cultures'. *Perspectives- Studies in Translatology*. 2. 243-248.

Knowles, F. 1998. ' 'New' versus 'Old''. In Hickey, L. (ed). *The Pragmatics of Translation*. 103-113. Clevedon: Multilingual Matters.

Koskinen, K. 2000. 'Institutional Illusions: Translating in the EU Comission'. *The Translator*. 6 (1). 49-65.

Kostouli, T. 1989. [Κωστούλη, Τ. 1989. 'Οι χρονικές προτάσεις και η συμβολή τους στη δόμηση του κειμένου'. *Studies in Greek Linguistics, 10th Annual Meeting of the Department of Linguistics*. Faculty of Philosophy. Aristotle University of Thessaloniki. 339-358.]

---. 1992. 'On the Structure of Textual Rhetoric: Some evidence from Greek narratives'. *Text*. 12 (3).

Kress, G. 1985/1989/1990. *Linguistic processes in sociocultural practice*. Oxford: OUP.

---. 1996. 'Representational Resources and Production of Subjectivity -Questions for the theoretical development of Critical Discourse Analysis in a multicultural society'. In Caldas-Coulthard, C.R. and M. Coulthard (eds). *Texts and Practices – Readings in Critical Discourse Analysis*. 15-31. London: Routledge.

Labov, W. 1972. *Language in the inner city*. Philadelphia: University of Pennsylvania Press.

Lakoff, G. and M. Johnson. 1980. *Metaphors we live by*. Chicago: University of Chicago Press.

Lakoff, R. 1975. *Language and Woman's place*. New York: Harper and Row.

Lakoff-Tolmack, R. 1990. *Talking Power*. USA: Basic Books.

Lambert, J. 1998. 'Language and Social Challenges for Tomorrow: Questions, Strategies, Programs''. In Gambier, Y. (ed.) *Translating for the Media*. 13-34. University of Turku: Centre for Translation and Interpreting.

Lee, D. 1992. *Competing Discourses: Perspective and Ideology in Language*. London: Longman.

Leech, G. 1983. *Principles of Pragmatics*. London: Longman.

Lefevere, A. 1998. 'Acculturating Bertolt Brecht'. In Bassnet, S. and A. Lefevere (Ed). *Constructing Cultures*. 109-122. Clevedon: Multilingual Matters.Levin, H. and P. Garett. 1990. 'Sentence Structure and Formality'. *Language in Society*. 19 (4). 511-520.

Levin, H. and P. Garrett. 1990. 'Sentence Structure and Formality'. *Language in Society*. 19 (4). 511-520.

Levinson, S. 1983. *Pragmatics*. Cambridge: CUP.

Levinson, S. 1987. 'What's Special about Conversational Inference' (Paper presented to the Annual Conference of the British Psychological Society, University College Swansea, April 1st, 1985). In Horn, L and S. Levinson. *Linguistic Institute Pragmatics Seminar Reader – Stanford University, June 29 – August 7, 1987*. 167-177. Palo Alto, California.

Leppihalme, R. 1997. *Culture Bumps*. Clevedon: Multilingual Matters.

Mac Cormac, E.. 1985/1988. *A Cognitive Theory of Metaphor*. Cambridge: MIT Press.

Machill, M. 1998. 'Euronews: the first European news channel as a case study for media industry development in Europe and for spectra of transnational journalism research'. *Media, Culture and Society*. 20. 427-450.

Makri-Tsilipakou, M. 1998. 'Breaking Through the Silencing: Strategies of Emergence'. In Cacoullos A. R. and M. Sifianou (eds). *Anatomies of Silence*. Parousia 44. 258-268.

Malmkjaer, K. 1999. *Contrastive Linguistics & Translation Studies*. Utrecht: Platform Vertalen & Vertaal-wetenschap.

Marmaridou, A. S. S. 1987. 'Semantic and Pragmatic Parameters of Meaning-On the Interface between Contrastive Text Analysis and the Production of Translated Texts'. *Journal of Pragmatics*. 11. 721-736.

Marmaridou, A. S. S. 1994. 'Conceptual Metaphor in Greek Financial Discourse'. In Philippaki-Warburton I., Nikolaidis L. and M. Sifianou (eds). *Themes in Greek Linguistics – Current Issues in Linguistic Theory*. 117. 247-252.

---. 1996. 'Directionality in Translation Processes and Practices'. *Target*. 8 (1). 49-73.

---. 2000. *Pragmatic Meaning and Cognition*. Amsterdam: John Benjamins.

Mason, I. 1994. 'Discourse, Ideology and Translation'. In Beaugrande R., Shunnaq A. and M. Heliel (eds). *Language, Discourse and Translation in the West and Middle East*. 23-34. Amsterdam: John Benjamins.

---. 1998. 'Discourse Connectives, Ellipsis and Markedness'. In Hickey, L. (ed.) *The Pragmatics of Translation*. 170-184. Clevedon: Multilingual Matters.

Mateo M. 1995. 'Translation Strategies and the Reception of Drama Performances: a mutual benefit'. In Snell-Hornby M., Jettmarová Z. and K. Kaindl (eds) *Tranalation as Intercultural Communication*. 99-110 Amsterdam: John Benjamins.

Mey, J. 1993. *Pragmatics*. Oxford: Basil Blackwell.

Milapides, M. 1994. 'Negative Appearances-Positive Effects'. In Douka-Kabitoglou, E. (Ed). *Logomachia – Forms of Opposition in English Language/ Literature*. 401-413. Thessaloniki.

Munday, J. 2001. *Introducing Translation Studies*. London: Routlegde.

Newmark, P. 1981. *Approaches to Translation*. Oxford: Pergamon.

---. 1988. *A Textbook of Translation*. London: Prentice Hall.

Nida, E. 1964. *Toward a Science of Translating with Special Reference to Principles and Procedures Involved in Bible Translating*. Leiden: E. J. Brill.

Nikiforidou, K. 1998. 'Metaphors of Silence'. In Cacoullos, A. R. and M. Sifianou (eds). *Anatomies of Silence*. Parousia 44. 277-287.

Nilsen, D. L. F. 1989. 'Better than the Original: Humorous Translations that Succeed'. *Meta – Translators' Journal*. 34 (1). 112-124.

Nord, C. 1995. 'Text-Functions in Translation: Titles and Headings as a Case in Point'. *Target*. 7 (2). 261-284.

---. 1997. *Translating as a Purposeful Activity*. Manchester: St. Jerome.

Pauwels, P. 1995. 'Levels of Metaphorization'. In Goossens, L. *et al* (eds). *By Word of Mouth – Metaphor, Metonymy and Linguistic Action in a Cognitive Perspective*. 123-158. Amsterdam: John Benjamins.

Papaefthimiou-Lytra, S. 1991. [Παπαευθυμίου-Λύτρα, Σ. 1991. 'Ο Ρόλος της Μετάφρασης στην Ενωμένη Ευρώπη: Εισαγωγή'. *Πρακτικά Ε' Στρογγυλής Τραπέζης.* Τμήμα Αγγλικής Γλώσσας και Φιλολογίας. Πανεπιστήμιο Αθηνών. I-III].

Puurtinen, T. 1992. 'Dynamic Style as a Parameter of Acceptability in Translated Children's Books'. In Snell-Hornby Pöchhacker F. and K. Kaindl (eds). *Translation Studies – An Interdiscipline.* 82-90. Amsterdam: John Benjamins

Quirk, R., Greenbaum, S., Leech, G and J. Stvartvik. 1972. *A Grammar of Contemporary English.* London: Longman.

Raftopoulos, D. 1996. [Ραυτόπουλος, Δ. 1996. *Αρης Αλεξάνδρου ο Εξόριστος.* Αθήνα: Σόκολη].

Richardson, B. 1998. 'Deictic Features and the Translator'. In Hickey, L. (ed.) *The Pragmatics of Translation.* 124-142. Clevedon: Multilingual Matters.

Robinson, D. 1997. *Translation and Empire.* Manchester: St. Jerome.

Roeh, I. and R. Nir. 1990. "Speech presentation in the Israel radio news: ideological constraints and rhetorical strategies". *Text.* 10 (3). 225-244.

Rose, G. M. 1997. *Translation and Literary Criticism.* Manchester: St. Jerome.

Rotzoll, K. 1985. 'Advertisements'. In van Dijk, T. (ed). *Discourse and Communication.* Berlin: Walter de Gruyter.

Schäffner, C and B. Herting. 1992. ' "The Revolution of the Magic Lantern": A cross-cultural comparison of translation studies'. In Snell-Hornby Pöchhacker F. and K. Kaindl (eds). *Translation Studies – An Interdiscipline.* 27-36. Amsterdam: John Benjamins

Schäffner, C. 1997. 'Strategies of Translating Political Texts'. In Trosborg, A. (ed.) *Text Typology and Translation.* 119-143. Amsterdam: John Benjamins.

---. 1997. 'Hedges in Political Texts: A Translation Perspective'. In Hichey, L. (ed.) *The Pragmatics of Translation.* 185-202. Clevedon: Multilingual Matters.

---. 2003. 'Third Ways and New Centres – Ideological Unity or Difference?' in Calzada Pérez, M. (ed.), *Apropos of Ideology.* 23-41. Manchester: StJerome.

Scollon, R. 1993. Maxims of Stance: channel, relationship and main topic in discourse. Report No 26. City Polytechnic of Hong Kong. Department of English.

Séguinot, Candace. 1994. 'Translation and Advertising: Going Global'. *Current Issues in Language and Society.* 1 (3). 249-265.

Sidiropoulou, M. 1989. [in Greek: 'Αιτία-υπόθεση/Εναντίωση: Παρατηρήσεις για τον Σημασιολογικό Χαρακτήρα των Συνδετικών' *Studies in Greek. Linguistics 10th Annual Meeting.* Department of Linguistics. Faculty of Philosophy. Aristotle University of Thessaloniki].

---. 1994. *Variation in Translation – English vs. Greek.* Parousia 31. Athens.

---. 1995a. 'Headlining in Translation: English vs. Greek Press'. *Target.* 7 (2). 285-304.

---. 1995b. 'Causal Shifts in News Reporting: English vs. Greek'. *Perspectives – Studies in Translatology.* 1. 83-98.

---. 1995c. 'Abstract Writing: English-speaking Countries vs. Greece'. *Meta – Translators' Journal.* 40 (4). 579-593.

---. 1995d. 'Time Reference in Translation'. In Milapides, M. (ed). *Proceedings, 9ᵗʰ International Symposium on the Description and/or Comparison of English and Greek.* School of English. Department of Theoretical and Applied Linguistics. Aristotle University of Thessaloniki. 61-74.

---. 1997. 'Reasoning in Interpreting'. In Taylor-Torsello, C. *et al.* "Linguistics, Discourse Analysis and Interpretation". 168-171. In Gambier Y., Gile D. and C. Taylor (eds). *Conference Interpreting: Current Trends in Research.* 167-186. Amsterdam: John Benjamins.

---. 1998a. 'Ad Translating: Silence in Advertising'. In Cacoullos, A. R. and M. Sifianou (eds). *Anatomies of Silence.* Parousia 44. 288-298.

---. 1998b. 'Advertising in Translation: English vs. Greek'. *Meta – Translators' Journal.* 43 (2). 191-204.

---. 1998c. 'Quantities in Translation: English vs. Greek Press'. *Target.* 10 (2). 319-334.

---. 1998d. 'Offensive Language in English-Greek Translation'. *Perspectives –Studies in Translatology.* 6 (2). 183-200.

---. 1999. *Parameters in Translation – English vs. Greek.* Parousia 46. Athens.

---. 2002. *Contrastive Linguistic Issues in Theatre and Film Translation.* Athens: Typothito.

---. 2003. *Options in Translation.* Athens: Sokolis.

---. .2004a. 'Sticky Captions: Genre-Internal Variation in Print-based Ad Translating'. *The Translator.* (forthcoming)

---. 2004b. ⌐'Marking' in News Translation vs. Linguistic Identity Inscription'. Proceedings of the *Choice and Difference in Translation* Conference. National and Kapodistrian University of Athens 3-6 December 2003 (forthcoming)

Sifianou, M. 1992. *Politeness Phenomena in England and Greece.* Oxford: Clarendon.

Simon, S. 1996. *Gender in Translation – Cultural Identity and the Politics of Transmission.* London: Routledge.

Simon-Vandenbergen, A-M. 1995. 'Assessing Linguistic Behaviour – A Study of Value Judgements'. In Goossens, L. *et al* (eds). *By Word of Mouth – Metaphor, Metonymy and Linguistic Action in a Cognitive Perspective.* 71-124. Amsterdam: John Benjamins.

Simpson, P. 1993. *Language, Ideology and Point of View.* London: Routledge.

Snell-Hornby, M. 1988. *Translation Studies – An Integrated Approach.* Amsterdam: John Benjamins.

Steiner, G. 1975/1992. *After Babel – Aspects of language & translation.* Oxford: OUP.

Sweetser, E. 1990. *From Etymology to Pragmatics.* Cambridge: CUP.

Tahir-Gürçağlar, Ş. 2003. 'The Translation Bureau Revisited – Translation as Symbol. in Calzada Pérez, M. (ed.), *Apropos of Ideology.* 131-129. Manchester: StJerome.

Tannen, D. 1984. *Conversational Style: analyzing talk among friends.* Norwood NJ: Ablex Publishing Corporation.

Thornborrow, J. 1993. 'Metaphors of security: a comparison of representation in defence discourse in post-cold-war France and Britain'. *Discourse & Society.* 4 (1). 99-119.

Tirkkonen-Condit, S. 1995. 330-332. In Schäffner, C and A. Beverly 'Translation as Intercultural Communication – Contact as Conflict'. In Snell-Hornby M., Jettmarová Z. and K. Kaindl (eds) *Translation as Intercultural Communication.* 325-337. Amsterdam: John Benjamins.

Toolan, M. J. 1991. *Narrative – A Critical Linguistic Introduction.* London: Routledge.

Torsello, C. *et al.* 'Linguistics, Discourse Analysis and Interpretation'. 168-171. In Gambier Y., Gile D. and C. Taylor (Eds). *Conference Interpreting: Current Trends in Research.* 167-186. Amsterdam: John Benjamins.

Toury, G. 1995. *Descriptive Translation Studies and Beyond.* Amsterdam: John Benjamins.

Trosborg, A. 1997. 'Translating Hybrid Political Texts'. In Trosborg, A. (ed,) *Text Typology and Translation.* 145-158. Amsterdam: John Benjamins.

Trudgill, P. 1972. 'Sex, covert prestige and linguistic change in the urban British English of Norwich'. *Language in Society.* 1. 179-195.

Turner, M. 1991. *Reading Minds –The Study of English in the Age of Cognitive Science.* Princeton: Princeton University Press

Tymoczko, M. 2003. 'Ideology and the Pisition of the Translator. In what Sense is a Translator 'In Between''. In Calzada Pérez, M. (ed.), *Apropos of Ideology.* 181-201. Manchester: StJerome.

Tytler, A. 1992. 'Discourse Structure and Specification of Relationships - A cross-linguistic analysis'. *Text.* 12 (1). 1-18.

Upton, C.-A. (Ed). 2000. *Moving Target.* Manchester: StJerome.

Valero-Garcés, C. 1995. "Modes of Translating Culture". *Meta –Translators' Journal.* 40 (4). 556-563.

Valiouli, M. 1996. 'ESP, Prospective Journalists and Language Awareness'. *Εφαρμοσμένη Γλωσσολογία* . 12. 91-99.

van Dijk, T. 1977. *Text and Context – Explorations in the Semantics and Pragmatics of Discourse.* London: Longman.

---. 1981. *Studies in the Pragmatics of Discourse.* The Hague: Mouton Publishers.

---. (ed.) 1985. *Discourse and Communication.* Berlin: Walter de Gruyter.

---. 1993. *Elite Discourse and Racism.* London: Sage Publications.

van Leeuwen, Th. 1996. 'The Representation of Social Actors'. In Caldas-Coulthard, C.R. and M. Coulthard (eds). *Texts and Practices – Readings in Critical Discourse Analysis.* 32-70. London: Routledge.

Venuti, L. 1995. *The Translator's Invisibility.* London: Routledge.

---. 1998. *The Scandals of Translation.* London: Routledge.

Vestergaard, T. and K. Schrøder. 1985. *The Language of Advertising.* New York: Blackwell.

von Flotow. 1997. *Translation and Gender.* Manchester: StJerome and University of Ottawa Press.

---. 1997. 'Mutual Pun-ishment? Translating Radical Feminist Wordplay: Mary Daly's 'Gyn/Ecology' in German'. In Delabastita, D. (ed.) *Traductio –*

Essays on Punning and Translation. 45-66. Manchester: St. Jerome and Presses Universitaires de Namur.

Wagner, E. Bech, S and J.M. Martínez. 2002. Translating for the European Union Institutions. Manchester: St Jerome.

Wegman, C. 1994. 'Factual argumentation in private opinions: Effects of rhetorical context and involvement'. *Text.* 14 (2). 284-312.

Weissbrod, R. 1996. '"Curiouser and Curiouser': Hebrew Translations of Wordplay in *Alice's Adventure in Wonderland*'. *The Translator – Studies in Intercultural Communication.* Special Issue. Wordplay and Translation. 2 (2). 219-234.

Wilson, J. 1990. *Politically Speaking.* Oxford: Basil Blackwell.

Wilss, W. 1999. *Translation and Interpreting in the 20th Century – Focus on German.* Amsterdam: John Benjamins.

Zabalbeascoa, P. 1996. 'Translating Jokes for Dubbed Television Situation Comedies'. *The Translator – Studies in Intercultural Communication.* Special Issue. Wordplay and Translation. 2 (2). 235-257.

Zlateva, P. 1998. 'Verb Substitution and Predicate Reference'. In Hickey, L. (ed.) *The Pragmatics of Translation.* 143-169. Clevedon: Multilingual Matters.

Appendix

QUESTIONNAIRE FRAGMENT:
News Testimonial Discourse in Translation:
High / Moderate/ Low Importance Topics.
Place yourself in the position of the average Greek newsreader and identify which items you would consider High (H), Moderate (M) or Low (L) importance topics.

....

30. ____
Γκονζάλες: ο ηττημένος νικητής των εκλογών. Δεν αποκλείεται η επάνοδός του στην πρωθυπουργία.

31. ____
Τα απόβλητα καθυστερούν την ένταξη. Η προστασία του περιβάλλοντος προϋπόθεση για ισότιμη συμμετοχή των Ανατολικών χωρών στην Ευρώπη.

32. ____
Ευρώπη. S.O.S. για το δημογραφικό. Αυξάνονται ιλιγγιωδώς οι συνταξιούχοι και μειώνονται δραματικά οι εργαζόμενοι, οι νέοι και τα παιδιά.

33. ____
Κόλαση στα κινέζικα ορφανοτροφεία. Υψηλός αριθμός θανάτων απο ασιτία. Καταγγελίες για διαχωρισμό σε «καλά» και «άχρηστα» παιδιά.

34. ____
Η σκοτεινή υπόθεση Ντιτρού. Υπόκοσμος νέου τύπου. Η μέχρι τώρα ατιμωρησία δημιουργεί υποψίες οτι διέθετε «υψηλή προστασία».

35. ____
Σε πέντε δισ. δολάρια ανέρχεται ο παγκόσμιος τζίρος της πορνείας ανηλίκων. Αναζητούν ακόμη πτώματα στο Βέλγιο.

36. ____
Σαράγεβο. Τα παιδιά της εθνοκάθαρσης. Στη διάρκεια του πολέμου στη Βοσνία πολλές γυναίκες έπεσαν θύματα βιαστών.

37. ____
Οι πολυεθνικές αγοράζουν τη ..Λατινική Αμερική. Θα καταφέρει η νέα γενιά να επιζήσει του ανταγωνισμού;

38. ____
Σε θέση απογείωσης οι τιμές των αεροπορικών εισητηρίων. Η αύξηση της τιμής του πετρελαίου θα έχει επιπτώσεις στα έσοδα των εταιριών.

39. ____
Η ανάσταση του Γέλτσιν. Ιατροπολιτικά παιγνίδια εξουσίας στη Μόσχα.

40. ____
Τα πυρηνικά όπλα ο μεγάλος κίνδυνος. Νέο υπόγειο στρατιωτικό κέντρο στα Ουράλια.

41. ____
Οχι χάδια στον Γέλτσιν. Η πολιτική της Ουάσινγκτον απέναντι στη Μόσχα και η νέα τάξη πραγμάτων.

42. ____
Ενας στρατός σε…ελεύθερη πτώση! Αν συνεχιστεί η κρίση, οι ένοπλες δυνάμεις της Ρωσίας κινδυνεύουν με ολοκληρωτική διάλυση.
....

Name Index

182 – *Linguistic Identities through Translation*

Labov, W. 21
Lakoff, G. 21, 63, 129
Lakoff, G. and M. Johnson 61, 73, 81,
    82, 84, 108, 130, 131
Lakoff, R. 41
Lakoff-Tolmack, R. 146
Lee, D. 21, 22, 49
Lefevere, A. 2, 3,
Levin, H. and P. Garrett 101
Levinson, S. 41, 81, 106, 160
Leppihalme, R. 145

Mac Cormac, E. 73
Machill, M. 61
Makri-Tsilipakou, M. 59
Malmkjaer, K. 18, 161
Marmaridou, A. S. 9, 11, 83, 85, 109
Mason, I. 21, 25, 29, 34, 35
Mateo M. 167
Mey, J. 73, 81, 82
Milapides, M. 58
Munday, J. 2, 17

Newmark, P. 4, 32
Nida, E. 2, 3
Nikiforidou, K. 112
Nilsen, D. L. F. 109, 110
Nord, C. 4

Pauwels, P. 129
Papaefthimiou-Lytra, S. 151
Puurtinen, T. 161

Quirk, R., Greenbaum, S., Leech, G.
    and J. Stvartvik, 44, 96

Raizis, M. B. 116, 122, 123
Reed, F. 156
Richardson, B. 105, 162
Robinson, D. 150
Roeh, I. and R. Nir 68
Rotzoll, K. 58

Schäffner, C and B. Herting 105
Schäffner, C. 21, 105, 165

Scollon, R. 37
Séguinot, C. 58
Sidiropoulou, M. 9, 11, 14, 15, 34,
    42, 46, 49, 57, 60, 61, 66,
    81, 106, 138, 139, 149, 162
Sifianou, M. 8, 41, 103, 106, 141, 160
Simon, S. 2, 5, 22, 59, 147
Simon-Vandenbergen, A-M. 128,
    129, 131
Simpson, P. 22, 57, 85
Snell-Hornby, M. 5
Sweetser, E. 73, 77

Tahir-Gürçağlar, Ş. 134
Tannen, D. 46, 49
Thornborrow, J. 73
Tirkkonen-Condit, S. 103
Torsello, C. 105
Toury, G. 2, 4, 5, 18, 55, 56, 61, 71,
    74-76, 83, 160
Trosborg, A. 87, 166, 168
Trudgill, P. 21
Turner, M. 114
Tymoczko, M. 159
Tytler, A. 42, 146

Upton, C.-A. 158

Valero-Garcés, C. 131
Valiouli, M. 86
van Dijk, T. 14, 41, 66, 86, 99, 139
van Leeuwen, Th. 86
Venuti, L. 2, 3, 5, 56, 133, 136, 147,
    148, 150
Vestergaard, T. and K. Schrøder 58,
von Flotow. 2, 59, 147, 148

Wagner, E. Bech, S. and J.M. Martín 87
Wegman, C. 71
Weissbrod, R. 6
Wilson, J. 74, 79
Wilss, W. 1

Zabalbeascoa, P. 81
Zlateva, P. 105

Subject Index

The visual is intended as a non-linguistic metaphor for translation. It draws on the analogy of projection between cognition and translation.

In cognition, "different people create different attributes and structures, and in different ways. As a result, the same environment can be conceptualized in radically different fashions" (Indurkhya, 1992: 127). The cognitive agent chooses one of the concept networks in the environment that respects his/her originally selected concept network and maps one on the other. Similarly, in translation, conceptual structures of one language are mapped onto those of another. Successful mapping occurs when an *appropriate* target structure is mapped onto the source one.

Diversified outlines of objects (in terms of size, prominence and orientation) may stand for different conceptualizations of the same environment, reflected in source and target texts, as a result of the process of identity inscription on TTs. In a translation context, the appropriate 'structure' of concepts is determined by the producer's cultural viewpoint. Shading may be taken to represent the "salience of domain" feature (Pauwels 1995) in cognitive studies of metaphorical mapping, or, in translation contexts, the tendency for certain languages to be absorbed by others in view of new world-map formations for languages (Lambert 1998).

Design - M. Sidiropoulou